ESSENTIAL
BUSINESS STATISTICS

Joanne Smailes
Angela McGrane

Newcastle Business School,
University of Northumbria

FINANCIAL TIMES
Prentice Hall

An imprint of **Pearson Education**

Harlow, England · London · New York · Reading, Massachusetts · San Francisco · Toronto · Don Mills, Ontario · Sydney
Tokyo · Singapore · Hong Kong · Seoul · Taipei · Cape Town · Madrid · Mexico City · Amsterdam · Munich · Paris · Milan

Pearson Education Limited

Edinburgh Gate
Harlow
Essex CM20 2JE
England

and Associated Companies throughout the World.

Visit us on the World Wide Web at:
www.pearsoneduc.com

First published 2000

ISBN 0 273 64333 9

British Library Cataloguing-in-Publication Data
A catalogue record for this book can be obtained from the British Library.

Library of Congress Cataloging-in-Publication Data
Smailes, Joanne.
    Essential business statistics/Joanne Smailes and Angela McGrane.
       p. cm.
    Includes bibliographical references and index.
    ISBN 0-273-64333-9 (alk. paper)
     1. Commercial statistics – Methodology. I. McGrane, Angela. II. Title.
  HF1017 .S58 2000
  519.5–dc21   99-085696

10 9 8 7 6 5 4 3 2 1
05 04 03 02 01 00

Typeset by 30
Printed and bound in Great Britain by Ashford Colour Press Ltd., Gosport

Trademark notice
Excel is a trademark of Microsoft Corporation.

CONTENTS

LIST OF FIGURES

LIST OF TABLES

INTRODUCTION

The authors of this book are both experienced lecturers at a university in the north-east of England. The book has evolved from material given to students on this university's first year quantitative methods unit for business studies and represents approximately 160 hours of study time. The intention of the book is to arm students with the basic essential quantitative skills required by similar courses. This is reflected in the design of the book which can, if required, be used as a self-study pack. Students are encouraged to make use of further texts in the subject area to enhance their understanding, and a selection of these are listed on page xvi. Page xvii also provides a rough cross-reference to the chapters in these texts which tally with the chapters in this book.

Overall aims of the book

The overall aims of *Essential Business Statistics* are as follows:

- to develop students' confidence in handling numerical data;
- to discuss the different ways in which primary data is collected and to consider some points in the formulation of questionnaires;
- to expose the reader to a wide range of introductory statistical techniques for use in the interpretation and analysis of business data;
- to explain the role of modelling as an aid to decision making;
- to introduce the importance of information technology as an aid to numerical analysis and the formulation of business models.

The book is split into 10 chapters, one main topic is covered in each chapter and these topics roughly represent two to three weeks of study. Each chapter gives an overview of the topic together with worked examples. Review activities are included at appropriate points, to encourage self-assessment. Each of these activities has a full worked solution given at the end of the book. There are also a number of additional exercises on the topic areas to further reinforce the understanding of the subject matter.

Suggested use of the book

Since this book has developed from teaching materials given to first year students, it is organized to suit the teaching methods employed on the original unit. These consisted of a weekly lecture covering the theory given in the chapter, a weekly computer workshop to complete the spreadsheet exercise and fortnightly seminar sessions where additional examples were attempted. Since this represented only 2.5 hours per week of formal contact time, students were also expected to undertake a reasonable amount of independent study (reading the notes, doing the review activities, trying the additional exercises etc.). For readers without access to formal teaching support, we suggest that an appropriate way to proceed would be:

1. Read the chapter material, completing the review activities and checking progress as necessary.

2. Attempt the additional exercises to further check and enhance understanding.

3. Attempt the spreadsheet exercise at the end of each chapter to gain a more practical understanding of the techniques presented.

Recommended further reading

This book does not claim to cater for every individual's needs. However, it is hoped that it will provide a starting point for the study of business statistics. More in-depth reading is recommended for a deeper understanding of the topics covered, so we have provided a list of some of the more popular texts below and a table that cross-references each of the book's chapters with the chapters in these texts (Table I.1).

- A. **Francis**, Business Mathematics and Statistics, 3rd edn, D.P. Publications, 1993

- M.L **Berenson** and D.M. **Levine**, Basic Statistics, 7th edn, Prentice Hall, 1998

- C. **Morris**, Quantitative Approaches in Business Studies, 5th edn, Pitman 2000

- J. **Curwin** and R. **Slater**, Quantitative Methods for Business Decisions, 4th edn, International Thomson Business Press, 1996

- F. **Owen** and R. **Jones**, Statistics, 4th edn, Pitman, 1994

- D.F. **Groebner** and P.W. **Shannon**, Business Statistics, 3rd edn, Maxwell MacMillan, 1990

- M. **Wisniewski**, Quantitative Methods for Decision Makers, 2nd edn, Financial Times Management, 1997

- G. **Bancroft** and G. **O'Sullivan**, Quantitative Methods for Accounting and Business Studies, 3rd edn, McGraw-Hill, 1993

- M.N.K. **Saunders** and S.A. **Cooper,** Understanding Business Statistics, D.P. Publications, 1993

Table I.1 **Schedule of topics and cross-references to texts**

Ch.	Topic	Francis	Berenson and Levine	Morris	Curwin and Slater	Owen	Groebner and Shannon	Wisniewski	Bancroft and O'Sullivan	Saunders and Cooper
1	Collecting Data	1, 2, 3	2	3	1	1, 15	1		6	1 ~ 6
2	Presenting Data	4, 5	3	5	2	2	2	3	7	7, 8, 9, 10
3	Summarizing data	7 ~ 12	4	6	3, 4	5, 9	3	4	8	11 ~ 14
4	Correlation and regression	15, 16, 18	16	13, 14	13, 14	23	13, 16	10	8	17, 18
5	Probability and expected value		5	8	6	11, 12		5	12, 13	
6	The normal distribution and confidence intervals	42	8, 10	9	8, 9	10	6	5	14	6, 25
7	Financial models	26, 27		17	15			15	3	
8	Linear programming	44		19	17			11		
9	Index numbers	22, 23, 24		7	5	8	1, 16	2, 4	11	20 ,21
10	Time based forecasting models	20	19	16	12	7	16, 17	9	10	

Spreadsheets

The use of information technology (IT) has become an integral part of data analysis (and some forms of data collection). For this book, the spreadsheet package Microsoft Excel (Excel 97 at time of press) has been chosen as the tool for the spreadsheet exercises given in each chapter.

A spreadsheet consists of rows and columns which divide the spreadsheet into cells. Each cell is referenced by its column and row labels. The cell in the extreme upper left corner is cell A1, this corresponds to column A and row 1. A spreadsheet contains thousands of cells, however only a small proportion can be viewed at any time due to the limitation imposed by screen size. To move around the spreadsheet and bring other parts into view the Cursor is employed. The cursor outlines a cell with a thick grey border and can be moved either by the arrow keys or the mouse.

A spreadsheet allows for three types of input: text, numbers and formulae. Text, unlike numbers or formulae, cannot be manipulated by the spreadsheet and hence is used only to augment the display. Numbers are not manipulated by the spreadsheet directly but by means of their cell references.

Example

Consider the multiplication of the numbers 2 and 3 in cells A1 and B1 respectively. The calculation of A1 times B1 can be done in another cell to give the answer 6. The advantage is that if the content of either cell is changed then the answer will change automatically.

Formulae are used to express relationships between cells and usually begin with the equals (=) sign. The arithmetic operations plus (+), minus (−), multiply (*), and divide (/) along with the power operator (^) can be used in formulae.

Example

Consider the multiplication of 2 times 3 squared. The value 2 is in cell A1 and the value 3 in cell B1 and the answer is to go into D1. This is achieved by moving the cursor to cell D1 and typing in =A1*B1^2. When the return key is pressed the answer 18 will appear in D1.

Each of the chapters within this book is accompanied by a spreadsheet exercise, and where necessary a brief set of instructions and illustrations are given to help in the completion of the exercise. For some of the more involved spreadsheet processes (e.g., graphs, linear programming) fairly detailed explanations accompanied by worked examples are given. However, it must be noted that this text has not been primarily written as an Excel manual. If you wish to learn more about the spreadsheet package you should refer to any of the numerous publications available commercially as well as the package's Help facility.

Numeracy

What constitutes basic numeracy in business education?

This textbook assumes a basic knowledge of mathematics (GCSE grade C or equivalent). Obviously, business studies students are not expected to be highly proficient mathematicians but there are certain areas where you should be competent. These are:

- addition, subtraction, multiplication, division and their order of manipulation;
- rounding;
- standard form/scientific notation;
- directed numbers;
- fractions;
- percentages and ratio;
- simple algebra.

Readers who feel that they are 'rusty' with their numeracy should develop their competence as quickly as possible and might consider working on sections of the following texts relating to the above skills:

- **Graham**, L. and **Sargent**, D. *Countdown to Mathematics*, Oxford University Press
- **Rowe**, R.N. *Refresher in Basic Mathematics*, D.P. Publications
- **Curwin**, J. and **Slater**, R. *Numeracy Skills for Business*, Chapman and Hall

To assess areas of strength and weakness we have supplied a test below. You should aim to complete all the questions without the aid of a calculator. The skills covered by each of these questions are given below the question in italic print.

Numeracy test

1. $5 - 1 * 3 + 16 \div 2^2 - 1 = ?$

   Addition, subtraction, multiplication, division and their order of manipulation

2. Estimate $(9.0382 - 1.0165) * 2.0329$ to the nearest whole number.

   Addition, subtraction, multiplication, division and their order of manipulation

3. Round 9.9935 to two decimal places.

   Rounding

4. Round 199201 to two significant figures.

   Rounding

5. Express 813000000 in scientific notation.

   Standard form/scientific notation

6. Express 0.000000024 in scientific notation.

   Standard form/scientific notation

7. $-3 * -7 * -4 - ?$

   Directed numbers

8. $-6 - (-7) + (-10 \div 2) - (-26 \div -2) = ?$

   Directed numbers

9. $\frac{1}{5} + \frac{2}{3} - \frac{1}{2} = ?$

   Fractions: addition and subtraction

10. $\frac{4}{27} * \frac{3}{16} \div \frac{1}{3} = ?$

    Fractions: multiplication and division

11. What is 12% of 450?

Percentages

12. A ex-catalogue store is selling trainers at £60 plus VAT @ 17.5%. They are presently also running a 10% off everything sale. How much would the trainers cost?

Percentages

13. A share price was £4.80 yesterday and is now £4.20. What is the percentage decrease in the share's price?

Percentage increases

14. A survey was recently conducted where 48 males and 16 females took part in interviews. What is the ratio of male to female participants expressed in its simplest form?

Ratios

15. A breakfast cereal is made up of cornflakes, dried apples and raisins in the ratio of 9:4:2. If 1.5 kg of cereal is to be made up, how many grammes of dried apple are required?

Ratios

16. Find r given that $4(r + 3) - 3(r - 1) = -5$

Simple algebra

17. Convert this number back from scientific notation $1.33 * 10^{-6}$

Standard form/scientific notation

18. A bracelet is bought for £3300 at an auction. This price includes the auctioneer's 10% commission. How much will the seller receive?

Percentages

19. Given $3 - \frac{2}{y} = 7$, what is y?

Simple algebra

20. Decrease 3600 by 11%

Percentages

Ideally each question should be answered correctly (see below). If you are unable to do the question or are repeatedly getting it wrong we suggest you use the recommended texts to update the particular skill.

Calculators

A calculator will be of use for any quantitative subject. If you are buying a calculator to use in conjunction with this book you should try to buy one with in-built functions to help calculate means, standard deviations and linear regression. Casio, Sharp and Texas Instruments all provide inexpensive calculators with statistical functions.

Numeracy test

Answers

1. 5	6. $2.4 * 10^{-8}$	11. 54	16. (-20)
2. 16	7. (-84)	12. £63.45	17. 0.00000133
3. 9.99	8. (-17)	13. (-12.5%)	18. £3000
4. 200,000	9. $1\frac{1}{30}$	14. 3:1	19. $(-\frac{1}{2})$
5. $8.13 * 10^8$	10. $\frac{1}{12}$	15. 400 g	20. 3204

Acknowledgements

Acknowledgement is given to the management of Newcastle Business School for allowing the inclusion of examination questions originally written by the authors.

In addition, we would like to thank colleagues in the Business Modelling Division of NBS and the many students who have been our guinea pigs.

Finally, thanks go to all of our friends and families. Too numerous to list, but you know who you are!

CHAPTER 1

Collecting data

LEARNING OBJECTIVES

- To introduce some elementary statistical concepts and discuss available information sources;
- To discuss the different ways in which primary data is collected;
- To introduce and discuss the importance of sampling in the design of a survey;
- To consider some points in the formulation of questionnaires.

Introduction

Businesses need information to make decisions; part of this information will be 'statistical'.

A dictionary definition states that statistics are numerical facts collected systematically, arranged and studied.

For decision makers, the primary role of statistics is to provide them with the methods for obtaining and converting data (values, facts, observations, measurements) into useful information. Diagrammatically this can be seen in Figure 1.1.

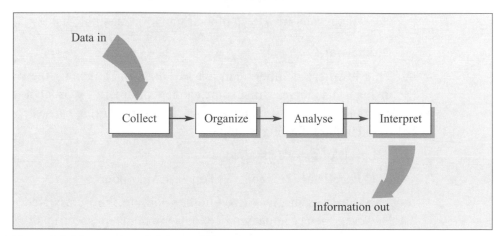

Figure 1.1 The process of data analysis

1.1 Types of data

Data comes in different forms, each of which is dealt with slightly differently on conversion to information. The main groups are shown in Figure 1.2 and further defined below.

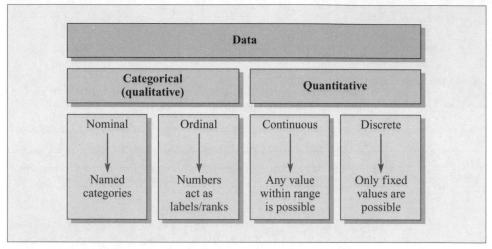

Figure 1.2 **Types of data**

Categorical (qualitative) data

Nominal data

These are data which can be divided into *non-measurable* named categories, for example colours of eyes, type of accommodation, makes of car and so on. Or the colours of shoes worn by 10 students in a lecture:

blue, brown, black, black, white, brown, red, black, black, white

Here, the results are shown in their raw form, a simple list.

Ordinal data

This is where numbers can act as labels or ranks. As the name suggests, it involves data representing some element of order. A year label would be a classic example. The classification of this type of data often causes confusion, as illustrated in the following example:

Levels of service are graded

1: Excellent   2: Good   3: Poor   4: Very poor

The words themselves (excellent, good etc.) are classified as nominal data. However, the accompanying codings are numbers specifically acting as ranks so these would be classified as ordinal data.

Note that there is a difference between ordering and coding. In the example opposite on shoe colours the colours could have been coded 1: black, 2: blue etc. but these numbers would *not* represent ordinal data because they do not give an order to the shoe colours.

Quantitative data

These are data which are measured, counted or quantified in some way. They can be divided into categories or classes according to their measurement. This type of data can be further subdivided into two types: continuous data and discrete data.

Continuous data

Continuous data are quantitative data for which any value within a continuous range of values is possible. It generally applies to data that are measured (e.g., heights, wages, times, weights). There is often debate about whether variables such as age and money should be classed as continuous data. In these cases common sense, with justification, prevails.

Table 1.1 A table to show the heights of 80 people

Height (cm)	Number* of people
150 to less than 160	12
160 to less than 170	24
170 to less than 180	28
180 to less than 190	16

Note: * The word 'frequency' is generally used to represent the number in each of the listed categories, and this term will be used from now on.

Consider Table 1.1. Here, height is the variable of interest.

Discrete data

These are quantitative data for which only certain fixed values (usually integers) are possible, for example counts, number of messages on an answerphone, number of visits to London and so on. Another example, with results shown in their raw form, follows:

Number of jewellery items worn by 15 students:

4, 5, 1, 0, 2, 3, 6, 2, 3, 0, 2, 4, 2, 0, 2

Table 1.2 shows the number of letters received each morning over a 30 day period. Here, the variable of interest is the number of letters.

Table 1.2 Number of letters received over a 30 day period

Number of letters each morning	Frequency
1	12
2	9
3	5
4	4

REVIEW ACTIVITY 1

State whether the following data are discrete, continuous, nominal or ordinal.

(a) Daily temperatures in central Newcastle.

(b) Days of the week.

(c) Number of products sold by each shop in a chain of supermarkets.

(d) Position in the music charts of UK singles.

Working:

Answers on page 215.

1.2 Sources of information

There are two basic sources of information, primary and secondary.

Primary data

These are data which have been collected specifically for a particular purpose.

Everyone at some time or other will have taken part in a data collection process. Every form filled in provides primary data to someone somewhere.

Often the information provided (say from questionnaires, interviews and feed-back forms) is only collected from a relatively small number of people. This is called a **sample**. In much rarer circumstances (for example the 10 yearly UK census) data may be collected from the population, or as many people in the country as it is possible to reach. A **population** need not be made up of every person living in the UK or even people themselves. Populations may be, for example, every chocolate bar produced by a factory using a batch of raw materi-als, salmon at a fish farm or all employees at a large firm.

The word **census** is used to describe the collection of data from the complete population.

The word **survey** describes the collection of data from a sample selected from a population. Samples are generally used as they are a more economical and practical method of data collection.

Data collected from a census or survey are known as **primary data**. The different ways in which such data are collected and how survey samples are determined will be discussed later in this chapter.

The gathering of primary data can be very costly and time consuming, particularly in the case of a census. Because of this census data is most commonly collected by governments or specialist market research companies who then make the information more widely available to others. It is at this stage that the data become known as **secondary data**.

Secondary data

These are data, originally collected for one project, but which then can be used for another purpose.

In the UK the Government Statistical Service holds most nationally published data. There are numerous government publications which include:

- *Social Trends*: an analysis and breakdown of many aspects of British life and work;
- *Financial Statistics*: key financial and monetary statistics within the UK;
- *Economic Trends*: a compilation of the main economic indicators.

Many other government publications are based on data which have been collected from surveys. Listed below are brief descriptions of some of these surveys.

- The *Family Expenditure Survey* (*FES*) investigates the income and spending patterns of about 7000 households in the UK. The population size is approximately 22 million and the survey is conducted annually.
- The *Survey of Retail Prices*, carried out by the Department of Employment, provides around 150,000 prices which are used in the calculation of the Retail Price Index (RPI). Population size is very difficult to estimate. The survey is conducted monthly.
- The *New Earnings Survey* (*NES*) collects information on the earnings of about 180,000 people. Population size is approximately 20 million and the survey is conducted annually.

Note that in the surveys where the population size is known the sample is less than 1% of the total population. The choice of sample size will be considered later in this chapter.

Other useful sources of secondary data include company and bank reviews, *The Employment Gazette*, *The Economist* and so on. Nowadays computing sources of secondary data are becoming ever more popular, for example Datastream, Prestel, the Internet and even Ceefax.

Of course secondary data can also be drawn from many other sources, and some of the spreadsheet exercises in this book will demonstrate that even a simple spreadsheet file can be a secondary data source.

1.3 Primary data collection methods

Data analysis often involves manipulation or work with data which have been collected from a survey: for that reason it is important to ensure that the collection of primary data is carried out in a statistically sound way, otherwise results may be biased. In the next sections, methods of collecting primary data will be examined.

Postal questionnaires

This is where a questionnaire is sent – usually through the post – to the desired sample. It is probably the most popular data collection method as it is very easy to make contact with respondents over a wide geographical area and is inexpensive to administer. Once the questionnaire has been received the respondents generally have a period of time in which to answer. This is particularly advantageous if 'non-instant recall' information is required. However, the method often results in very low return rates and, because there is no personal contact, it is impossible to probe for further information on interesting responses or to give clarification on any questions which may be misinterpreted.

Personal interviews

This procedure usually requires a trained interviewer going out and asking a prepared set of questions, either in a public place (for example stopping people on the street to take part in a political opinion poll) or at the respondent's home or place of work. Because of the involvement of a trained individual, some of the problems of postal questionnaires can be avoided. Ambiguous questions can be explained, interesting responses can be followed up and as the interviewer can encourage participation, the response rates are generally higher. But, because of the human contact, this method is very expensive (salary, training, transport), especially if a wide geographical cover is required. Also, accurate results rely heavily on the interviewer's expertise.

Telephone interview

This could be considered as almost a compromise between a postal questionnaire and a personal interview. There is still personal contact, with the added bonus of being able to directly enter responses on to a computer, if such facilities are available. But, in this case, there is an immediate bias as people who do not own a phone are excluded from the sample; also one is never sure who is responding at the other end of the telephone line.

Observation

This is the main method employed when the population of interest does not consist of people or require people's responses. An example of an observational survey is a traffic survey. Again, the method relies heavily on the skills of the observer, and owing to its nature can be the most time consuming (in terms of human participation) when observation of irregular events is required.

1.4 Estimation of sample size

As mentioned previously, the sample size may be very small in relation to the overall population. In fact there is no precise way in which an optimal sample size can be calculated for any particular survey. However, there are two useful statistical facts which should be kept in mind:

- the larger the size of the sample, the more *accurate* the information on the population will be;
- above a certain size, little *extra* information about a population can be gained yet costs in time and money increase.

Without becoming too technical, common sense is used in conjunction with any information already known and details about the information sought to estimate an appropriate sample size. This will be illustrated with some scenarios and suggestions of appropriate sample sizes.

EXAMPLE 1.1

The IT resource manager of a large company wishes to do a quick market research exercise on employees' attitudes towards the printing facilities provided.

In this case, no particular specialist information is required, the results will probably have no major impact on the employees themselves and, knowing that they all use the IT facilities regularly, a sample size of, say, between 50 and 100 would be sufficient.

EXAMPLE 1.2

A university is considering extending the teaching week to include Saturday mornings and wishes to receive some staff and student views on this.

In this case, the outcome of the survey could bring about a major change in the university's working environment. Because of this it would be advisable to find out the population size and select between 20% and 30% of the population (staff and students) to be canvassed.

1.5 Choosing a suitable, representative sample

In the same way as selecting a suitable sample size, common sense is the most important factor in ensuring a sample is representative.

EXAMPLE 1.3

You are working for a building society and have been asked to find out the current average selling price for a three bedroom, semi-detached house in the north-east of England.

In this case you could *not* simply go into the nearest estate agent and pick up details on say 20 (or even 70) such houses and expect to have a representative sample for the whole of the area of interest.

EXAMPLE 1.4

A students' union wishes to gauge students' opinions of the catering facilities provided in the union building.

In this case it would be reasonable to assume that asking, say, 50–100 students as they leave the union building would give a sufficiently representative sample as all would probably have an interest in the catering facilities.

1.6 Sampling methods

A number of methods are available to try and achieve a representative sample of the population and these are described below.

Simple random sampling

The key to this method is that every member of the population must have an equal chance of being included in the sample. For small populations, a method such as 'drawing from a hat' would achieve this. For larger populations, each member of the population is usually given a unique identification number and then random numbers are generated (often using a computer). The sample is then made up of the population members whose numbers match those generated. The method 'feels' fair, and has no bias. However, it might be difficult to contact all of the chosen sample (say if there is a wide geographical spread in the data) and (simply through chance) an unrepresentative sample may occur.

Stratified random sampling

This method is very similar to simple random sampling, but is used where it is thought that the population contains distinct groups who might have different views about the issues of interest (for example it might be thought that car owners and cyclists/pedestrians would have different views about the introduction of car control measures in a city centre). To overcome the danger of a sample accidentally being unrepresentative, the sample can be stratified according to these groups so that it has approximately the same proportions as the population (e.g., if there are 80% car owners and 20% cyclists/pedestrians in the population then the ratio of 4:1 should be reflected in the sample). For each 'stratum', the sample members are selected randomly (as above for simple random sampling). It is a comparatively unbiased sampling method and should give a representative sample. Again, however, it is necessary to have good access to the population of interest and stratification will add costs to the survey process.

Systematic sampling

Again this is similar to simple random sampling except that instead of picking a member of the sample by using a random number generator, the data are assumed to be in random order and every nth member is selected where n is given by

$$\text{(population size)} \div \text{(desired sample size)}$$

For example if a sample of 5 were required from a list of 30 people every 6th person could be chosen. Note that it is not necessary to start with the first person on the list – the start point should be chosen randomly. Thus the sample might contain the people numbered 1, 7, 13, 19 and 25 – or 2, 8, 14, 20 and 26 – or 3, 9, 15, 21 and 27 etc. It is an easy method to use, and can be useful if the exact population is not known (e.g., all users of a bank's cash machines on a particular day would be hard to define in advance, but every 15th customer could easily be questioned). Care must be taken to ensure that the sample is not biased (e.g., if every 5th item is taken from a production line with 5 machines, does that mean that the same machine is sampled each time?).

Cluster sampling

This method is frequently used when the population items of interest are widely spread and it is desirable to ensure that the sample elements are grouped together in some way (perhaps geographically or over a short period of time).

For example, if a retailer wanted to interview a sample of shopkeepers it would make sense to randomly select two or three sales areas first. Every shopkeeper within those areas could then be interviewed: this would avoid the selection of a number of isolated shopkeepers scattered across the country. Clearly this is a useful method for widely spread geographical data where the population is not defined exactly. Again care must be taken to ensure that bias does not occur.

Quota sampling

Quota sampling is usually used where interviewing is the main method of data collection; the aim is similar to that for stratified sampling in that it is desirable to make sure the composition of the sample matches that in the population. The interviewer is given a 'predetermined' sample profile where the numbers of inter-viewees in each category are chosen to match the population proportions. The interviewer then selects people from the passing population to match the required numbers in each category. For example, on the basis of Table 1.3 an interviewer for a political opinion poll is required to sample 40 people in total: two of these will be professional females (social class A/B aged between 45 and 64, etc.). This will have been chosen so that the proportion in the sample ($\frac{2}{40}$ = 5%) is similar to that in the original population.

Table 1.3 Interview quotas for a political opinion poll

Social class	A/B		C		D/E	
Age/Sex	M	F	M	F	M	F
18–29	0	0	3	1	2	2
30–44	1	1	2	1	4	3
45–64	2	2	3	1	2	2
65 or over	1	1	2	1	3	0

This method tends to have good response rates because the interviewer achieves the quota set – non-respondents are ignored and other people are chosen to replace them. However, it is very reliant on the interviewer, and bias could occur as it is a non-random technique.

Multistage sampling

Multistage sampling is a technique which is used for producing a representative sample from a widespread population – in similar situations to those discussed earlier for cluster sampling. However, in this case the process continues down to selection of the individual sampling units (rather than groups as for cluster sampling). This is done by splitting the sampling process into stages and using the most relevant of the sampling techniques already listed to each of these different stages. For example, a large food manufacturer wishing to conduct a national survey into the lifestyle and eating habits of consumers, to provide information for the possible launch of a pre-prepared food range, might use a three-stage survey to cover the whole of the country.

- *Stage 1* (*primary sampling units*): Split the UK into a number of regions (e.g. TV regions) and then randomly select a small number of these.

- *Stage 2* (*secondary sampling units*): Taking each of the selected regions, randomly sample sub-regions (perhaps parliamentary constituencies).

- *Stage 3* (*tertiary sampling units*): Individual households could then be selected by using systematic sampling from the electoral register.

This is another technique (like cluster sampling) which is very useful for widely spread data. Careful thought is necessary at the various sample stages to avoid the risk of bias.

REVIEW ACTIVITY 2

Table 1.4 is a seminar group listing for students on the AR101 Introduction to Aromatherapy unit. With the aid of the list of random numbers below you are required to select a sample of 5 people, who will be given a free massage by the tutor, using:

(a)   Simple random sampling.

(b)   Stratified random sampling based on gender.

(c)   Systematic random sampling.

Table 1.4 Seminar group listing for students on Aromatherapy unit

Surname	Forename	Surname	Forename
Black	Lynn	North	John
Kirk	Tim	Fox	Malcolm
Hughes	Jim	Peters	Sue
Hobson	Anne	Howe	Roy
Dixon	Patrick	Morris	Karen
Carr	Bill	Philipson	Gail
Murray	John	Plant	Vicki
Smith	Alan	Stewart	Angela
Thompson	Ivor	Ward	David
Swallow	Adam	Smith	Liz

Random numbers:

11	14	05	16	18	12	18	19	15	03	07
17	13	09	01	07	13	08	11	14	10	14
13	14	11	06	12	15	02	15	18	19	13

11

> **Working:**
>
>
>
>
>
> *Answers on pages 215–16.*

1.7 Questionnaire design

Most primary data collection methods make use of questionnaires. Good questionnaire design is crucial to the success of a survey. Because of this it is very important to 'pilot' the questionnaire on a small number of respondents to check for inaccuracies in wording of a question, whether all possible answers of interest will be covered, etc.

Question types

There are three basic types of question used in questionnaires: dichotomous questions, multiple choice questions and open-ended questions. Here each will be examined in turn.

Dichotomous questions

These allow for two answers only. For example, yes or no; male or female; true or false; like or dislike.

EXAMPLE 1.5

1. Are you living in halls of residence?   Yes ☐   No ☐
2. Is your personal tutor: Male ☐   Female ☐ ?
3. 7 * 3 = 20   True ☐   or   False ☐ ?
4. Do you   Like ☐   or Dislike mathematics ☐ ?

It is important that questions of the type shown in (4) above are not overused where there may be 'middle ground', that is, they must allow for don't know; no opinion etc.

In such cases it is more appropriate to use multiple choice questions.

Multiple choice questions

Respondents can choose from several indicated possibilities. Included in this category are those questions which may ask the respondent to rank choices.

It is important to make sure that the possibilities are both 'comprehensive' and 'mutually exclusive' (that is every respondent should, unless otherwise stated, be able to pick one and only one of the possibilities).

EXAMPLE 1.6

You never know – someone could be living in a tent!

What type of accommodation are you living in during this year of study?

Halls of residence ☐	Own/parents' house or flat ☐
Rented house/flat ☐	Lodgings ☐

Other (please specify) _____

The *other* category provides for any types which may have been missed, but care must be taken to make sure that this category does not end up being the most popular choice.

EXAMPLE 1.7

Grey, green, violet and hazel eyes would all have to be put in the *other* category

What colour are your eyes ?

Blue ☐

Brown ☐

Other (please specify) _____

When using questions which require a level of opinion, make sure there are the same number of potential answers 'for' as 'against'.

EXAMPLE 1.8

3 choices on the 'for' side

Do you think the students' union catering facilities overall are:

Excellent ☐	OK ☐
Very good ☐	Bad ☐
Quite good ☐	

Only 1 on the 'against'

Whenever it is appropriate, remember to account for the don't knows or the don't haves.

EXAMPLE 1.9

How many doors does your car have?

(include the boot, if it is a hatchback)

One ☐		Four ☐	
Two ☐		Five ☐	
Three ☐		More than five ☐	
Don't own a car ☐			

Open-ended questions

Respondents are left to answer these in any manner they choose.

The main advantage for this type of question is that it allows for an infinite number of divergent answers. This, however, is also their greatest disadvantage, as the responses to such questions are the hardest to process and analyse. Therefore, one needs to be wary not to use too many on any one questionnaire.

However, open-ended questions can be very useful in three particular areas:

1. On pilot surveys. Here they can be used to try and gauge all possible responses to a particular question so that this question can then become a well designed multiple choice question in the full survey.

EXAMPLE 1.10

How do you get to and from work on an average day?

---

2. Probing – to get extra information depending on a choice made by a previous response.

EXAMPLE 1.11

Was this university your first choice of place to study for your degree?

Yes ☐   No ☐   If No please briefly explain why _____

---

3. Used at the end of a questionnaire or section they can be a means of giving the respondent the chance to add anything they feel is important but is not covered by the questions given.

Note that open-ended questions can add weight and credibility to a final report by the use of actual responses as direct quotes.

In summary, when looking at the overall design of a questionnaire the following should be kept in mind:

- Questionnaires should be as short as possible.
- The questions themselves should:
  - avoid using complex words and phrases in their construction;
  - be meaningful;
  - not be too technical or involve too much calculation;
  - not be too personal or offensive;
  - not tax the memory;
  - be unambiguous.
- Questions should be arranged in a logical order.
- Questionnaires should be attractively laid out and constructed.
- How the responses will be analysed should be considered at the questionnaire design stage (i.e., appropriate coding should be considered).

1.8 Sources of error

No survey of any population can ever be 100% accurate. (One notable disaster was the predicted outcome of the 1992 general election when opinion polls stated that the Labour Party would win comfortably and, in fact, the Conservatives were returned to power.) There are several different ways in which errors can occur and there are steps which can be taken to try and avoid them.

Sampling errors

These errors arise from the sample not being representative of the population concerned. They are generally avoided by careful consideration of the sampling method to be used. With random samples, the size of these sampling errors can be usefully estimated.

Non-sampling errors

These arise from a variety of causes including:

- the incorrect recording of responses (e.g. by interviewers);
- transferring data incorrectly onto a computer for processing;
- sample members refusing to co-operate (non-respondents);
- failure to make initial contact with sample members (non-respondents);
- badly designed questions.

Non-sampling errors are generally avoided by good training of the individuals involved in the data collection and processing process; also, carrying out a pilot survey helps to minimize their occurrence.

1.9 Overall survey design

To summarize, here is a checklist of the main stages in survey design:

Planning

1. Define the survey aims.
2. Define the population.
3. Identify each member of the population.
4. Identify the sampling scheme (how to choose the sample and how large it should be).
5. Decide upon the method of data collection (postal questionnaire, interviews etc.).
6. Design a questionnaire (equally appropriate for personal interviews and observation).
7. Select and train any people involved in the data collection process.

Fieldwork

1. Select the sample.
2. Collect the data.
3. Follow up non-responses wherever possible.
4. Collate and code information (particularly if a computer is to be used for the analysis).

Analysis and interpretation

1. Screen data for recording errors and extreme values (known as outliers).
2. Carry out any statistical computations.
3. Identify and note any possible sources of error and/or bias.

Publication

Generally in two sections:

1. Written results and conclusions.

2. Detailed statistical section which includes:
   (a) details of the questionnaires used;
   (b) sampling details;
   (c) background statistical theory;
   (d) summary of data collected.

REVIEW
ACTIVITY 3

The following questions are taken from a questionnaire issued to new car owners by a local car showroom:

(a) What is the colour of your new car?

   Red ☐   Blue ☐   White ☐   Other ☐

(b) Did you use cash to pay for the car?

   Yes ☐   No ☐

(c) How much did you pay for the car?

   £5000 – £7000 ☐   £7000 – £9000 ☐   £9000 – £11,000 ☐

(d) Do you feel that the service you received from our staff was

   Excellent ☐   Very good ☐   Good ☐   Poor ☐ ?

Considering each of the questions in turn state whether you think the question could be improved. If so suggest an alternative.

Working:

Answers on page 216.

Key points to remember

1. Data may be defined as categorical (qualitative) or quantitative.

2. Categorical data can be further divided into nominal data and ordinal data.

3. Quantitative data can be further divided into continuous data and discrete data.

4. Data comes from either a primary or a secondary source.

5. A census involves collecting data from a population (all items/people of interest), while a survey collects data from a sample (a carefully chosen small group).

6. Primary data may be collected through a postal questionnaire, a personal interview, a telephone interview or by observation.

7. Common sense must be used to decide on a suitable sample size.

8. Samples may be chosen through the use of simple random sampling, stratified random sampling, systematic sampling, cluster sampling, quota sampling or multistage sampling.

9. Good questionnaire design is essential to the success of a survey.

10. The basic question types used in questionnaires are dichotomous, multiple choice and open-ended.

11. The categories in multiple choice questions should be comprehensive and mutually exclusive.

12. The answers to open-ended questions are difficult to process and analyse, hence care should be taken not to overuse these sorts of questions.

13. Sampling or non-sampling errors may arise from the survey process. Non-sampling errors are generally avoidable.

ADDITIONAL EXERCISES

Question 1   The following are some commonly used sources of secondary data:

- Annual Abstract of Statistics
- Social Trends
- Economic Trends
- Regional Trends
- Family Spending
- Key Data
- Guide to Official Statistics.

Find a copy of one of these publications and prepare a summary of the information provided, giving appropriate examples. Can you think of managerial situations where such information could be valuable?

Question 2   State whether the following data are discrete, continuous, nominal or ordinal.

(a) Petrol consumption rates for a range of cars.

(b) Exam grades (A, B, C etc.) for a group of students.

(c) Corresponding percentage exam marks for the same students.

(d) Types of cheese sold in a supermarket.

Question 3   Suggest a suitable sampling method that could be used to obtain information on:

(a) The attitude of passengers to smoking on local bus services.

(b) The percentage of unsatisfactory components produced each week on a production line.

(c)   The attitudes toward the provision of a workplace nursery in a large company.

(d)   The views of car drivers to traffic calming measures on a residential road.

(e)   The likely sales figures for a new type of tea bag.

Question 4   You have been commissioned, by an independent national daily newspaper, to undertake a national survey of people's reactions to a number of issues including the government's recent handling of the economy. You have been instructed that for the survey to retain any credibility, it will be necessary to survey a representative cross-section of at least 5000 people. Consider, in detail, the sampling and data collection methods you would use to carry out this survey, paying particular attention to the requirements for a large, representative group of respondents.

Question 5   A fast food company has many franchised outlets throughout the UK. An executive wants to survey the opinions of the franchise holders towards the current distribution system for raw materials. Suggest a sampling method the executive may use, giving reasons for your choice.

Question 6   Table 1.5 is a seminar group listing for students on a first year Business Studies course. With the aid of the list of random numbers below you are required to select a sample of 4 people using:

(a)   Simple random sampling.

(b)   Stratified random sampling based on sex.

(c)   Systematic random sampling.

Table 1.5 Seminar group listing for Business Studies students

First name	Surname	First name	Surname
Steven	Adams	Andrea	Cross
Clare	Anderson	John	Davidson
Graham	Buckley	Jacqui	Hobson
Glen	Burden	Iain	McLeod
Angela	Dean	Anne	Smith
Susan	Dixon	Elizabeth	Swift
Sarah	Gray	Stuart	Trainer
Joanne	Keane	Philip	Twist
Henry	Ross	Graham	West
David	Wright	Zoe	Wilkinson

Random numbers:

12	15	06	15	17	13	17	20	14	02
18	14	10	02	09	13	07	12	16	12
15	16	10	07	13	16	01	14	19	18

Question 7   The deputy manager of a local department store has asked her marketing assistant to conduct a survey on the possibility of late night opening on Tuesdays and Thursdays. The deputy manager does not have a list of the store's customers but estimates there must be over 10,000 of them with 90% living locally. She does, however, have a breakdown of storecard holders based on age and gender and shown in Table 1.6.

Table 1.6 Estimated proportion of customers by age and gender

Age/Gender	Male	Female
Under 20	3	6
20–29	6	14
30–44	9	21
45–59	7	20
60 or over	4	10

Given that the marketing assistant only has a small budget for printing and stationery, and that the survey results are required in two weeks, suggest a suitable sample size and a sampling method. Give reasons for the choices made.

Question 8   One hundred dairy farms in four European countries have been surveyed to collect information about their size, amount of livestock and number of employees.

(a) The intention is to use this survey as a pilot study, with the eventual survey covering farms across the EEC. Suggest a suitable sampling technique that could be used to decide which farms should take part in the larger study. Give reasons for your choice.

(b) In this wider study information on the *number* of different breeds of cows kept by the farmers is also to be collected. Suggest a question to be included in the study which would allow this.

SPREADSHEET EXERCISE

This first spreadsheet exercise is designed to give an introduction to the spreadsheet package used throughout this book – Microsoft Excel. Some of the basic functions and features will be reviewed. Readers with no previous spreadsheet knowledge will find a basic guide to Excel useful if more information about the specific features of the package is required.

(a) Load up the file AROMA.XLS.
   This file contains a listing of the marks for a group of students who studied the unit AR101 'Introduction to Aromatherapy' last semester. Table 1.7 shows the marks for five students missing from the list.

Table 1.7 Marks for Aromatherapy students missing from AROMA.XLS

Name		Seminar group	Assignment 1	Assignment 2	Exam
West	Nick	B	54	42	35
Bell	Joan	B	62	64	65
Book	Iain	A	54	43	47
Philips	Tracey	B	72	72	65
Oliver	Paul	A	41	43	37

(b) *Add the details* for these five students to the spreadsheet.

(c) *Change the width* of columns D and E so that the headings fit into one cell.

(d) *Right justify* all of the column headings.

(e) Given that the final exam mark is made up as follows:

$$(0.8 * \text{exam mark}) + (0.1 * \text{assignment 1 mark}) + (0.1 * \text{assignment 2 mark})$$

Type a formula into cell G6 to calculate the overall mark for the first student on the list. *Copy this down* to give a full column of final marks.

(f) *Format* the overall marks so that they are displayed to *one decimal place* and give column G a suitable heading.

(g) A student fails if they have less than 40% for the unit. *Enter an IF statement* in cell H6 and *copy it down* to show whether each student has passed or failed.

(h) *Save* your file onto a disk (but do not close it).

(i) *Sort* the data by seminar group and name so that group A are listed before group B and the student names are displayed alphabetically within their groups.

(j) *Copy* the headings from cells A6–G6 to a new area on your spreadsheet, then *move* the marks for group B so that there are two separate tables of marks (i.e., one table for each seminar group).

(k) Nick West (group B) has withdrawn from the course, so *delete* his name and marks.

(l) Use the *Help facility* on Excel to find a suitable *function* which would work out the average overall mark for each seminar group.

(m) Using this function, *make up a table* showing the average mark for each seminar group and add the *percentage* of students failing (*Hint*: *count* how many fails there are in each group first, using a *function*).

(n) *Save and close* your file, and *exit* Excel.

CHAPTER 2

Presenting data

LEARNING OBJECTIVES

- To look at the different ways in which collected data can be summarized for presentation purposes;
- To provide guidelines which can aid in the selection of the appropriate graphical representation of various data types.

Introduction

The first stage in transforming raw data into useful information is to simplify and present it.

To illustrate this, the data in Table 2.1 comes from a survey used to find out information on student accommodation. A simple questionnaire was issued to each of 36 students on a BA Ceramics course, asking their gender, number of distinct post-16 qualifications held (eg, number of A levels, foundation course), present accommodation, monthly accommodation payments and their age.

Immediately it can be seen how difficult it is to obtain, from raw data, simple information such as the number of students of each sex. Raw data, left as it is, is not particularly useful. To improve its usefulness, it is necessary to provide summaries in the form of tables and/or graphs.

2.1 Tabulation

The simplest form of tabulation is where one particular piece of data is taken, say gender from the list above. Allocate categories (or classes) to that data i.e., Male and Female and then count how many pieces of the data fall into each of these classes (in statistical terms the word 'frequency' is used for count).

In other cases this classification might not be quite so clear cut. The following guidelines will be helpful in undertaking appropriate classification.

Table 2.1 Data on students' accommodation

Sex	Q'L	Accommodation	Rent	Age	Sex	Q'L	Accommodation	Rent	Age
M	3	Lodgings	125	18	M	3	Rented Flat/House	157	18
M	2	Rented Flat/House	130	20	M	3	Caravan	100	18
F	5	Own/Parents' Home	120	18	F	2	Rented Flat/House	146	19
F	1	Halls of Residence	128	19	M	1	Rented Flat/House	135	19
F	3	Halls of Residence	137	18	F	4	Halls of Residence	115	18
F	2	Rented Flat/House	141	21	F	1	Halls of Residence	110	18
M	4	Own/Parents' Home	162	25	M	2	Own/Parents' Home	134	20
F	1	Lodgings	153	18	F	3	Halls of Residence	127	20
M	2	Halls of Residence	136	18	M	1	Halls of Residence	132	18
M	2	Halls of Residence	143	18	F	1	Rented Flat/House	135	18
F	1	Rented Flat/House	129	19	F	3	Lodgings	126	20
F	5	Rented Flat/House	138	18	F	3	Own/Parents' Home	110	35
F	3	Rented Flat/House	135	19	M	2	Own/Parents' Home	112	18
F	2	Rented Flat/House	141	19	M	3	Rented Flat/House	130	19
F	1	Halls of Residence	152	20	F	2	Lodgings	140	21
F	4	Lodgings	140	18	M	2	Halls of Residence	135	28
F	3	Lodgings	133	20	F	1	YWCA	145	18
M	1	Lodgings	129	21	M	3	Lodgings	132	20

Note: Q'L (qualifications) represents the number of post-16 qualifications held

Classification of data

1. The categories chosen must be comprehensive so that *every* response can be included.

   For nominal data, if necessary, a class for 'other' may have to be created to account for those responses otherwise omitted (but with care taken so that it doesn't become too big!).

   For discrete and continuous data this may mean the inclusion of open-ended categories. For example, when classifying the age of the UK population the last category might be '90 or over'.

2. The categories must be distinct and unambiguous to avoid uncertainty as to where to put an observation. This is particularly relevant to numerical data in groups, for instance age groupings of under 20, 20 to 30, 30 to 40, etc. would *not* be acceptable. This is because there would be doubt as to the class in which to place a person who is 30 years old.

3. The categories should not be too numerous – generally aim for around five to 10 classes. This is recommended to provide a succinct visual impact. However, note that it is easier (assuming later use) to combine classes than to separate data which has been classified into too few groups.

Construction of the table

Tables of data are an almost everyday occurrence and there are no real hard and fast rules which govern their construction. But as with many visual forms of presentation there are some elements of good practice to be considered:

- Be clear about what you wish the table to show.
- Give the variable of interest prominence by listing it first.
- If you have large amounts of data, two or three simple tables are better than one large complicated one.
- Every table should be given a clear explanatory title.
- Each row/column should be given a clear heading.
- Whenever useful include row/column totals.
- The source of information used should be noted at the bottom of a table.
- Include any other information considered to be useful in a footnote (e.g., units of measurement).

In the student accommodation survey data there are five variables of interest. The responses themselves along with the data type should help suggest suitable classifications and hence lead to the construction of appropriate summary tables.

Each variable will be looked at in turn.

Gender of the students

This is *nominal* data and can simply be put into two categories Male and Female, which form the first column (or row, if preferred) in the table (see Table 2.2). A quick count of the 'M' and 'F' responses gives the frequency of each group.

Table 2.2 Gender of students on BA Ceramics course

Sex	No. of students
Male	15
Female	21
Total	**36**

Source: Student questionnaire

Note how the table is given a clear title and source so that it can be interpreted in isolation of any other information.

Post-16 qualifications

As these data are a *count* of the number of higher qualifications held by each person they are classified as *discrete*. Examination of the data shows that the minimum value given in response was one post-16 qualification with a maximum of five. Therefore classes of 1, 2, 3, 4 and 5 post-16 qualifications may be used for the table. A quick count or tally table (see Figure 2.1 for an example) gives a frequency for each of the classes. Table 2.3 shows the resulting table for the data on post-16 qualifications.

Table 2.3 Number of distinct post-16 qualifications held by students on BA Ceramics

Number of post-16 qualifications	Frequency
1	10
2	10
3	11
4	3
5	2
Total	**36**

Source: Student questionnaire

Accommodation

Again, these are *nominal* data which can be classified by the four common responses given – Halls of Residence, Rented Flat/House, Own or Parents' Home, Lodgings, and the two unusual observations of YWCA and Caravan can be put into an Other category. See Table 2.4.

Table 2.4 Present accommodation of BA Ceramics students

Accommodation	Frequency
Halls of Residence	10
Rented House/Flat	11
Own/Parents' Home	5
Lodgings	8
Other	2
Total	**36**

Source: Student questionnaire

Monthly rent

This is classified as *continuous*, even though the values have been given to the nearest £. This is because it would be possible to convert the data to (say) daily rent which would be an amount with a number of decimal places. Data of this type is perhaps the most difficult to summarize as it is more wide ranging. To help, the data are usually gathered together into groups. (However, it should be noted that by collecting values into groups the accuracy of the individual observations will be lost.)

Unless the classification into groups is self-evident, an attempt to have around 10 groups means a group interval width of about

$$(\text{maximum value} - \text{minimum value}) / 10$$

As the monthly rent data ranges from 100 to 162, to give around 10 groups the interval width would be $(162 - 100)/10 = 6.2$ which for convenience is rounded to 10.

So the interval starting points will be 100, 110, 120 etc.

To ensure the intervals are mutually exclusive, these intervals are taken as '100 to less than 110', this means values of 100 up to and *not* including 110 are placed in this interval.

Having decided on the intervals, the observations are taken one by one and **tally** marks used to count the number of values in each interval (e.g., using a 'five bar gate' system). The result would be as shown in Figure 2.1, which gives Table 2.5 overleaf.

Monthly rent (£) (continuous classes)	Tally 'five bar gate'
100 to less than 110	I
110 to less than 120	IIII
120 to less than 130	JHT II
130 to less than 140	JHT JHT III
140 to less than 150	JHT II
150 to less than 160	III
160 or more	I

Figure 2.1 Tabulation of grouped data via five bar gate

Age of the students

Age is a funny variable which can be classified in a number of ways, depending on personal viewpoint. Some people consider it to be *ordinal* data as the numbers can act as ranks, some feel it is *continuous* as it can be measured down to

Table 2.5 Monthly rent paid by students on BA Ceramics

Monthly rent (£)	Frequency
100 to less than 110	1
110 to less than 120	4
120 to less than 130	7
130 to less than 140	13
140 to less than 150	7
150 to less than 160	3
160 or more	1
Total	**36**

Source: Student questionnaire

seconds, others say it is discrete as it is usually stated as a whole number of years. All of these have become generally acceptable as long as they are justified. However, technically the data are in fact *continuous* as we can measure our age in years, months, days, hours and so on.

When deciding on the classes for these data it is necessary to consider what the expected responses would be. Most undergraduate students are between 18 and 21 years old, so classes for each of these ages, i.e., 18, 19, 20 and 21 are appropriate. In order to account for the continuous nature of the data these classes become 18 to less than 19, 19 to less than 20 and so on.

Note that these categories do not cover anyone under 18 or over 21. No students under 18 are expected, so this category can be viably excluded, but there is a chance of having mature (over 21) students. As the number of these are small and ages more wide ranging an open-ended 22 or above category is included to ensure all responses are covered. A quick count or, if preferred, a five bar gate system can then be used to find the frequency for each category with the result being Table 2.6.

Table 2.6 Age of students on BA Ceramics

Age	Frequency
18 to less than 19	16
19 to less than 20	7
20 to less than 21	7
21 to less than 22	3
22 or above	3
Total	**36**

Source: Student questionnaire

2.2 Cross-tabulation of two or more data variables

There are many occasions when it is useful to construct tables that summarize more than one variable at the same time.

For example, Table 2.7 shows a cross-tabulation of the age and gender of students. (The table also shows sub-totals for the numbers in each age category and number of each gender.)

Table 2.7 Age and gender of students on BA Ceramics

Age	Number of students		
	Male	**Female**	**Total**
18 to less than 19	7	9	16
19 to less than 20	2	5	7
20 to less than 21	3	4	7
21 to less than 22	1	2	3
22 or above	2	1	3
Total	**15**	**21**	**36**

Source: Student questionnaire

This method could be extended so that more categories are cross-tabulated (refer to page 10 for an example of three-way cross-tabulation, showing a data breakdown by age, social class and sex). However, there comes a point with cross-tabulation when increasing the amount of information included in the table makes it so complicated that it becomes difficult to understand. It is then beneficial to use several smaller tables.

REVIEW ACTIVITY 1

(a) Thirty students agreed to record how long they spent revising for a statistics exam. The times taken in hours were:

15, 12, 13, 21, 18, 11, 4, 16, 12, 15, 9, 15, 18, 14, 15
9, 6, 12, 11, 12, 19, 13, 13, 11, 16, 13, 10, 9, 20, 18

Construct a frequency distribution from these data.

(b) Using the questionnaire responses from the BA Ceramics course, cross-tabulate the data relating to gender and number of post-16 qualifications held.

Working:

Answers on page 217.

2.3 Graphical presentation of data

As well as using tables to summarize a set of data, graphs provide a useful alternative visual impact.

When constructing any type of graph it is important to ensure that (as with tables) the graph is given an appropriate title, each of the axes should be labelled, and a sensible scale used. This is so that a graph is meaningful and easily understood if no data accompanies it.

In this chapter the more common forms of graphical representation used will be considered. This will be done initially by considering a single data set and matching the most appropriate graph with data types (ie, nominal, ordinal, discrete, continuous).

Bar/column chart

This is the most commonly used type of graphical representation. Each category is represented by a distinct rectangular bar where frequency is shown by the length/height of the bar.

This graph can be used for all data types excluding *continuous* data and *ordinal* data which is in the form of a time series.

Figure 2.2 uses a bar chart to present the information on the gender of students (from Table 2.7).

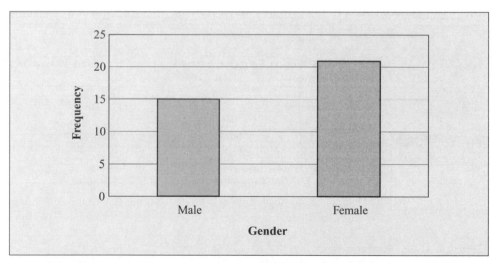

Figure 2.2 Illustration of bar/column chart, showing gender of students on BA Ceramics course
Source: Student questionnaire

Pie chart

Here the total data set is represented by a circle and each category is represented by a part of that circle (i.e., a 'slice' of the pie). Frequency is represented by the angle, where 360° represents the total data.

In a similar way to a bar/column chart the pie chart can be used for most data types. However, as a pie chart is used to show what proportion of the whole is taken up by a category, it is only useful if the number of categories is small and each is a significant proportion of the total data. It is also possible to emphasize a particular category by 'cutting away the slice' from the main chart.

In the case of the student survey this feature could be used to emphasize the respondents with five post-16 qualifications, as shown in Figure 2.3.

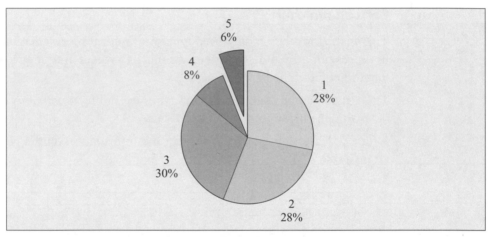

Figure 2.3 Illustration of pie chart, showing number of post-16 qualifications held by BA Ceramics students

<table>
<tr><td>REVIEW
ACTIVITY 2</td><td>Name the graph which could be used to illustrate the proportion of students in the survey living in each type of accommodation.

Working:

Answer on page 217.</td></tr>
</table>

The histogram

The histogram is used to give the equivalent of a bar chart for *continuous* data that has been grouped into a frequency distribution table, i.e., it provides a comparative representation of the data.

It should be noted that there are many situations where histograms are inaccurately represented and few computer packages have the ability to represent them accurately. Take great care when histograms are referred to; often it is in fact a bar chart that has been used.

Although a histogram looks very similar to a bar chart, there are two main differences:

1. The axis across the bottom (the *x*-axis) has a continuous scale and the blocks are joined together.

2. Most importantly, the *area* of each block represents the frequency.

   If the class intervals for the data are all the same width this doesn't present any problems and the height of a block is equal to the frequency. However, *where class widths are unequal*, constructing a histogram is achieved by making the height of the block equal to a measurement known as frequency density where:

   frequency density = frequency divided by width of category

The construction of a histogram under both of these circumstances is illustrated in the next two examples.

EXAMPLE 2.1

Rowell Graphics is a small business enterprise employing 25 permanent graphic artists. The company operates on a flexible working hours basis. Under this system, each month an employee can carry up to 10 hours credit or four hours debit through to the next working month. Table 2.8 summarizes the number of hours carried forward into the month of January this year.

Table 2.8 Hours of credit for Rowell Graphics' employees

Hours of credit carried forward	Number of employees
−4 to less than −2	2
−2 to less than 0	3
0 to less than 2	5
2 to less than 4	8
4 to less than 6	4
6 to less than 8	2
8 to less than 10	1
Total	**25**

Note: Debit shown as negative amount of credit
Source: Flexible time records

In this case all of the categories cover the same time band of two hours. Therefore when constructing the histogram, the frequency (i.e., number of employees) for each group may be used to represent the height of a single block (remembering that given the data is continuous the blocks are joined together across the *x*-axis representing time).

The resulting histogram is shown in Figure 2.4.

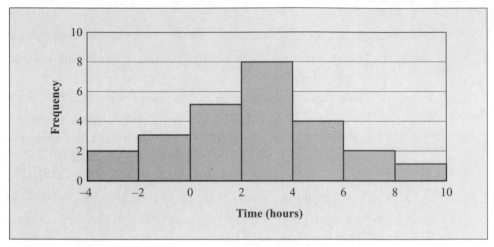

Figure 2.4 Histogram with groups of equal width, showing flexible working hours carried forward from January by Rowell Graphics' staff
Source: Flexible time records

EXAMPLE 2.2

Rowell Graphics also employs around 50 home workers on a casual basis during particularly busy periods. These artists are paid on an hourly basis with payment being made retrospectively at the end of each month. Table 2.9 summarizes the number of hours submitted by these workers at the end of January this year. Illustrate this data on a histogram.

Upon examining the table it can be seen that the number of hours covered by the first two categories in the table differ both from each other and from the following four categories. Also, the final category has been left open-ended.

As the width of the categories is uneven, the calculation of frequency density to represent the height of each block is required. As this calculation is made by dividing the frequency by the width of the categories, finding the value for the last open-ended category is not possible at present.

Table 2.9 Hours claimed by Rowell Graphics' home workers

Hours claimed	Number of employees
Less than 30	3
30 to less than 50	5
50 to less than 75	8
75 to less than 100	10
100 to less than 125	15
125 to less than 150	7
150 or over	2
Total	**50**

Source: Company records

It is quite common for data to be presented in this way and there are no hard and fast rules about the way in which it is dealt with. Within this text, it is recommended that the width of an open-ended category should be twice that of the most common category used to summarize the data.

Therefore, for this example the width of the last category will be 50 giving an end point of 200 hours. Table 2.10 illustrates the calculations required for finding the frequency density.

Table 2.10 Finding the frequency density

Hours claimed	Number of employees	Class width	Frequency density
Less than 30	3	30	$^3/_{30} = 0.1$
30 to less than 50	5	20	$^5/_{20} = 0.25$
50 to less than 75	8	25	$^8/_{25} = 0.32$
75 to less than 100	10	25	$^{10}/_{25} = 0.4$
100 to less than 125	15	25	$^{15}/_{25} = 0.6$
125 to less than 150	7	25	$^7/_{25} = 0.28$
150 to less than 200	2	50	$^2/_{50} = 0.04$

The histogram is then constructed by plotting the hours claimed on the *x*-axis with the values of frequency density being plotted on the *y*-axis (Figure 2.5).

Example 2.2
continued

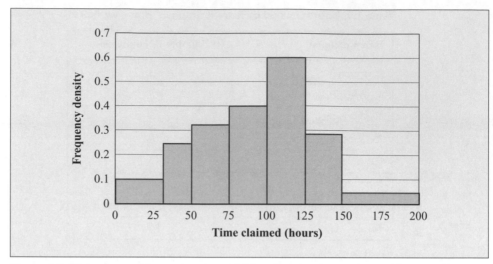

Figure 2.5 Histogram with uneven class widths, showing hours claimed by Rowell Graphics' casual workers in January
Source: Company records

REVIEW ACTIVITY 3

Illustrate the data given in Table 2.11 on a histogram

Table 2.11 Monthly rent paid by students on BA Ceramics course

Monthly rent (£)	Frequency (f)
100 to less than 110	1
110 to less than 120	4
120 to less than 130	7
130 to less than 140	13
140 to less than 150	7
150 to less than 160	3
160 or more	1

Source: Student questionnaire

Working:

Answers on pages 217–8.

The cumulative frequency graph

The cumulative frequency graph, or ogive, is another graph which is used in particular with *continuous* data. The graph gives a proportional representation of the data and its main use is for finding statistical measures such as the median and inter-quartile range, the calculation of which will be discussed in Chapter 3.

In order to construct a cumulative frequency graph it is often necessary to change the way in which the data have been tabulated. This is in order to calculate cumulative frequencies (i.e., the total number of observations which are less than a stated observation). These cumulative frequency values become the data points on the y-axis. This is explained in Example 2.3.

EXAMPLE 2.3

Construct an ogive for the student monthly rent data shown in Table 2.11 in Review activity 3 above.

Two additional columns are added, resulting in Table 2.12. These last two columns of data are plotted on the horizontal (x) and vertical (y) axes respectively, then joined together with straight lines or curves to produce the ogive. This is shown in Figure 2.6.

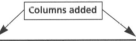
Columns added

Table 2.12 **Expanding on the data in Table 2.11**

Monthly rent (£)	Frequency(f)	Monthly rent less than	Cumulative frequency
	–	100	0
100 to less than 110	1	110	1
110 to less than 120	4	120	5
120 to less than 130	7	130	12
130 to less than 140	13	140	25
140 to less than 150	7	150	32
150 to less than 160	3	160	35
160 or more	1	180*	36

Note: *Remember, for an open-ended category it is usual to choose an appropriate end point. Here the last category has been made twice the width of the others.

Example 2.3
continued

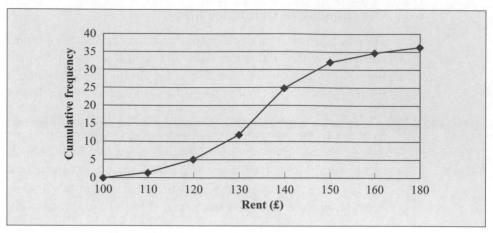

Figure 2.6 Ogive, showing students' monthly rent
Source: Student questionnaire

Figure 2.7 demonstrates how the ogive can be used to make various estimations about the distribution, such as how many students pay less than £125 per month. This would be done by drawing a line from £125 on the *x*-axis to meet the curve. From that point another line would be drawn across to the *y*-axis and the appropriate reading taken. In this case, the estimate is that 8 of the 36 students pay less than £125 per month.

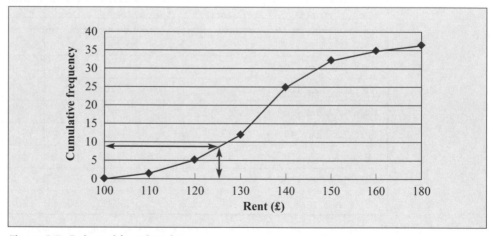

Figure 2.7 Ogive with estimation
Source: Student questionnaire

The line graph

Again this is a graph which is normally used for one specific purpose i.e., presenting time series data. It simply consists of the time variable plotted on the horizontal (*x*) axis and the second variable (be it sales, profits, production costs etc.) plotted on the vertical (*y*) axis. Each individual point is represented by a cross or a dot, and each of these points is joined to the next by a straight line. So, for example, if the average monthly rent paid by students had been collected over a 10 year period then a line graph would be the most appropriate presentation choice.

Figure 2.8 shows such a line graph. Note that even though a data table has not been provided, information from the graph should be easily attainable.

For example, what was the average monthly rent paid by the BA Ceramics students in 1992? (*Answer: £120*)

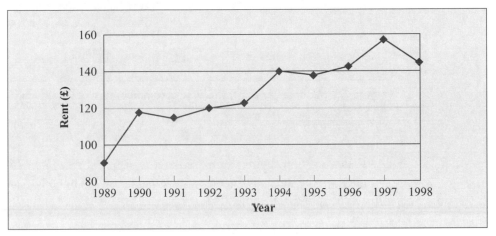

Figure 2.8 Line graph, showing average student rent
Source: BA Ceramics student records

For line graphs, if two or more separate sets of data are being shown then different patterns, colours and point indicators can be used to distinguish between them and an accompanying key or legend given. This naturally leads us on to looking at the other alternatives that are available for displaying more than one set of data.

For nominal and discrete data, there are two alternatives which are based on the bar/column chart, and, for continuous data, a graph known as a frequency polygon is used.

Multiple (or component) bar chart

A multiple bar chart is used when a comparison of the *distribution* of two or more data groups is needed. On many occasions the total number of observations in each of the groups will differ, therefore the frequencies cannot be compared directly. If this is required, percentage frequencies are calculated and the resulting figures are plotted on the graph.

Figure 2.9 is a multiple bar chart which has been used to show data on the accommodation and gender of the students on the BA Ceramics course.

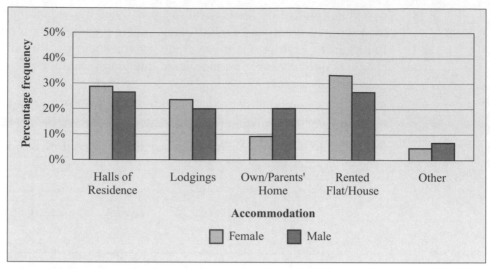

Figure 2.9 Multiple bar chart, showing accommodation of BA Ceramics students by gender
Source: Student questionnaire

As the two groups being compared are of different sizes i.e., 15 males versus 21 females, percentage frequencies have been used. The calculations required for this are displayed in Table 2.13.

Table 2.13 Accommodation of BA Ceramics students showing percentage frequencies

Accommodation	Male	Male % frequency	Female	Female % frequency
Halls of Residence	4	$\frac{4}{15} * 100 = 27$	6	$\frac{6}{21} * 100 = 29$
Lodgings	3	20	5	24
Own/Parents' Home	3	20	2	10
Rented Flat/House	4	27	7	33
Other	1	7	1	5
Total	**15**	**101%***	**21**	**101%***

Note: Percentage frequencies do not equal 100 owing to rounding errors.
Source: Student questionnaire

Stacked (compound) bar chart

In a similar way to pie charts for a single data set, a stacked bar chart is used to illustrate proportional representation within a data set. Stacked bar charts are most effective when there are a small number of subdivisions (two or three) within a category. In those cases where the comparison is between a number of subdivisions, a simple line graph or multiple bar chart is more appropriate.

Therefore for the data cross-tabulating accommodation by gender, both forms of representation are equally valid. However, the stacked bar chart has the slight advantage of not requiring the calculation of percentage frequencies. A stacked bar chart of this data can be seen in Figure 2.10.

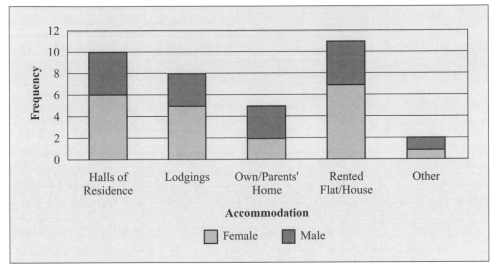

Figure 2.10 Stacked bar chart, showing accommodation of BA Ceramics students by gender
Source: Student questionnaire

The frequency polygon

As a histogram uses a continuous scale along the x-axis, it is not possible to draw two histograms on the same graph because they would be superimposed on one another. Therefore, to compare the distribution of two or more groups of continuous data, a frequency polygon (similar to a line graph) is used.

From the BA Ceramics questionnaire data a frequency polygon would be required to compare the distribution of age within each gender. See Table 2.14.

Table 2.14 Age and gender of students on BA Ceramics

Age	Number of students		
	Male	**Female**	**Total**
18 to less than 19	7	9	16
19 to less than 20	2	5	7
20 to less than 21	3	4	7
21 to less than 22	1	2	3
22 or above	2	1	3
Total	**15**	**21**	**36**

Source: Student questionnaire

The two groups of students are of different sizes (Male: 15, Female: 21) so, in order to carry out a direct comparison, it is necessary to first calculate percentage frequencies, as in Table 2.15.

Table 2.15 Age of students on BA Ceramics, showing percentage frequencies

Age	Male % frequency	Female % frequency
18 to less than 19	$7/_{15} * 100 = 47$	$9/_{21} * 100 = 43$
19 to less than 20	13	24
20 to less than 21	20	19
21 to less than 22	7	10
22 or above	13	5

These percentage frequencies are then plotted against the class mid-points to produce the frequency polygon diagram – see Figure 2.11.

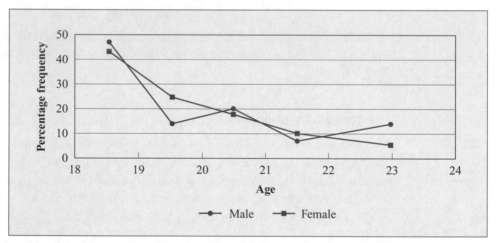

Figure 2.11 Frequency polygon, comparing age and gender of BA Ceramics
Source: Student questionnaire

To account for the open-ended final category (22 or more) an end point of 24 has been selected.

In this chapter, only the most common ways in which data can be presented have been covered. One only needs to look through a newspaper, watch the news on television, or look at publications such as *Social Trends*, to see the wide variety available.

REVIEW ACTIVITY 4

Construct an appropriate graph of the table produced in Review activity 1(b) (Table S.2.2.) page 217.

Working:

Answers on page 219.

Key points to remember

Tables

1. Categories must be comprehensive and mutually exclusive.

2. Aim to use between five and 10 classes/categories.

3. The word 'frequency' is used to represent the number of responses in each category.

4. All tables must be given a clear explanatory title plus row/column headings.

5. Remember to include a source (particularly if secondary data have been used).

Graphs

6. As with tables, ensure graphs have an appropriate title and label the axes.

7. Graphs should be compatible with their data type:

   (a) bar/column chart – suitable for all excluding continuous and time series data;

   (b) pie chart – as above, good to emphasize proportions;

   (c) histogram – for a single set of continuous data;

   (d) ogive – continuous data;

   (e) line graph – time series data.

8. For uneven continuous categories use frequency density when constructing a histogram.

9. Using spreadsheets to construct tables and graphs is not as easy as it seems. Think ahead!

ADDITIONAL EXERCISES

Question 1   The local authority have commissioned a study to examine the distances which car drivers travel to the city centre as part of a feasibility study into a proposed park and ride scheme. A batch of 50 results (distances in miles) is given below.

15	21	8	3	7	9	2	3	20	15
9	9	11	14	19	2	3	6	9	17
17	6	8	2	5	9	32	5	23	40
18	19	8	8	22	7	8	4	8	3
23	12	4	9	10	8	3	6	13	2

Construct a frequency distribution from these data, using eight class intervals of equal width.

Question 2   In 1985 there were 219,000 people unemployed in the north of England, 280,000 in Yorkshire, 729,000 in the south-east and 191,000 in the south-west. In 1990 the corresponding figures were 123,000 in the north, 161,000 in Yorkshire, 372,000 in the south-east and 97,000 in the south-west. By mid-1993 the figures were 170,000 unemployed in the north, 244,000 in Yorkshire, 928,000 in the south-east and 217,000 in the south-west. Tabulate these data and draw a graph to illustrate them. Comment briefly on your results. What might be the problems with comparing these sorts of figures in this way? (*Adapted from Regional Trends*)

Table 2.16 Population estimates in mid-1997

Region	Population (millions)	
	Male	**Female**
United Kingdom	29.0	30.0
Great Britain	28.2	29.2
England	24.3	25.0
Wales	1.4	1.5

Adapted from Office of National Statistics

Question 3   Using the data shown in Table 2.16:

(a) Draw an appropriate graph to compare the *number* of males in England, Northern Ireland, Scotland and Wales.

(b) Draw an appropriate graph to compare the *percentage* of females in England, Northern Ireland, Scotland and Wales.

Question 4   The following figures relate to visitor numbers at a local museum:

Year	1991	1992	1993	1994	1995	1996	1997
Visitors (10,000's)	34.5	33.6	39.9	40.7	40.6	46.5	57.8

Draw a suitable graph to represent these data and comment on any distinguishing features of the graph.

Question 5   Table 2.17 shows the results of a random sample of 100 daily expense claims made by a firm's executives.

Table 2.17 Expenses claims made by a firm's executives

Amount of claim (£)	Frequency
Under £15.00	12
£15.00 to under £17.50	23
£17.50 to under £20.00	26
£20.00 to under £22.50	18
£22.50 to under £25.00	13
£25.00 to under £30.00	8

(a) Draw a histogram to represent these data.

(b) Construct a cumulative frequency diagram (ogive) and use it to estimate the percentage of claims which were above £21.00.

Question 6   Table 2.18 shows GCSE performance by region in 1995/96. Portray these data on a suitable graph which clearly compares the male and female sub-totals for each region.

Table 2.18 GCSE performance by region

Region	Male: five or more A*–C grades	Female: five or more A*–C grades
North-east	33.6	42.7
North-west and Merseyside	38.8	48.2
Yorkshire and the Humber	34.7	43.4
East Midlands	38.3	47.5
West Midlands	37.2	46.3
Eastern	42.7	53.1
London	38.2	47.4
South-east	45.6	55.5
South-west	44.6	55.3

Measure: Percentage of pupils by examination achievement
Adapted from Department for Education and Employment

SPREADSHEET EXERCISE

The construction of both tables and graphs is one of the most common features used within Excel. In both cases, there is a tool known as a wizard which attempts to simplify the process by breaking it down into a number of steps. Unfortunately this is not a very instinctive process for most users. What follows is a relatively detailed worked example which illustrates the process. This is followed by an exercise to attempt for yourself.

Worked example

A utility company operates a workers' share scheme. Each year employees are allowed to apply for shares in the company. The data shown in Figure 2.12 relates to 20 of these employees.

	A	B	C	D	E
	Staff grade	Years with Company	Shares Owned	Additional shares requested	
1	Retail	3	70	0	
2	Operational	10	135	250	
3	Retail	4	122	1250	
4	Management	20	122	750	
5	Operational	12	126	1250	
6	Operational	15	104	1250	
7	Operational	9	111	1500	
8	Operational	27	202	250	
9	Retail	23	154	0	
10	Retail	9	128	500	
11	Operational	19	142	1000	
12	Management	15	113	1500	
13	Retail	12	116	0	
14	Operational	23	142	1250	
15	Management	20	173	1500	
16	Operational	23	163	750	
17	Operational	16	120	1000	
18	Retail	23	178	1000	
19	Retail	2	114	500	
20	Retail	7	115	1250	

Figure 2.12 Demo data for spreadsheet exercise

Column A is the employee's staff grade; column B indicates the time the employee has been with the company; column C shows the number of shares already owned by the employee; and column D indicates the number of additional shares applied for this year. What follows will illustrate how tables and graphs, similar to those described above, are constructed in Excel.

Table to show the number of each staff from each grade plus associated pie chart.

Table: For the majority of summary tables it is possible to make use of one of Excel's tools known as the PivotTable Wizard. This is selected by clicking on the PivotTable icon ⊞ or selecting Data, PivotTable Report from the menu. This will display a wizard window consisting of four easy steps, the first of which is to simply state that your data comes in the form of an Excel data list (top option). Clicking on the next button to continue, the second step requires all the data (including column headings) to be highlighted. The third step will then present you with a table layout similar to the one shown in Figure 2.13.

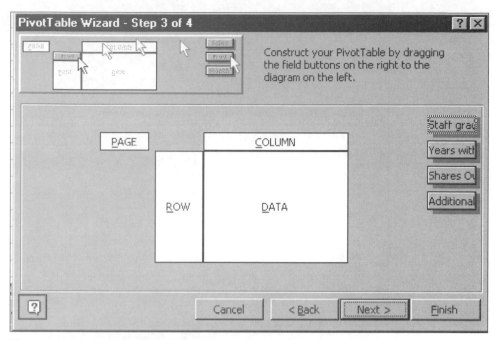

Figure 2.13 **Spreadsheet demo: step 3 of PivotTable**

The main section of this window consists of a blank table layout. To the right-hand side there are four buttons showing each of the column headings in the selected list. A table is constructed by dragging the required fields into position. In this case the Staff grade heading was dragged into both the Row and Data section. Moving on to the final step, a blank portion of the spreadsheet where the resulting table will be deposited is required. For this example the resulting table is shown in Figure 2.14.

Graph: Graphs, in a similar way to tables, are constructed by following a number of steps within a chart wizard, using the Graph icon ▦. Alternatively, Insert, Graph may be selected from the menu. The first of the chart wizard steps is to choose, by clicking, the type of graph required from the list supplied to the left of the window and the preferred layout shown to the right. For this example a 3D pie chart was picked. The next step requires the selection of the data to be graphed. This requires careful thought on the part of the user, for this example just the staff grading labels and frequencies (not total) are required – as shown in Figure 2.15 (the selected data being surrounded by a dotted line).

As an aid, a sample graph is shown within the wizard window.

The opportunity to add an appropriate title and (if required) labels to the graph forms the third step. Finally, the choice of either superimposing the graph onto the existing worksheet or creating a new worksheet for the chart is given. For this example the former option was selected and Figure 2.16 illustrates the result.

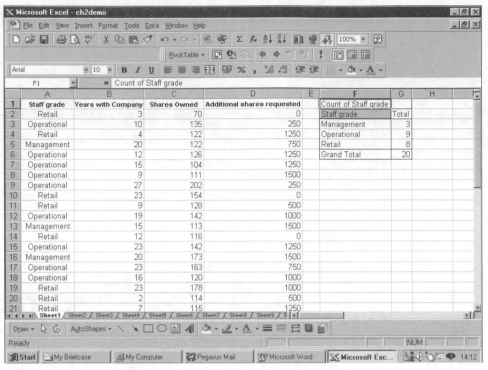

Figure 2.14 Resulting table

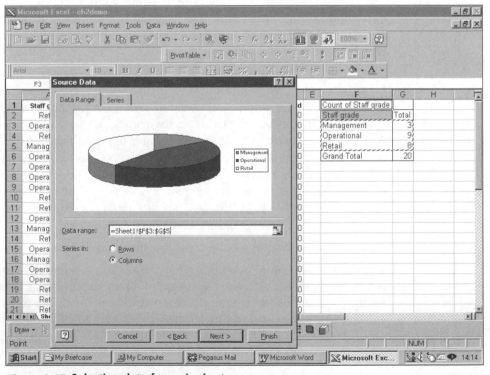

Figure 2.15 Selecting data for a pie chart

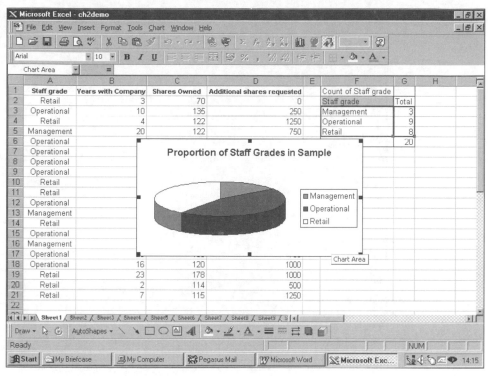

Figure 2.16 Finished pie chart

Summary table and graph for number of years an employee has been with the company

Table: If the data covers a wide range of differing values, as in the number of years an employee has been with the company, the method described in the previous section would produce a table with too many categories (one for each of the possibilities). In this case it is better to preset the categories and use a function called Frequency to count the number of responses within the required range. To start with, the number and widths of the categories must be decided. To help with this decision, it is useful to know the minimum

Excel function: =MIN(data range)

and maximum

Excel function: =MAX(data range)

values. The minimum for this data was found to be 2 with a maximum of 27 (see Figure 2.17). Based on this information it was decided to construct categories covering five years. These categories (remembering time is a continuous variable) are then typed across three columns of the spreadsheet. Three columns have been used as a spreadsheet cannot distinguish between text and numbers within one cell. Again, this is illustrated in Figure 2.17. To use the Frequency command, first (and importantly) the blank cells to the right of the table layout – see Figure 2.18 – are highlighted. Then the first part of the function is typed i.e., =FREQUENCY(

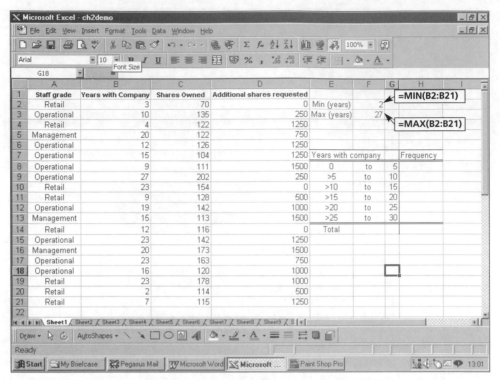

Figure 2.17 Set-up for using Frequency command

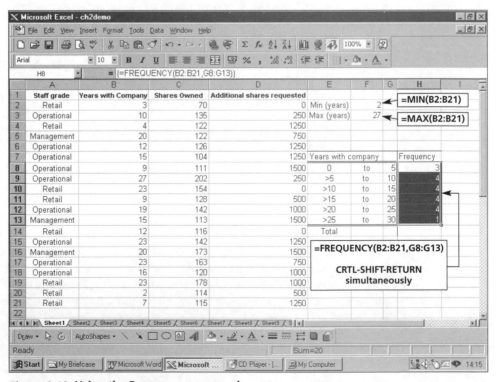

Figure 2.18 Using the Frequency command

Next, using the mouse and excluding the column heading, the original data (for Figure 2.18 cells B2 to B21 relating to age) are highlighted. This is followed by a comma, and the numbers which make up the upper limits of the categories (in Figure 2.18 this would be G8 to G13) are highlighted. The final and most vital stage is to finish off the function by typing in a closing parenthesis and pressing simultaneously the Ctrl, Shift and Return buttons.

(*Note*: Many students encounter various types of difficulties when first attempting this procedure. In instances of error delete the Frequency area and start again. For further instruction, consult specialist Excel texts.)

Graph: The number of years an employee has been with the company is an example of continuous data. The graph required to illustrate this data is a histogram. As already stated in the main text spreadsheets are unable accurately to construct a histogram (even though they claim they can). However, with a little extra calculation it is possible to construct another graph associated with continuous data i.e., a cumulative frequency diagram.

Before using the chart wizard, the cumulative frequencies need to be added to the frequency table created. The formulae involved in this are shown in Figure 2.19.

To construct a cumulative frequency graph (ogive) through the chart wizard, at the first stage the *X-Y* scatter diagram joined by lines is selected. At the second stage, care must again be taken to think exactly what data will make up the graph. These data are then selected. For an ogive the *x*-axis values are the upper limits of the group classifications with the *y*-axis values being the cumulative frequencies (i.e., in Figure 2.19 the ranges G8:G13 and I8:I13 respectively).

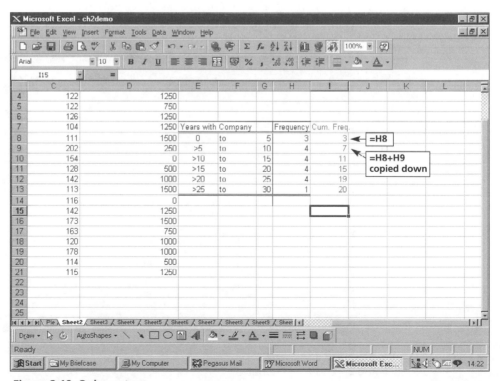

Figure 2.19 Ogive set-up

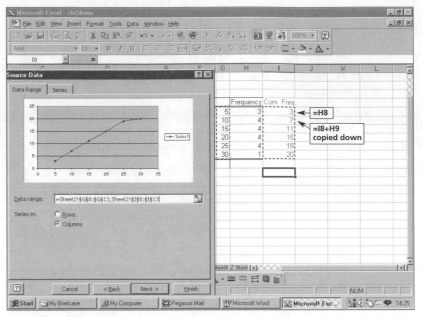

Figure 2.20 Ogive data selection

To select data for two non-adjoining columns (as in this case) – the first set of data (to go along the *x*-axis) is highlighted, the Ctrl key is then pressed and then the *y*-axis data is selected with this key held down. Once again a sample graph is displayed as an aid (Figure 2.20). At the next stage titles and labels are added; the completed graph is illustrated in Figure 2.21.

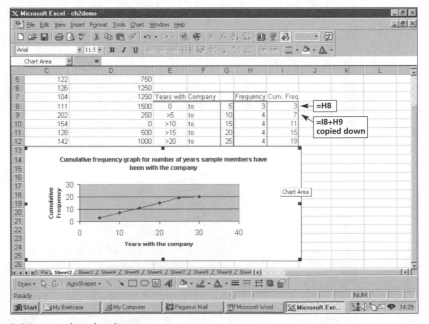

Figure 2.21 Completed ogive

Cross-tabulation of staff grade and value of shares applied for

Table: For the majority of cross-tabulations the PivotTable Report feature is used as described on pages 44–5. For cross-tabulation, the variables are set down into the Row, Column and Data sections as required (see Figure 2.22). Figure 2.23 shows the resultant table.

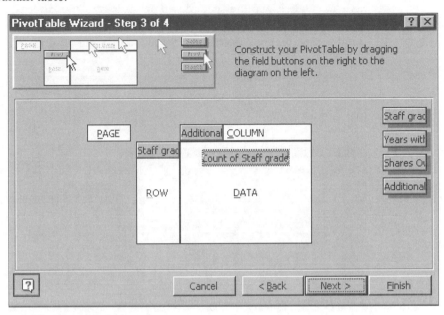

Figure 2.22 Cross-tabulation

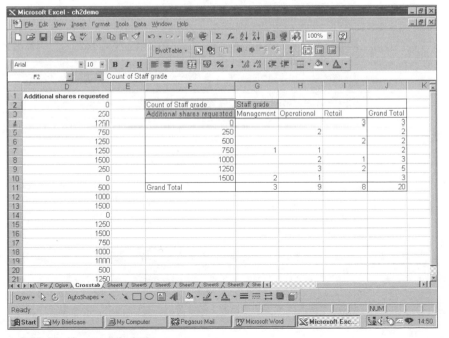

Figure 2.23 Final cross-tabulation

Graph: As these data contain a mixture of *discrete* – additional shares applied for – and *nominal* – staff grade – data a multiple bar chart would be an appropriate representation. Using the chart wizard this selection is made in the first step. For the second step the data needs to be selected in a slightly different manner than before. Two different sets of data are to be represented by titles – one will be used as *x*-axis labels and the second will act as a key. The latter is selected first with the data to be plotted; for this example this was the counts plus the three different staff grades. See Figure 2.24 (data surrounded by a dotted line).

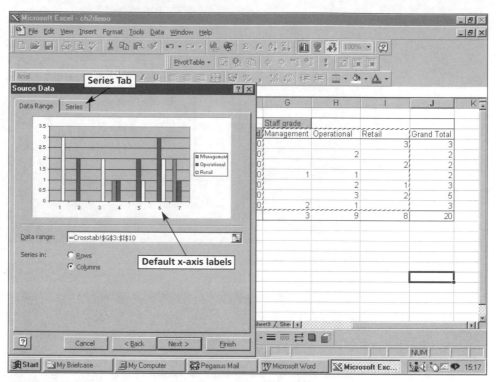

Figure 2.24 Constructing a multiple bar chart: stage one

Within the Chart Wizard window to the left of Figure 2.24 it can be seen that by default numbered categories (1–7) are given to the *x*-axis labels. These are generally meaningless and require replacement. This is achieved by clicking on the tab in the existing window named Series. At the bottom of the window in Figure 2.25 is a box where the replacement *x*-axis labels (in this case, the additional share amounts) can be selected.

On the next step, title and axis labels are added as usual with Figure 2.26 illustrating the final graph.

For further information on how graphs and tables can be enhanced and amended consult either Excel's Help facility or textbooks dealing solely with Excel.

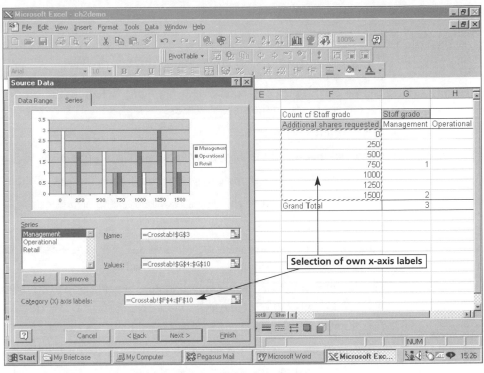

Figure 2.25 Defining *x*-axis labels for multiple bar chart

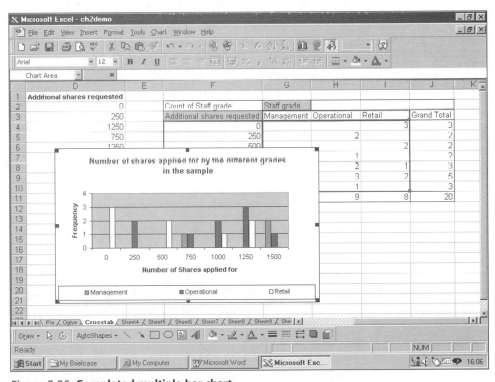

Figure 2.26 Completed multiple bar chart

Now attempt to put these techniques into practice.

Exercise

The owners of a large department store in the UK have authorized their marketing department to make a study of their customers who have been issued with a store charge card. Forty customers were randomly selected and the following variables were recorded from the store's records:

- age of the customer;
- annual income of the customer (in thousands of pounds);
- number of purchases made by the customer over the last 12 months;
- number of other store charge cards owned by the customer;
- sex of the customer.

This information is stored in the form of an Excel file STORE.XLS. The variables above are stored in columns A to E respectively.

For the following construct an appropriate table and graph (if possible) to summarize the data provided in STORE.XLS:

(a) Number of additional store cards owned by the customer.

(b) Age of the customer (using six categories of equal width).

(c) Annual income for male and female customers using the following categories: less than £15,000; £15,000 up to £25,000; £25,000 up to £35,000; £35,000 up to £45,000; £45,000 up to £65,000. (Construct a cumulative frequency graph for the male data.)

(d) Proportion of male and female customers in the sample.

(e) Number of storecards owned cross-tabulated by gender.

CHAPTER 3

Summarizing data

LEARNING OBJECTIVES

- To consider a number of statistical measures which provide a measure of the central tendency of a set of data;
- To consider a number of statistical measures which provide a measure of the spread of a data set;
- To suggest when the application of each of the measures is appropriate.

Introduction

Measures of central tendency (or average) refer to values of a variable that are typical or representative of a data set, i.e., they are a value around which a large proportion of other values are centred.

It is also important to know how the data are spread or how varied the observations are and the statistics used to do this are often called measures of dispersion. Both types of statistic will be examined in this chapter.

The three main measures of central tendency are:

- the mode (the most popular observation);
- the median (the middle observation);
- the mean (generally referred to as the average).

There are several different methods of measuring variation, the most commonly used being:

- the range (measure of the extremes of a data set);
- the inter-quartile range (measure of the middle 50% of a data set);
- the variance/standard deviation (measure of average distance of an observation from the mean).

The calculation of each of these measures will be looked at in turn. The method of calculation depends on the format of the data (i.e., whether it is raw or tabulated) and the different approaches will be explained by example.

3.1 Measures of central tendency: the mode

The mode is defined as the most frequently occurring value (or values) in a data set.

EXAMPLE 3.1: Raw data

Find the mode for the following salaries:

£6000   £10,000   £8000   £12,000   £8000

Mode = £8000, since it occurs more often than any other value.

When discrete data have been presented in a table then the mode is the value which has the highest frequency.

EXAMPLE 3.2: tabulated data

The table below shows the number of times students have been absent from lectures in a particular week. Find the mode.

Missed lectures in a week	Number of times (Frequency)	
0	8	
1	10	
2	12	(highest)
3	6	

The mode is 2, the number of classes most commonly missed in a given week.

For data which have been grouped together in class intervals it is usual to identify the modal group. If the class intervals are all of equal width, the modal group is simply the class interval which has the highest frequency.

EXAMPLE 3.3: grouped tabulated data (equal width)

The table on page 57 gives the heights of a sample of 60 people. Identify the modal group.

Height (cm)	Frequency
150 to < 160	9
160 to < 170	18
170 to < 180	21
180 to < 190	12

The modal group is 170 to < 180 cm, since this is the group with the largest frequency (and the groups are of equal width).

If unequal groups are used for collecting the data, then it is necessary to carry out the calculation required for the construction of a histogram. The modal group is identified as the class interval with the highest frequency density.

EXAMPLE 3.4: grouped tabulated data (unequal width)

The table below shows the number of weeks that business properties were on the market before being sold. Identify the modal group.

Number of weeks	Frequency
0 up to 10	3
10 up to 15	7
15 up to 20	12
20 up to 30	15
30 up to 50	5

Frequency density = Frequency divided by Class width

So the required calculations are:

Number of weeks	Frequency	Class width	Frequency density	
0 up to 10	3	10	$\frac{3}{10} = 0.3$	
10 up to 15	7	5	$\frac{7}{5} = 1.4$	
15 up to 20	12	5	$\frac{12}{5} = 2.4$	← (highest frequency density)
20 up to 30	15	10	$\frac{15}{10} = 1.5$	
30 up to 50	5	20	$\frac{5}{20} = 0.25$	

The modal group is 15 up to 20 weeks, as this group has the largest frequency density.

The mode is not generally regarded as the most efficient measure of central tendency because there are many situations where multiple or no distinct modal values occur, as shown by the examples below.

EXAMPLE 3.5

Find the mode for the following salaries:

£6000   £10,000   £8000   £10,000   £8000

There are two modes in this case: £8000 and £10,000.

EXAMPLE 3.6

Find the mode for the following salaries:

£6000   £10,000   £8000   £12,000   £9000

No distinct mode exists – all of the values are different.

3.2 Measures of central tendency: the median

This is the middle value, when the values have been placed in order. In other words, the median is that value which divides a data set into two equal parts. In general

$$\textbf{Median} = \frac{(\textbf{\textit{n}}+1)}{2} \textbf{ th ordered value}$$

If there are an even number of values, then the median is located in the centre of the middle two ordered observations.

EXAMPLE 3.7: raw data

What is the median for the following salaries?

£6000   £10,000   £8000   £12,000   £8000

Ordering the salaries gives:

£6000   £8000   £8000   £10,000   £12,000

The median is the middle $(n+1)/2 = 6/2 = 3$rd ordered value, which is £8000.

EXAMPLE 3.8: tabulated data

The table below shows the number of times students have been absent from lectures in a particular week. Find the median.

Number of times	Frequency	
0	8	← (person 1 to person 8)
1	10	← (person 9 to person 18)
2	12	← (person 19 to person 30)
3	6	← (person 31 to person 36)
Total	**36**	

There are 36 items in the data set and the median would be the number of classes missed by the middle person.

$$\frac{(36+1)}{2} \text{ th} = 18\tfrac{1}{2}\text{th}$$

This is found by calculating the value in between the 18th and 19th people in the data set. The 18th person missed one class and the 19th person missed two classes.

Therefore the median is given as the centre of those two values ie, 1.5 missed classes.

For a continuous or grouped data set the median is generally estimated rather than an exact value calculated. This is achieved by using a cumulative frequency graph (the construction of this was discussed in detail in Chapter 2). Once the graph has been drawn, the y-axis represents the order of the values. A line is drawn from the median's position across to the curve. The line is then dropped down from the curve until it meets the x-axis – this point is the median.

EXAMPLE 3.9: continuous data

The table below shows the cumulative frequency of the heights of a sample of 60 people. By drawing an appropriate graph estimate the value of the median.

Height (cm)	Cumulative frequency
less than 150	0
less than 160	9
less than 170	27
less than 180	48
less than 190	60

The resulting cumulative frequency graph is shown in Figure 3.1. There are 60 people in the group so the median is found at 30.5 on the cumulative frequency axis. (*Note*: as the graph can only provide an estimate, it is quite acceptable to use $^n\!/_2$th observation as the median.)

A horizontal line is drawn from this position on the y-axis across to meet the curve. A vertical line is then drawn from the curve to meet the x-axis. This value is the estimated median.

From Figure 3.1 it can be seen that the median height is 172 cm.

Example 3.9
continued

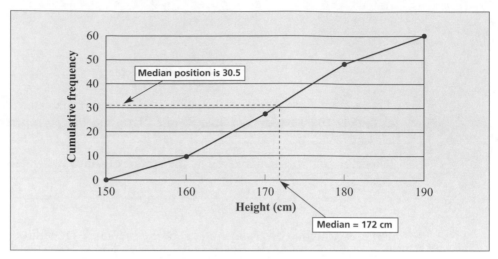

Figure 3.1 Cumulative frequency graph, showing heights of 60 people

3.3 Measures of central tendency: the mean

The (arithmetic) mean is the statistical name for what is commonly called an average and is calculated by simply adding up all possible values in a data set and dividing this by the number of items in the data set. In general this is expressed by the formula:

$$\textbf{Mean} = \frac{\sum x}{n}$$

where: x refers to the individual values within a data set

n represents the number of items in the data set

$\sum$ is a Greek symbol meaning 'sum of'.

It should be noted that this is a truncated form of the notation. In other formats letters and numbers (showing the limits) appear above and below the 'sum of' symbol. Even though these can look confusing they mean the same thing i.e., add all of the values together.

In statistics it is often necessary to deal with data that have originated from either a population or a sample. For certain calculations, knowing whether the mean comes from a population or a sample is vital. Even though the way in which they are calculated is the same, in order to distinguish between them, two separate symbols are used:

● $\bar{x}$ (x bar) indicates that the data have originated from a sample;

● μ (Greek letter mi/mu) indicates that the data have originated from a population.

EXAMPLE 3.10: raw data

Find the mean of the following sample of salaries:

£6000   £10,000   £8000   £12,000   £8000

$$\text{Mean} = \bar{x} = \frac{6000 + 10,000 + 8000 + 12,000 + 8000}{5} = \text{£8800}$$

When data have been presented in a table the formula for calculating the mean is:

$$\textbf{Mean} = \frac{\Sigma fx}{\Sigma f}$$

Here each of the individual values (represented by x) is multiplied by its frequency (f) before adding the resulting values (fx) together. This result is then divided by the number of items in the data set (i.e., the sum of the frequencies, Σf).

EXAMPLE 3.11: tabulated data

Find the mean for the data below, which considers the number of lectures missed by a class of students in a particular week.

Classes missed (x)	Number of students (f)
0	8
1	10
2	12
3	6

In order to find the mean a column of frequency(f) multiplied by the number of classes missed (x) needs to be calculated i.e.,

Classes missed (x)	Number of students (f)	fx
0	8	$8*0 = 0$
1	10	$10*1 = 10$
2	12	$12*2 = 24$
3	6	$6*3 = 18$
	$\Sigma f - 36$	$\Sigma fx = 52$

$$\text{Mean} = \mu = \frac{\Sigma fx}{\Sigma f} = \frac{52}{36} = 1.44 \text{ classes missed}$$

to two decimal places, or d.p

The method used to estimate the mean for continuous or grouped data sets is similar to that above, but only one value to represent the class interval is used. That value is the *interval mid-point*.

EXAMPLE 3.12

Find the mean height for the following sample of 60 people.

Height (cm)	Frequency (*f*)	Mid-point (*x*)	*fx*
150 to < 160	9	155	1395
160 to < 170	18	165	2970
170 to < 180	21	175	3675
180 to < 190	12	185	2220
	$\Sigma f = 60$		$\Sigma fx = 10{,}260$

$$\text{Mean height} = \bar{x} = \frac{\Sigma fx}{\Sigma f} = \frac{10{,}260}{60} = 171 \text{ cm}$$

If the interval mid-point is not obvious it can be found by adding together the lower and upper limits of a class interval and dividing the result by two.

3.4 Choosing the appropriate measure of central tendency for a data set

The mode is the value which occurs most often or the value about which most of the other values are concentrated in a data set; therefore it may be assumed to be typical of the data. However, it may prove to be inappropriate since there may be more than one in a data set (or none). The mode can easily change from one value to another if small samples are involved and is therefore not very consistent.

The median may be considered to give a true middle of the data set. It is not affected by extreme observations within the set. Its disadvantage is that for grouped data it cannot be calculated easily.

Unlike the mode and median, the mean uses every data value equally in its calculation. However, because of this, the mean is influenced by exceptionally high or low values in a data set (since it takes all values into account).

When selecting which summary measure to use for a particular data set the mean (as the most commonly used measure of average) is selected in most cases. The median is preferable if there are extreme values in the data set.

EXAMPLE 3.13

Given the following annual salaries for a sample of five freelance journalists, calculate the mean, median and mode. Which measure of central tendency provides the most suitable summary measure?

£17,000   £18,000   £20,000   £23,000   £65,000

Mode: no distinct modal value exists

Median: middle value i.e., £20,000

Mean: $(17,000 + 18,000 + 20,000 + 23,000 + 65,000)/5 = £28,600$

The extreme value of £65,000 gives a high mean value which is not truly representative of the whole data set. In this case the median provides the more suitable summary measure.

To help in the decision-making process for larger sets of data a histogram, bar chart or frequency polygon (as appropriate to data type) is drawn to illustrate the general distributional shape of the data. If this shape is fairly symmetrical then this indicates there are no extreme measures.

REVIEW ACTIVITY 1

(a) The following table is the frequency distribution table created in Review activity 1, Chapter 2. It shows the revision times of students taking a statistics exam. Use this table to calculate the mean number of hours a sample of 30 students spent revising for the exam.

Time in hours	Frequency
Under 5	1
5 up to 10	4
10 up to 15	13
15 up to 20	10
20 up to 25	2

Source: Student survey

(b) The original data before tabulation were as follows:

15, 12, 13, 21, 18, 11, 4, 16, 12, 15, 9, 15, 18, 14, 15
 9, 6, 12, 11, 12, 19, 13, 13, 11, 16, 13, 10, 9, 20, 18

Using these data, calculate the mean, median and mode.

Compare your two answers for the mean, are they different? If so, offer an explanation as to why.

(c) Which measure do you feel is most appropriate? Why?

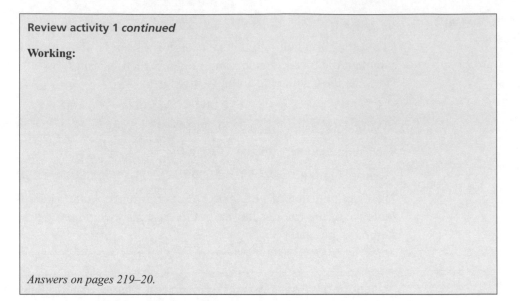

Review activity 1 *continued*

Working:

Answers on pages 219–20.

3.5 Measures of dispersion: the range

This is the easiest measure of spread to find and is given by:

Range = Maximum value – Minimum value

EXAMPLE 3.14: raw data

Find the range for the following sample of salaries:

£6000   £10,000   £9000   £8000

Maximum value = £10,000   Minimum value = £6000

Range = £10,000 – £6000 = £4000

If the data have been grouped together then the range is found as follows:

Range = Upper limit of last group – Lower limit of first group

EXAMPLE 3.15: grouped tabulated data

The table on page 65 shows the number of weeks that business properties were on the market before being sold. Find the range.

Number of weeks	Frequency
0 up to 10	3
10 up to 15	7
15 up to 20	12
20 up to 30	15
30 up to 50	5

Upper limit of last group = 50

Lower limit of first group = 0

Therefore Range = 50 – 0 = 50 weeks

The range is actually a poor measure of dispersion because it only considers extreme values and says nothing about the distribution of the values in-between. Consider the following two sets of data.

A: 3 4 5 6 8 9 10 12 15 Range = 15 – 3 = 12

B: 3 7 7 7 8 8 8 10 15 Range = 15 – 3 = 12

The range for the two groups of data is the same but it can be seen that the distributions are very different.

3.6 Measures of dispersion: the inter-quartile range

Previously the median was described as the measure which splits a data set into two equal halves. Using a similar approach, the data can be further split into quartiles. Between them

- the lower quartile (Q1), which is the $(n+1)/4$ value when the data are placed in order;

- the median, which is the $(n+1)/2$ value when the data are placed in order; and

- the upper quartile (Q3), which is the $3(n+1)/4$ value when the data are placed in order

divide a distribution into four equal parts. The distance between the upper and lower quartiles measures the spread of the middle half of the observations and is known as the inter-quartile range.

(*Note*: If there are an even number of items in the data set, using $n/4$ and $3n/4$ to find the lower and upper quartile positions is an acceptable approximation.)

Inter-quartile range = Upper quartile – Lower quartile

EXAMPLE 3.16: tabulated data

The table below shows the annual salaries of 25 workers. What is the inter-quartile range for these data?

Salary (£000s)	Frequency	
8	7	◄— (person 1 to 7)
10	12	◄— (person 8 to 19)
15	4	◄— (person 20 to 23)
18	2	◄— (person 24 to 25)

Median = middle value (ordered value $(n+1)/2$)

$$= \frac{(25+1)}{2}$$

= 13th ordered value = £10,000

Lower quartile (Q1) = $(n+1)/4$ ordered value

$$= \frac{(25+1)}{4}$$

= 6½th ordered observation

= £8000

Upper quartile (Q3) = $3(n+1)/4$ ordered value

$$= \frac{3(25+1)}{4}$$

= 19½th ordered observation

= £12,500 (midway between 10,000 and 15,000)

Inter-quartile range = Q3 − Q1 = £12,500 − £8000 = £4500

For data which have been grouped together, the lower and upper quartiles are estimated from a cumulative frequency graph (ogive) in a similar way to the median, as discussed in Example 3.9.

The lower quartile is located approximately one-quarter of the way along the distribution and the upper quartile three-quarters of the way along the distribution. How this works in practice is demonstrated in the next example.

EXAMPLE 3.17: grouped tabulated data

The table below shows the heights of a sample of 60 people. Using a cumulative frequency graph (Figure 3.2), estimate the upper and lower quartiles and hence find the inter-quartile range.

Heights (cm)	Frequency
150 up to 160	9
160 up to 170	18
170 up to 180	21
180 up to 190	12

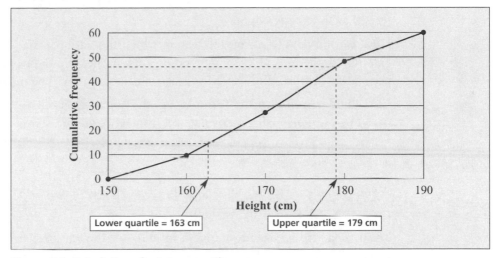

Figure 3.2 Calculations for inter-quartile range

A quarter of the way along the distribution in this case is approximately the 15th observation – this gives a height of about 163 cm. Three-quarters of the way along the distribution, in this case the 45th observation, gives a height of 179 cm.

Thus, inter-quartile range = 179 – 163 = 16 cm

By definition, the inter-quartile range measures the spread of the middle 50% of values in a data set. Since the bottom 25% and top 25% of values are excluded from its calculation, its value is not affected by extreme values in the data set. As a consequence, the inter-quartile range is a more robust measure of dispersion than the range.

3.7   Measures of dispersion: variance and standard deviation

Variance and standard deviation are the most commonly applied measures of dispersion, and are related to each other as the variance is the standard deviation squared. The variance considers the position of each observation relative to the mean value of the data set, and is defined as the average squared deviation from the mean.

As with the mean, for certain calculations knowing whether the data are from a population or a sample is vital.

Again, two separate symbols are used:

- σ^2 (variance) and σ (standard deviation) indicate that the data are from a population;

- s^2 (variance) and s (standard deviation) indicate that the data are from a sample.

(σ is the Greek letter sigma.)

However, unlike the mean, the way in which the variance/standard deviation is calculated changes slightly depending on whether the data originated from a population or a sample. The differences in calculation will be made clear later.

First the derivation of the formula and the calculations involved will be illustrated by example, using a raw data set from a population.

EXAMPLE 3.18

A small business, which employs only five staff pays the following salaries:

6, 10, 8, 12, 8   (£ thousands):

These data will be used to derive a formula for the variance from the definition supplied.

Definition: Variance = Average squared deviation from the mean

Step 1: Find the mean of the data

$$\text{Mean } (\mu) = \frac{6 + 10 + 8 + 12 + 8}{5} = 8.8$$

Step 2: Find the deviation of the individual value from the mean i.e., $(x - \mu)$

x	$(x - \mu)$
6	$6 - 8.8 = -2.8$
10	$10 - 8.8 = 1.2$
8	$8 - 8.8 = -0.8$
12	$12 - 8.8 = 3.2$
8	$8 - 8.8 = -0.8$

Step 3: Find the squared deviation of each individual value from the mean i.e., $(x - \mu)^2$

x	$(x - \mu)$	$(x - \mu)^2$
6	−2.8	7.84
10	1.2	1.44
8	−0.8	0.64
12	3.2	10.24
8	−0.8	0.64

Step 4: Find the average of the squared deviations from the mean (the variance) i.e., $\dfrac{\Sigma(x - \mu)^2}{n}$

$$\frac{\Sigma(x - \mu)^2}{n} = \frac{7.84 + 1.44 + 0.64 + 10.24 + 0.64}{5} = 4.16$$

So the formula for finding the variance for a population is

$$\sigma^2 = \frac{\Sigma(x - \mu)^2}{n}$$

where σ^2 is the notation used for a population variance.

However, it should be noted that because the differences between the observations and the mean have been squared (hence the notation σ^2), the units of measurement for the variance are not the same as the original data.

By taking the positive square root of the variance a measure of dispersion which is in the same units as the original data is obtained. This measure is known as the standard deviation (and for a population is denoted by σ).

In short, *the standard deviation is simply the positive square root of the variance.*

There are other ways in which the formula for the population variance can be rewritten in order to simplify its calculation. The most common of these is

$$\sigma^2 = \frac{\Sigma x^2}{n} - \left[\frac{\Sigma x}{n}\right]^2$$

and if the data has been grouped together into a frequency distribution table, then the formula is amended slightly to become

$$\sigma^2 = \frac{\Sigma f x^2}{n} - \left[\frac{\Sigma f x}{n}\right]^2$$

Note: In both of the above formulas n can also be replaced by Σf.

The following example illustrates the different way in which a problem is approached when calculating the variance using the above formula.

EXAMPLE 3.19: tabulated data

Calculate the variance and hence find the standard deviation for the data below, which gives the number of lectures missed by a class of students in a particular week.

Classes missed (x)	Number of students (f)
0	8
1	10
2	12
3	6

In order to use the formula quoted above it is necessary to construct a table with columns which contain the calculation of frequency times observation (fx), and frequency times observation squared (fx^2).

Classes missed (x)	Number of students (f)	fx	fx²
0	8	$8*0 = 0$	$8*0^2 = 0$
1	10	$10*1 = 10$	$10*1^2 = 10$
2	12	$12*2 = 24$	$12*2^2 = 48$
3	6	$6*3 = 18$	$6*3^2 = 54$
	$\sum f = 36$	$\sum fx = 52$	$\sum fx^2 = 112$

$$\sigma^2 = \frac{\sum fx^2}{n} - \left[\frac{\sum fx}{n}\right]^2 \text{ (where } n = \sum f)$$

$$\sigma^2 = \frac{112}{36} - \left[\frac{52}{36}\right]^2 = 3.11111111 - 1.4444444^2$$

$$\sigma^2 = 3.1111111 - 2.0864198 = 1.0246913 = 1.02 \text{ (to 2 d.p.)}$$

Hence, as standard deviation = √ variance

$$\sigma = \sqrt{1.0246913} = 1.0122704 = 1.01 \text{ (to 2 d.p.)}$$

Earlier in this chapter a distinction was made between x bar – the mean of a sample – and μ – the mean of a population. As mentioned previously, the calculation of the variance/standard deviation is another situation where this must be taken into account.

If data have been taken from a sample, then common sense suggests that the values are likely to be more bunched together than data from a population. For instance, asking 20 friends how much they spend each week on eating out will probably result in values which are much more closely bunched together than asking every household in the UK.

Data that have originated from a sample (for practical reasons) is generally used to provide an estimate for what takes place in an entire population. Pioneering mathematicians have found that the variance from a sample will slightly underestimate what takes place in a population but, fortunately, they have also found a method of accounting for this.

When calculating a variance from data that has originated from a sample, the population variance formula is used and an adjustment is made to this resulting value to find the sample variance.

$$s^2 = \frac{n}{(n-1)} * \sigma^2$$

Note: To distinguish between the two, the adopted notation is

s^2 = sample variance   and s = sample standard deviation

σ^2 = population variance   and σ = population standard deviation.

As with the population variance, there are several ways in which the formula for sample variance may be written – these may be found in the textbooks listed as supplementary reading. Each will yield the same result.

The calculation of a sample variance and standard deviation is illustrated in the following example.

EXAMPLE 3.20: grouped tabulated data

Calculate the variance and hence find the standard deviation for the heights of a sample of 60 people.

Height (cm)	Frequency (f)
150 up to 160	9
160 up to 170	18
170 up to 180	21
180 up to 190	12

First, in this example the data are in continuous groups, therefore (as with the mean) the mid-point of each of the groups is required to be used as the value of x in the formula.

Example 3.20
continued

Height (cm)	Frequency (f)	Mid-point (x)	fx	fx^2
150 up to 160	9	155	$9*155 =$ 1395	$9*155*155 =$ 216,225
160 up to 170	18	165	2970	490,050
170 up to 180	21	175	3675	643,125
180 up to 190	12	185	2220	410,700
	$\Sigma f = 60$		$\Sigma fx = 10,260$	$\Sigma fx^2 = 1,760,100$

$$\sigma^2 = \frac{\Sigma fx^2}{n} - \left[\frac{\Sigma fx}{n}\right]^2 \quad \text{where } n = \Sigma f$$

$$\sigma^2 = \frac{1,760,100}{60} - \left[\frac{10,260}{60}\right]^2 = 29,335 - 171^2$$

$$\sigma^2 = 29,335 - 29,241 = 94$$

Data are from a sample therefore apply correction factor:

$$s^2 = \frac{n}{(n-1)} * \sigma^2 = \frac{60}{59} * 94 = 95.59322$$

Hence, as standard deviation = $\sqrt{}$ variance

$$s = \sqrt{95.59322} = 9.7771785 = 9.78 \text{ (to 2 d.p.)}$$

When making any interpretation of a set of data, it is usually the standard deviation rather than the variance that is used. By definition, the standard deviation is a measure of how the data is spread around the mean, therefore the bigger the standard deviation the more spread out the data is.

Calculation of the standard deviation has the reputation of causing difficulty with many statistics students but, fortunately, these days most scientific calculators have functions that have the ability to calculate means and standard deviations automatically. The manufacturer's handbook should be consulted to find out how this is achieved.

3.8 Using the measures

In this chapter three measures of central tendency have been examined: the mode, the median and the mean, along with three different measures of dispersion: the range, the inter-quartile range and the variance/standard deviation.

The range is a very easily calculated measure which simply takes into account the smallest and largest values of a data set. Therefore it is often quoted along with, not instead of, the other two measures of dispersion considered. These two

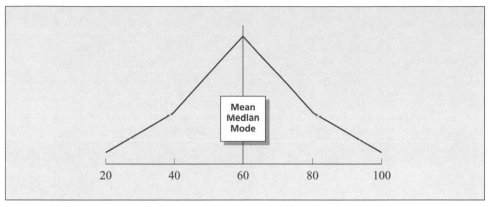

Figure 3.3 Symmetrical distribution

measures can actually be paired up with a measure of central tendency i.e., the mean is paired with the standard deviation/variance and the median is paired with the inter-quartile range.

In most cases the choice of which set of measures to use to represent a set of data depends on the distributional shape of the data set. In general, the construction of a histogram or bar chart will provide sufficient evidence to suggest whether a data set is symmetrical or skewed in shape.

For a unimodal data set which is symmetrically distributed, the mode, median and mean coincide as shown in Figure 3.3 and any of the three measures is suitable but it is the mean which is generally used. If the mean is used, then the standard deviation would be selected to accompany it.

This is also the case if the data set is almost symmetrical in shape.

If the data is asymmetrically distributed, then it is said to be skewed in shape. Typically, a skewed distribution is characterized by a short tail on one side of the modal value and a longer tail on the other side. There are two types of skewed distribution: positive or right skewness (Figure 3.4) where the long tail lies to the

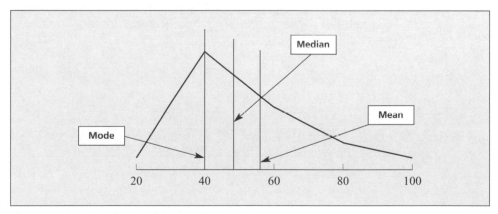

Figure 3.4 Positively skewed distribution

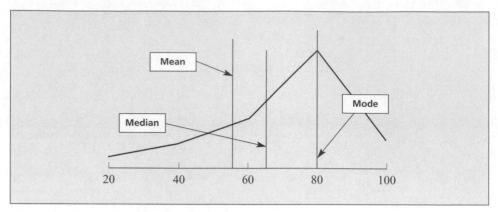

Figure 3.5 Negatively skewed distribution

right of the mode, and negative or left skewness (Figure 3.5) where the long tail lies to the left of the mode. If a data set is skewed, then the mean (and the standard deviation) will be influenced by the extreme values. As a consequence, the median or mode may provide more suitable measures of central tendency and the inter-quartile range a better measure of dispersion.

Generally it is the median and inter-quartile range which are used unless the data set is very highly skewed and in these cases it is the mode which is more suitable (assuming a distinct mode exists).

REVIEW ACTIVITY 2

(a) Use the data provided in Review activity 1 on page 63 to calculate the following measures of dispersion for both the raw and tabulated data:

   (i)   inter-quartile range;

   (ii) standard deviation.

(b) Compare your answers for the raw and tabulated data sets. Are they different? If so, say why.

(c) Which measure of dispersion is the most appropriate for this data set? Why?

Working:

Answers on page 220.

Key points to remember

1. The mode is defined as the most popular observation. For grouped continuous data in uneven categories this is determined by choosing the category with the highest frequency density. Otherwise, the group with the highest frequency is selected.

2. The median is defined as the middle observation. In general this is the $(n+1)/2$th ordered value. For continuous data this is found from an ogive (where, as only an estimate can be found, it is quite acceptable to use the $n/2$th observation).

3. The mean – commonly referred to as the average – is found using the general formula:

$$\text{Mean} = \frac{\sum fx}{\sum f} \quad \text{(for ungrouped data } f = 1\text{)}$$

4. Two separate symbols are used to represent the mean depending on the origin of the data:

   $\bar{x}$ indicates that data have originated from a sample;

   μ indicates that data have originated from a population.

5. For grouped data the mid-point of the group is used to represent x.

6. The range is a measure of the extremes of the data set and is found by taking the minimum value from the maximum value.

7. The lower quartile is the $(n+1)/4$th observation in a data set when placed in order. (For an even number of values $n/4$ is an acceptable approximation.) For continuous data this is estimated from an ogive.

8. The upper quartile is the $3(n+1)/4$th observation in a data set when placed in order. (For an even number of values $3n/4$ is an acceptable approximation). For continuous data this is estimated from an ogive.

9. The inter-quartile range is a measure of the middle 50% of the data set and is calculated by taking the lower quartile value from the upper quartile value.

10. The variance is defined as the average squared deviation from the mean. As with the mean, two symbols are used to represent the origin of the data:

    σ^2 indicates that data are from a population;

    s^2 indicates that data are from a sample.

11. The general formula for finding a population variance is

$$\sigma^2 = \frac{\sum fx^2}{n} - \left[\frac{\sum fx}{n}\right]^2 \quad \text{(for ungrouped data } f = 1\text{)}$$

In the above formula n can also be replaced by $\sum f$. For grouped data the mid-point of the group is used to represent x.

12. To calculate the sample variance the following adjustment is made to the population variance:

$$s^2 = \frac{n}{(n-1)} * \sigma^2$$

13. The standard deviation is the positive square root of the variance, where:

σ = population standard deviation;

s = sample standard deviation.

14. The mean and variance/standard deviation are paired together as a set of measures. The median and inter-quartile range form another separate set of measures. For a particular set of data only one of these pairs is usually quoted as the most appropriate measure of central tendency and dispersion. This depends on the distributional shape of the data. For data which are almost symmetrical in shape the mean and variance/standard deviation are quoted. For data which are asymmetrical (skewed) the median and inter-quartile range are used.

ADDITIONAL EXERCISES

Question 1 Calculate the mean, median, mode, range, inter-quartile range and standard deviation for the following set of data:

2   1   3   7   2   1   6   8   4   3   9   2   4   6   5

Assume the data are from a population.

Question 2 A group of students was asked how long they spent per week working part-time. A sample of the replies (recorded in hours) was as follows:

5   9   4   12   3   8   4   10

(a) Calculate the mode, mean and median times.

(b) Calculate the range, inter-quartile range and standard deviation for these data.

(c) Another student responded by saying he worked 30 hours per week. Recalculate the six summary measures for the nine students.

(d) If you had to quote an average time and measure of spread for the nine students, which measures would you use?

Question 3 In 14 consecutive weeks a salesman's commissions in £s were:

35   47   48   31   30   94   98   10   15   120   73   60   184   13

(a) Calculate the mean weekly commission.

(b) Calculate the range and standard deviation for the weekly commission.

(c) If his mean commission for a 30 week period (including the 14 weeks above) was reduced by £3.10, what is his mean commission for the other 16 weeks?

Question 4   Calculate the mean, median, mode, range, inter-quartile range and standard deviation of the following frequency distribution which represents the number of errors made per day by the computer system in an auditing department, recorded over a period of 100 days. Treat the data as coming from a sample.

Errors	0	1	2	3	4	5	6	7	8	9
Days	15	18	19	19	10	8	7	2	1	1

Which is the most appropriate set of measures?

Question 5   The following data relate to lot size (in acres) for a sample of 40 pieces of building land being sold by a national land agent.

Lot size (acres)	< 0.5	0.5 up to 1	1 up to 1.5	1.5 up to 2	2 up to 2.5
Frequency	19	8	8	2	3

(a) Draw a histogram to represent the data.

(b) Establish the modal class for the data set.

(c) Determine the mean and standard deviation for the lot size.

(d) Determine the median and inter-quartile range for the data set.

(e) Comment on the distributional shape of the data and state the most appropriate measure of central tendency

Question 6   The JFS chemical solvent manufacturer records data for all employees relating to the number of years they have been with the company. This is shown in the table below. For the purposes of calculation assume that no one has been with the company for more than 50 years.

Years of service	0 to < 5	5 to < 15	15 to < 25	25 to < 35	35+
No. of employees	105	231	173	85	31

(a) Draw a histogram to represent the data, first establishing the class limits.

(b) Establish the modal class for the data set.

(c) Determine the mean and standard deviation of the number of years of service with the company.

(d) Also find the median and inter-quartile range for these data.

(e) Comment on the distributional shape of the data and state the most appropriate measures of central tendency and dispersion.

Question 7   A study was conducted in a shopping centre in which 81 people were asked how much they spent on luxury goods per week. No respondent spent more than £100.

Amount (£)	up to 15	15 to < 25	25 to < 40	40 to < 60	60 +
Number of respondents	10	20	25	15	11

(a) Calculate the mean and standard deviation for expenditure.

(b) Calculate the median and inter-quartile range for expenditure.

(c) Replies from a further 12 respondents have been received and the data relating to them is as follows:

    35   34   49   12   29   30
    57   13   25   18   31   29

    (i)   Reconstruct the frequency distribution table to account for the additional respondents.

    (ii)   Present the data in (i) using an appropriate graphical display.

    (iii)   Recalculate the most suitable measures of central tendency and dispersion.

SPREADSHEET EXERCISE

This exercise will introduce the Excel functions for summarizing data.

The Quick Bite chain of restaurants run a pizza delivery service. The data located in file QUICK.XLS relates to a sample of 250 delivery distances. Use these data to calculate the following summary measures:

(a) Median

(b) Mean

(c) Range

(d) Inter-quartile range

(e) Variance

(f) Standard deviation.

The following table summarizes the value of individual orders received over the last week by one of the shops in the chain. Treat these data as a population and calculate or estimate, where appropriate, the six summary measures listed above.

Value of order (£)	Number of orders
0 to less than 8	120
8 to less than 15	310
15 to less than 20	430
20 to less than 25	530
25 to less than 35	150
35 to less than 50	60

Hints for completion

In Chapter 3 you should have become aware that when summarizing data it can be presented initially in two forms i.e., a data list and a frequency table. Generally spreadsheets assume that the data will be in the former style. Therefore the statistical functions only cater for this type of data.

In Excel the functions for summarizing data are as follows:

=MAX(Data Range)	Returns the maximum value from a data set
=MIN(Data Range)	Returns the minimum value from a data set
=AVERAGE(Data Range)	Returns the mean value from a data set
=MEDIAN(Data Range)	Returns the median value from a data set
=MODE(Data Range)	Returns the mode from a data set. Note: This is used with caution as when there is more than one mode in a data set the command will result in an error or a #NA message
=QUARTILE(Data Range, Q_No.)	Returns the quartile values for a data set where a quartile number of 1 gives the lower quartile and 3 an upper quartile
=STDEV(Data Range)	Returns the *sample* standard deviation value from a data set
=VAR(Data Range)	Returns the *sample* variance from a data set
=STDEVP(Data Range)	Returns the *population* standard deviation value from a data set
=VARP(Data Range)	Returns the *population* variance from a data set

Figure 3.6 shows the formulae required to find the standard six summary measures used in Chapter 3.

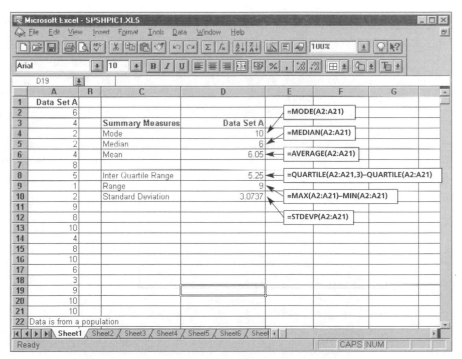

Figure 3.6 Finding summary measures for raw data on Excel

However, if the data have already been tabulated there are no specific functions available. In this case, formulae are constructed to carry out calculations as you would on a calculator. This is illustrated in Figure 3.7.

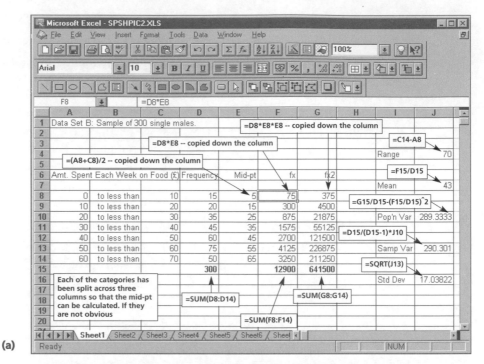

Figure 3.7 Calculation of summary measures for tabulated data on Excel

CHAPTER 4

Correlation and regression

LEARNING OBJECTIVES

- To identify, by diagram, whether a possible relationship exists between two variables;
- To quantify the strength of association between variables using the correlation coefficient;
- To show how a relationship can be expressed as an equation;
- To identify linear equations when written and when graphed;
- To examine regression, a widely used linear model, and to consider its uses and limitations.

Introduction

In many business situations, it is reasonable to suggest that relationships exist between variables. For example, it would be logical to assume that the sales of a mass-produced good are related to its price and advertising expenditure.

For decision making purposes it is useful to identify whether a linear relationship exists between two variables and, if appropriate, quantify its strength. A relationship can be identified using a graph called a **scatter diagram**, and its strength can be quantified using a statistical measure called the **correlation coefficient**.

Once such an association has been found, it can often be very useful to produce a forecasting **model** which can be used to predict one variable if the other is known (e.g., it may be possible to predict sales if advertising expenditure is known).

In this chapter, two methods of quantifying the strength of the relationship (the correlation) between two variables will be presented. This will be followed by a section discussing how a linear model for forecasting can be constructed and used once a relationship has been discovered.

Before proceeding with the theory relating to the development of a forecasting model it is worth considering what is actually meant by the use of the word 'model' in this context.

A model may be used in several different ways: the idea of scale models as used by engineers or architects, a kit used to make an aeroplane or car or even someone who shows off clothes on a catwalk may come to mind. In each of these situations the model is used to demonstrate or show people how something will look or behave. In the context of this unit, a model may mean an equation or specially prepared spreadsheet but it is still meant to be some sort of representation of the real world which helps the user to experiment – seeing the effect of changes, making forecasts or making decisions.

4.1   The scatter diagram

A scatter diagram is simply a plot of data points on an *X–Y* graph.

The *y*-axis is used to represent the dependent variable of interest to the decision maker, whilst the *x*-axis is used to represent a variable which can be controlled or measured by the decision maker (often called the independent variable). Each pair of values is subsequently represented on the graph by a point or cross.

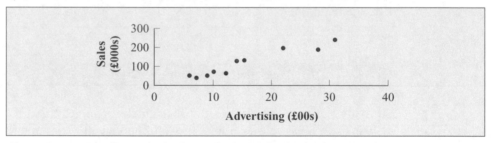

Figure 4.1 Scatter diagram of sales and advertising expenditure

In the scatter diagram shown in Figure 4.1, the *y* variable is the value of sales, whilst the *x* variable is advertising expenditure for a certain mass-produced good. This is because sales would be the variable that a decision maker may be interested in predicting (i.e., *y*), whilst advertising expenditure may be changed to suit the decision maker (i.e., *x*). Weekly sales and advertising expenditure are recorded and each pair is represented on the graph by a point (•). The overall pattern of the points on this graph suggests that a relationship may exist between sales and advertising costs. In particular, the scatter diagram suggests the more money spent on advertising, the greater the value of sales. The pattern of the points roughly form a straight line suggesting that there is possibly a linear association between the two variables.

Depending upon the variables being considered, the relationship suggested by the scatter diagram may be strongly linear, non-linear or even non-existent. Therefore, a scatter diagram is a useful first indication of whether an association exists between two variables.

Causal relationships

Before performing further analysis, it is important to be able to hypothesize on whether a cause and effect relationship might exist between the variables concerned, and to clearly identify which is the dependent variable.

A scatter diagram of pairs of data, showing business failures against graduating students, might suggest a strong positive relationship, since both groups have increased over the past years. But clearly there is nothing to suggest a direct relationship between the two; it is mere coincidence that both have increased.

Hence it is very important to be able to justify in advance that variable y is the *effect* resulting from changes in x, the *cause* variable.

In the case above, it seems sensible to say that changes in sales are *caused* by changes in advertising expenditure so it is safe to proceed with the next stage – quantifying the strength of the relationship through correlation analysis.

4.2   Correlation coefficients

Correlation analysis is a mathematical technique which is used to measure the *strength* of association between two variables. This measurement takes into account the 'degree of scatter' between the data values. Obviously, the less scattered the data, the stronger the relationship (correlation) is between the two variables.

The correlation coefficient is denoted by the symbol r and can *only* take a value between -1 and $+1$ inclusive.

Before looking at the details of how r is calculated, its meaning in relation to various scatter diagrams will be discussed.

In Figure 4.2, r equals $+1$ which indicates that there is perfect positive correlation between the two variables. This means all of the data lies on a straight line sloping upwards, showing that as the value of x increases so does the value of y (which is why correlation can be said to be positive) and for every known value of x, the value of y can be predicted exactly.

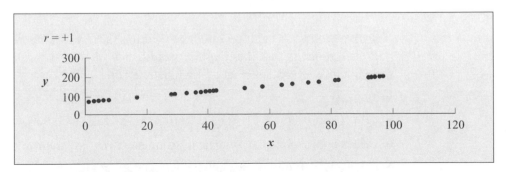

Figure 4.2 Scatter diagram where r = 1

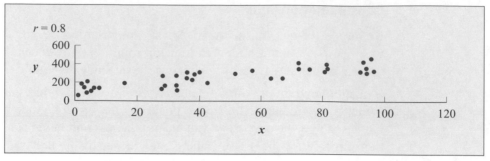

Figure 4.3 Scatter diagram showing *r* of around 0.8

In Figure 4.3, it can be seen that as *x* increases *y* still increases, and that the data are quite closely grouped together. In this case it can be said that there is evidence of strong positive correlation between the two variables and this would yield a value of *r* around 0.8.

Now consider the further scatter diagrams shown in Figure 4.4. In the diagram on the left it can be seen that the value of *x* is not influencing the value of *y* in any way (*y* is constant), in this case the value of *r* = 0 shows there is no correlation (association) between the two variables. In the diagram on the right there is some scatter but there is no particular association between the value of *x* and the value of *y*. Therefore it can be said there is very little correlation between the two variables. Here the value of *r* would be somewhere between –0.3 and +0.3.

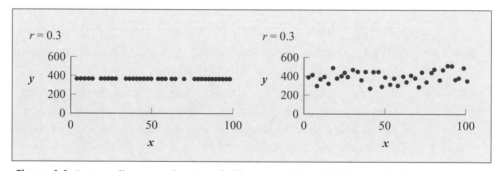

Figure 4.4 Scatter diagrams showing (left) zero and (right) little correlation

Negative values of *r* can be interpreted in the same way as positive values – the only difference is that the diagram would show that as the value of *x* increases the value of *y* decreases. Figure 4.5 illustrates this.

In summary:

- values approaching +1 suggest a strong positive association;
- values approaching –1 suggest a strong negative association;
- values near 0 suggest possibly no association at all.

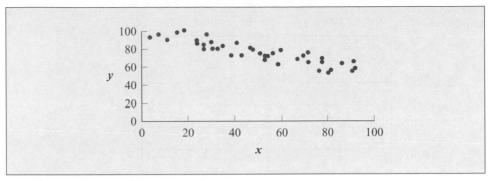

Figure 4.5 Scatter diagram showing strong negative correlation

The next point to consider is the calculation of r.

4.3   Calculating the correlation coefficient

Pearson's product moment correlation coefficient measures the strength of a possible linear relationship between the variables. The formula for its calculation is:

$$r = \frac{n\sum xy - \sum x \sum y}{\sqrt{\left[n\sum x^2 - (\sum x)^2 \right]\left[n\sum y^2 - (\sum y)^2 \right]}}$$

This formula looks complicated and tends to cause difficulties with many statistics students (luckily many scientific calculators and spreadsheets have automatic built-in functions for its calculation). However, in an attempt to overcome this, Example 4.1 will illustrate the method of calculation step by step.

EXAMPLE 4.1

The table overleaf shows advertising expenditure and associated sales of a particular product. By examining a scatter diagram and calculating Pearson's product moment correlation coefficient, comment on the association between the two variables.

Step 1: **Establish the independent (*x*) and dependent (*y*) variables and graph them**

It is very likely that expenditure would affect sales. Therefore expenditure is defined as the independent variable and is plotted on the *x*-axis with sales as the dependent variable plotted on the *y*-axis. This produces the scatter diagram shown in Figure 4.6.

▶

Example 4.1
continued

Sales (£000s)	Expenditure (£00s)
25	8
35	12
29	11
24	5
38	14
12	3
18	6
27	8
17	4
30	9

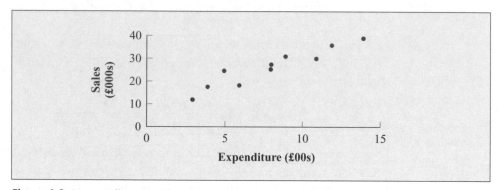

Figure 4.6 Scatter diagram, showing expenditure versus sales

Step 2: Examine the graph

The graph indicates that as expenditure increases sales increase, it also appears that the data are quite closely grouped together. This would suggest there is strong positive correlation between the two variables. To back up these observations the value of r can be calculated.

Step 3: Calculate the correlation coefficient

Looking at the formula more closely, the individual elements required are:

$\sum x$ – the sum of all the x values;

$\sum y$ – the sum of all the y values;

$\sum x^2$ – the x values squared then added together;

$\sum y^2$ – the y values squared then added together;

$\sum xy$ – the sum of the x values multiplied by the y values;

n – the number of (expenditure, sales) pairs.

In order to calculate these a table is needed:

Sales (y)	Expenditure (x)	x^2	y^2	xy
25	8	$8*8=64$	$25*25=625$	$8*25=200$
35	12	$12*12=144$	1225	420
29	11	$11*11=121$	841	319
24	5	25	576	120
38	14	196	1444	532
12	3	9	144	36
18	6	36	324	108
27	8	64	729	216
17	4	16	289	68
30	9	81	900	270
$\Sigma y = 255$	$\Sigma x = 80$	$\Sigma x^2 = 756$	$\Sigma y^2 = 7097$	$\Sigma xy = 2289$

and $n = 10$.

The summary values are substituted into the correlation coefficient formula and worked through:

$$r = \frac{n\Sigma xy - \Sigma x \Sigma y}{\sqrt{[n\Sigma x^2 - (\Sigma x)^2][n\Sigma y^2 - (\Sigma y)^2]}}$$

$$r = \frac{(10*2289) - (80*255)}{\sqrt{[(10*(756)) - 80^2][(10*7097) - 255^2]}}$$

$$r = \frac{(22890 - 20400)}{\sqrt{(7560 - 6400)(70970 - 65025)}}$$

$$r = \frac{2490}{\sqrt{6896200}} = \frac{2490}{2626.0617}$$

So $r = 0.948$ (to 3 d.p.)

The value of r is close to $+1$, so this suggests that a very strong positive relationship exists between the two variables.

Since it is such a widely used statistic, most spreadsheet packages and many scientific calculators have in-built functions which can be used to find the value of r once the two sets of data have been entered. This is the way in which the correlation coefficient is usually calculated in practice.

4.4 The rank correlation coefficient

With Pearson's product moment correlation coefficient the two sets of data need to be numeric. It is also possible to measure the association between numeric and non-numeric variables if the non-numeric data have been given in the form of **ranks** (for example, product names ranked in order of preference).

The most common rank coefficient is derived from Pearson's coefficient and is known as **Spearman's rank correlation coefficient**. The formula for this is:

$$r = 1 - \frac{6 * \sum d^2}{n(n^2 - 1)}$$

where: n = number of pairs of observations

d = difference between the rank of x and y.

The value of r is interpreted in a similar way to Pearson's correlation coefficient, however it is not really possible to say that one variable is affecting the other. The value of r is used to indicate the *level of agreement* between the two variables.

EXAMPLE 4.2

A large travel company produces a list of its top 10 travel destinations for the previous year every January. In the same month each year a national women's magazine also produces a similar list based on their annual reader survey. Calculate a suitable correlation coefficient and make appropriate comments on your result. The data collected are shown in the table below:

Destination	Travel company rank	Magazine rank
Florida	2	1
Canary Islands	5	6
Greek Islands	3	2
Germany	4	4
Spain	6	5
Caribbean	10	7
Australia	7	9
France	9	10
Canada	8	8
Russia	1	3

In order to calculate r a table that calculates the square of the differences between the ranks (d^2) is needed. Note that as the values are squared it does not matter which way round the differences are calculated.

Destination	Travel company rank	Magazine rank	d	d^2
Florida	2	1	1	1
Canary Islands	5	6	−1	1
Greek Islands	3	2	1	1
Germany	4	4	0	0
Spain	6	5	1	1
Caribbean	10	7	3	9
Australia	7	9	−2	4
France	9	10	−1	1
Canada	8	8	0	0
Russia	1	3	−2	4
				$\sum d^2 = 22$

$$r = 1 - \frac{6 * \sum d^2}{n(n^2 - 1)} = 1 - \frac{(6 * 22)}{10(100 - 1)}$$

$$r = 1 - \frac{132}{990}$$

$$r = 1 - 0.1333 = 0.867 \text{ (to 3 d.p.)}$$

As $r = 0.867$ this indicates there is quite a high level of agreement between the two publications.

In Example 4.2 both sets of data were already ranked. It is very likely that one set of data may require conversion into ranks. In such cases it is also very likely that the ranking will produce ties. An adjustment must be made so that the tied values equally share the ranks they would have occupied. This is shown by the following data:

Data:	39	28	28	20	17	17	17	15	13
Rank given:	1	2½	2½	4	6	6	6	8	9
		(share 2,3)			(share 5,6,7)				

Once ranked, the calculation would proceed as above, as shown in Example 4.3.

EXAMPLE 4.3

A florist franchise has recently set up an Internet site for the sale of its top five rated arrangements. Recorded in the table below are the numbers of orders received via the Internet for each of these arrangements. By calculating a suitable correlation coefficient, comment on the level of association between overall sales of the arrangements and sales made solely on the Internet.

Rating	Arrangement	Internet sales (£00s)
1	Lemon posy	29
2	Mixed blooms	35
3	Blue symphony	18
4	Pink carnival	29
5	Lover's knot	16

In this case only one set of data has been presented in the form of ranks, therefore before proceeding the data relating to Internet sales needs to be ranked appropriately.

For Internet sales it can be seen that the 'Mixed blooms' arrangement has the largest number of sales, thus a rank of 1 is allocated. There are then two arrangements with 2900 sales each, namely the 'Pink carnival' and the 'Lemon posy'. This means that in terms of ranks they are required to share 2 and 3 between them, giving the two arrangements a rank of 2½. The 'Blue symphony' arrangement is next with 1800 sales. As the second and third ranks have been allocated through the shared rank of 2½ 'Blue symphony' is given a rank of 4, with the final arrangement taking the rank of 5.

This information along with the subsequent differences (d) and values of d^2 is shown below:

Arrangement	Internet sales (£00s)	Internet rank	d	d^2
1: Lemon posy	29	2.5	−1.5	2.25
2: Mixed blooms	35	1	1	1
3: Blue symphony	18	4	−1	1
4: Pink carnival	29	2.5	1.5	2.25
5: Lover's knot	16	5	0	0
				$\sum d^2 = 6.5$

$$r = 1 - \frac{6 * \Sigma d^2}{n(n^2 - 1)} = 1 - \frac{(6 * 6.5)}{5(25 - 1)}$$

$$r = 1 - \frac{39}{120}$$

$$r = 1 - 0.325 = 0.675$$

Therefore we can see that there is a reasonable level of similarity between the best sellers on the Internet site and the florist's overall best sellers.

REVIEW ACTIVITY 1

Ten printers, suitable for use with personal computers and retailing at between £300 and £550, were evaluated by a number of volunteers. The volunteers were asked to award each printer percentage marks for 'speed' and 'print quality'. The assessments of these printers including an overall ranking are summarized as follows:

Model	1	2	3	4	5	6	7	8	9	10
Speed	20	45	25	10	30	25	35	30	20	25
Quality	65	35	55	85	15	25	45	25	55	35
Overall rank	5	3	8	7	4	10	1	2	9	6
Price (£)	410	396	350	530	399	353	430	404	350	375

(a) Calculate the product moment correlation coefficient between 'speed' and 'print quality' and interpret your answer.

(b) Calculate the rank correlation coefficient between overall ranking and retail price and interpret your answer.

Working:

Answers on pages 222–3.

4.5 Linear models

The construction of a linear regression model builds on a basic knowledge of linear equations. Hence to understand this work fully it is necessary to understand and to be able to construct linear equations. A brief summary of the knowledge required follows here, but readers may find it necessary to refer to other notes or textbooks to consolidate their skills before proceeding.

The general format for a simple linear equation is:

$$y = a + bx$$

(In some texts this is written as $y = mx + c$ where m is equivalent to b and c is equivalent to a).

- y is the *dependent* variable.

- x is the *independent* variable.

- a is a *constant* representing the point where the straight line cuts the y-axis (known as the *intercept*).

- b is a *constant* representing the *slope* (or gradient) of the straight line.

This is illustrated in Figure 4.7.

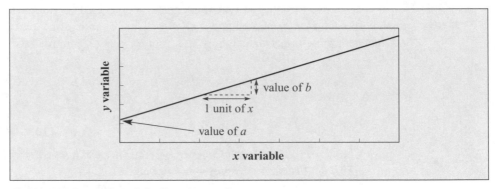

Figure 4.7 General straight line: $y = a + bx$

To consider how a linear model (as opposed to linear regression) is constructed, look at the following example.

EXAMPLE 4.4

An electricity company has a standing charge of £17.50 per quarter plus 8p per unit for electricity used. Find and graph a linear equation to model this situation for usage of up to 1500 units per quarter.

The equation will have the general form:

$$y = a + bx$$

- y must be *electricity charges* since this is the variable of interest.

- x must be *number of units used* since this determines the electricity charges.

(Also it may be said that charges *depend on* units used so electricity charge is *dependent* and number of units used is *independent*.)

To find a and b it is helpful to consider how the charges which arise at various levels of usage are made up.

For instance, if 10 units of electricity are used the charge is £17.50 + £0.08 * 10.

standing charge   unit charge   no. of units used

And if 20 units of electricity are used the charge is £17.50 + £0.08 * 20 ... and so on.

In general, therefore,

$$\text{Electricity charges} = £17.50 + £0.08 * \text{units used}$$

or, in the usual notation where y = electricity charges (£) and x = number of units used:

$$y = 17.5 + 0.08x$$

which is a linear model representing electricity charges in terms of units used.

There are a number of ways in which a known model can be presented on a graph. Perhaps the easiest of these is simply to choose a few values for x (two are sufficient but three allow a check for mistakes!), calculate the corresponding values of y and then plot the resulting pairs of points and join them together. Here the x values chosen are 0, 750 and 1500.

x	0	750	1500
$y = 17.5 + 0.08x$	$17.5 + 0.08 * 0 = 17.5$	$17.5 + 0.08 * 750 = 77.5$	$17.5 + 0.08 * 1500 = 137.5$

The resulting graph is shown in Figure 4.8.

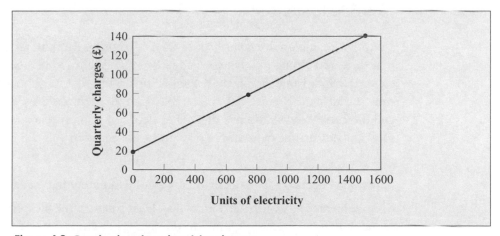

Figure 4.8 Graph, showing electricity charges

In order to check your understanding of linear models have a go at Review activity 2 before considering linear regression.

Two local retailers are offering mobile telephones at different tariffs. Phoneyvode charge £15 per month plus 50p per minute for calls, while Purplecom charge £17.25 for rental but only 35p per minute for calls.

(a) Formulate equations for the call charges in each case.

(b) Produce a *single* graph showing the costs of each option if between 0 and 40 minutes of calls are made per month.

(c) Determine the level of calls at which Purplecom's tariff becomes the cheaper option.

(d) What is the overall cost per month at this level of calls?

Working:

Answers on page 224.

The linear equations in Example 4.4 and Review activity 2 are examples of a **deterministic** model i.e., if electricity usage were known then charges could be predicted exactly with no room for variation. In real life, it is often necessary to build a **probabilistic** model to deal with uncertainty. Simple linear regression, the technique which is described below, is an example of this latter type of model.

4.6   Simple linear regression

Consider Example 4.1 again (the sales and advertising data). It has been established that there is a strong link between advertising and sales, with a correlation coefficient of 0.948. However, due to the variability in the data it is impossible to find an exact linear model, as we did in Example 4.4 above. Nevertheless, given Figure 4.6 and the correlation coefficient there is evidence of a linear relationship between the sales and advertising expenditure. Therefore, the equation will still have the format

$$y = a + bx$$

but what is needed is a mathematical way of estimating the a and b values.

Simple linear regression (also known as least squares linear regression) is a technique which has been developed to do this. In essence, the aim is to find values of a and b (remember these are just constant values) which give the line which best fits the points. To do this requires more mathematical formulae:

$$b = \frac{n\sum xy - \sum x \sum y}{n\sum x^2 - (\sum x)^2}$$

and

$$a = \frac{\Sigma y}{n} - \frac{b\Sigma x}{n} \quad \text{or} \quad a = \bar{y} - b\bar{x}$$

(Note that these two formulae for a are equivalent and either may be used).

As with Pearson's correlation coefficient, most spreadsheets and scientific calculators have in-built functions that can be used to find these two values automatically (and their use is recommended).

Example 4.5 illustrates finding the linear regression coefficients using the full formulae.

EXAMPLE 4.5

Using the previous data on sales and advertising expenditure:

Sales (£000s)	25	35	29	24	38	12	18	27	17	30
Advert. expend. (£00s)	8	12	11	5	14	3	6	8	4	9

find the linear regression equation, add it to the original scatter graph, and produce forecasts for sales if advertising expenditure is:

(a) £700

(b) £1800

The value of b must be calculated first (since it is needed to work out the value of a). To do this, various numbers are needed:

Σx – the sum of all the x values;

Σy – the sum of all the y values;

Σx^2 – the x values squared then added together;

Σxy – the sum of the x values multiplied by the y values;

n – the number of (expenditure, sales) pairs.

These were also required for the calculation of the correlation coefficient (r) which was completed in Example 4.1. Therefore the relevant figures can be extracted from that example i.e., $\Sigma x = 80$, $\Sigma y = 255$, $\Sigma x^2 = 756$, $\Sigma xy = 2289$ and $n = 10$.

(If r had not been previously calculated a similar table to the one in Example 4.1 would be required to calculate the summary values.)

Therefore

$$b = \frac{n\Sigma xy - \Sigma x\Sigma y}{n\Sigma x^2 - (\Sigma x)^2} = \frac{(10*2289) - (80*255)}{(10*756) - (80)^2}$$

$$b = \frac{22,890 - 20,400}{7560 - 6400} = \frac{2490}{1160}$$

$$b = 2.1465517$$

▶

Example 4.5 continued

(Note that b has been left with a large number of decimal places at this stage to avoid errors in subsequent calculations. This would be achieved in practice by making use of a calculator's memory.)

Then

$$a = \frac{\Sigma y}{n} - \frac{b\Sigma x}{n} = \frac{255}{10} - 2.1465517 * \frac{80}{10}$$

$$a = 25.5 - 17.172413 = 8.327587$$

The final answers (rounded to three decimal places) are:

$$a = 8.32 \qquad b = 2.147$$

(Note that three decimal places were chosen as the data supplied were in thousands and hundreds.)

These give the linear regression equation

$$y = 8.328 + 2.147x$$

or, if preferred,

$$\text{Sales} = 8.328 + 2.147 * \text{Advertising expenditure}$$

When adding this to the scatter graph, the procedure is exactly as for graphing any other straight line: choose three x values and calculate y, then add the pairs of points to the graph. Here $x = 0$, 10 and 15 have been used to cover all of the values of x supplied in the original data. See Figure 4.9.

x	0	10	15
$y = 8.328 + 2.147x$	8.328	29.798	40.533

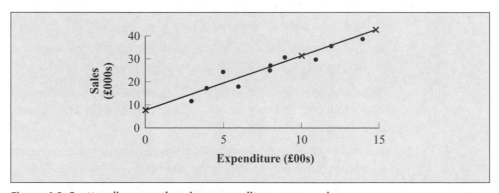

Figure 4.9 Scatter diagram, showing expenditure versus sales

To make forecasts, the values for x are simply substituted into the regression equation:

(a) Advertising expenditure = £700. As the figures used in the equation were given in hundreds, this means $x = 7$ giving

$$y = 8.328 + 2.147 * 7 = 23.357$$

As *y* is in thousands, 23,357 sales are forecast.

(b) Expenditure = £1800, so $x = 18$.

$$y = 8.328 + 2.147 * 18 = 46.974$$

i.e., 46,974 sales are forecast.

4.7 Assessing the accuracy of forecasts

Consider the two forecasts made at the end of the previous example in relation to the original data supplied.

In (a) the *x* value (7) fell within the range of the original data provided for *x* – which went from 3 to 14. This type of forecast is known as **interpolation**, and the forecast produced is likely to be accurate, since *r* is high and the model is considered to fit the data well.

However, in (b) the value of *x* used (18) falls outside the original data range, and it is not possible to be sure that the model continues to fit the data well. This is called **extrapolation** and it is necessary to be much more careful with forecasts made in this way. For instance, it might be that sales have reached a plateau level where more money spent on advertising has little or no effect. If this was the case the forecast would be inaccurate.

Therefore, when forecasts are made it is prudent to note whether interpolation or extrapolation is carried out and to consider the possible consequences.

As we have seen, the correlation coefficient (*r*) is often used as the first assessment of the model; a further measure, r^2, the **coefficient of determination**, can also be useful for further interpretation. Effectively, this is Pearson's correlation coefficient squared, but the term is generally used to describe the percentage of the variation in the *y* data that can be attributed to variation in the *x* data.

In the example above $r = 0.948$ so $r^2 = 0.899$. Thus it may be said that 89.9% of the variation in sales of the products is due to variation in the levels of advertising expenditure.

Finally, it should be noted that the sample size used may also have an important effect on the quality of the forecasts. In the example above only a small sample size – 10 pairs of points – were used, for ease of calculation. In reality, it is desirable to use at least 30 data points as, obviously, the larger the sample the more confidence can be placed in the accuracy of the model.

4.8 More complex regression models

The simple linear regression model discussed in this chapter has many other developments which are useful in modelling more complex situations. It may be desirable to add other factors which also have an effect on the dependent variable. For example, gas demand does not depend solely on the most obvious factor – temperature – but also on windchill and day of the week. It is possible to build **multiple regression models** which include all of these factors rather than just a single one.

In other situations the data may not exhibit the type of linear behaviour seen here (i.e., the graphs may be curved in some way) and so a **non-linear model** based on powers of x (x^2, x^3 etc.) or other transformations may be more appropriate. Although these developments are not discussed in detail here you should be aware that they exist and may be used in situations where simple linear models are inadequate.

REVIEW ACTIVITY 3

Mr Lillystone is the owner of a gift shop in a small town. He believes that the shop takings are related to the number of tourist coaches that stop in the town. He has collected the following data on takings and number of coach visits for a selection of recent days.

Day number	No. of coaches	Takings (£)
1	24	962
2	30	1181
3	9	578
4	48	1429
5	38	1324
6	15	752
7	5	542
8	38	1355
9	15	788
10	24	998
11	49	1462
12	10	650
13	17	862
14	11	719
15	16	828

(a) Determine which set of data represents the x (independent) and which the y (dependent) variable in this situation.

(b) Calculate values for a and b and write out the regression equation for this data.

(c) Forecast the takings for days where:

    (i) 27 coaches

    (ii) 55 coaches visit the town.

(d) How good do you expect the forecasts calculated in part (c) to be?

Working:

Answers on page 225.

Key points to remember

1. Correlation and regression are techniques which are used to see whether a relationship exists between two or more different sets of data. (In this book only two sets of data are considered.)

2. A graph known as a scatter diagram is used to identify the possibility and type of relationship. y is defined as the variable which it is believed is being influenced (dependent) and x is defined as the variable which is doing the influencing (independent).

3. The strength of a relationship between two sets of data is measured by Pearson's correlation coefficient (r). It is found by the following formula:

$$r = \frac{n\Sigma xy - \Sigma x \, \Sigma y}{\sqrt{[n\Sigma x^2 - (\Sigma x)^2] \, [n\Sigma y^2 - (\Sigma y)^2]}}$$

4. The value of r can only take a value of -1 to $+1$ inclusive. Brief guidelines on the interpretation of this value are as follows:

$+1$	Perfect positive correlation exists between the data. As x increases y increases. If x is known y can be predicted exactly.
$+0.8 < +1$	Strong positive correlation exists between the data. As x increases y increases.
$+0.4 < +0.8$	Moderate positive correlation exists between the data. As x increases y increases.

$-0.4 < +0.4$	Very little correlation exists between the data.
$-0.4 < -0.8$	Moderate negative correlation exists between the data. As x increases y decreases.
$-0.8 < -1$	Strong negative correlation exists between the data. As x increases y decreases.
-1	Perfect negative correlation exists between the data. As x increases y decreases. If x is known y can be predicted exactly.

5. Regression is a technique which builds a straight line relationship between two sets of data. This relationship is of the form $y = a + bx$ where a and b are found by the following formulae:

$$b = \frac{n\Sigma xy - \Sigma x \Sigma y}{n\Sigma x^2 - (\Sigma x)^2}$$

and

$$a = \frac{\Sigma y}{n} - \frac{b\Sigma x}{n} \quad \text{or} \quad a = \bar{y} - b\bar{x}$$

6. Forecasts may be made using the resulting model. If the x (independent) value used falls within the original data set then this forecast is known as interpolation. If the x value falls outside the bounds of the original data then this forecast is known as extrapolation and care must be taken in its use.

7. The coefficient of determination (r^2) is another measure which may be used to assess the appropriateness of a regression model. This is found by squaring Pearson's correlation coefficient and then expressing it as a percentage. The resulting figure is then used to describe the percentage variation in the y data that can be attributed to the variation in the x data.

8. Spearman's rank correlation coefficient is used to measure the agreement between two sets of data, at least one of which has been presented in the form of ranks. The formula for its calculation is:

$$r = \frac{1 - 6 * \Sigma d^2}{n(n^2 - 1)}$$

where: n = number of pairs of observations

d = difference between the rank of x and y.

If one of the sets of data is not ranked, they must be allocated ranks and any identical values are to be allocated a shared rank.

9. Finally, you should be aware that other more complex regression models do exist. These can be either in the form of non-linear or multiple regression models. More details of these can be found in the books listed in the further reading section of the Introduction.

ADDITIONAL EXERCISES

Question 1   Pemberton's slimming club has decided to illustrate a theoretical approach to how aerobic exercise and calorie intake can affect weight. Twelve of the established club members have carefully recorded the number of minutes of aerobic exercise they have undertaken in one week along with their weekly calorie intake. This data is presented in the table below.

Weight loss (lb)	Aerobic exercise (mins)	Calorie intake
0.6	112	9560
2.8	190	7552
1.4	171	11,981
1.4	148	8338
2.6	193	10,202
3.8	235	7252
3.3	237	8097
2.5	176	8121
2.6	185	8300
2.0	186	11,216
3.3	228	7212
1.1	65	7631

(a) Construct two scatter diagrams to illustrate the relationship between weight loss and aerobic exercise plus weight loss and calorie intake. Describe the main features of the graphs and hence *estimate* possible correlation coefficients.

(b) *Calculate* the correlation coefficient for the weight loss and aerobic exercise relationship. Using this figure, calculate the coefficient of determination and define its meaning in this context.

(c) Given the following summary values for the relationship between weight loss and calorie intake, calculate *r*. By comparing this with the correlation coefficient found in (b) determine which of the two factors is the better contributor to weight loss, giving appropriate reasons for your choice.

$$\sum x^2 = 9.5461103 * 10^8 \qquad \sum xy = 232{,}639.3 \qquad \sum x = 105{,}462$$

Question 2   A group of students and a group of senior citizens were asked to consider seven yellow paint shades and rank them in order of preference. Using the results in the table:

Paint shade	Students preference	Senior citizens' preference
Luscious lemon	1	2
Mellow mustard	3	4
Buttercup	4	3
Sunrise	7	7
Mexican spice	6	5
Lemon sherbet	2	1
Banana boat	5	6

(a) Calculate a suitable correlation coefficient.

(b) Comment on the agreement between the two groups taking part in the survey.

Question 3 Parker's IT recruitment services hold regular interview days where candidates are required to undergo an interview and an IT aptitude test. The results for one particular session are presented below.

Candidate	A	B	C	D	E	F	G	H
Interview rank	5	1	3	2	6	8	7	4
IT aptitude score (out of 100)	70	85	80	75	60	60	60	80

Calculate a suitable correlation coefficient and use this to comment on the level of agreement between the interview and testing process.

Question 4 (This question assumes you have completed Question 1.)

Calculate a linear regression model which describes the relationship between weight loss and amount of aerobic exercise. Use this equation to predict the expected weight loss of a club member who has undertaken 150 minutes of aerobic exercise in the week.

Question 5 A transport company has provided the following data relating to a sample of journeys made, giving distance travelled and time taken. The company is interested in developing a model to predict time taken for a journey if distance to be travelled is known.

Distance (km)	Time (hours)
200	3.2
120	2.0
175	3.0
150	2.0
300	4.7
320	5.5
240	3.8
180	2.8
210	3.4
260	4.5

$\Sigma x = 2155$

$\Sigma y = 34.9$

$\Sigma x^2 = 501625$

$\Sigma y^2 = 133.67$

$\Sigma xy = 8175$

(a) Present the data using a suitable scatter diagram.

(b) Find the correlation coefficient and the equation of the line of regression and state them clearly.

(c) Two lorries are just about to leave the depot. One is to make a journey of 90 km while the other is to travel 220 km. Using your regression equation estimate the journey times for each lorry. How much confidence would you have in each of these answers?

Question 6 A supermarket chain is about to launch its own range of batteries and wishes to base its marketing on a campaign emphasizing that the price of a battery is not the most important factor in determining its reliability.

To assist in their publicity they have commissioned a small study into battery life. A sample of 50 batteries of various ages bought at varying prices have been tested (each under the same conditions) to see how long they would last.

Graphs and statistics as shown in Figure 4.10 have been produced.

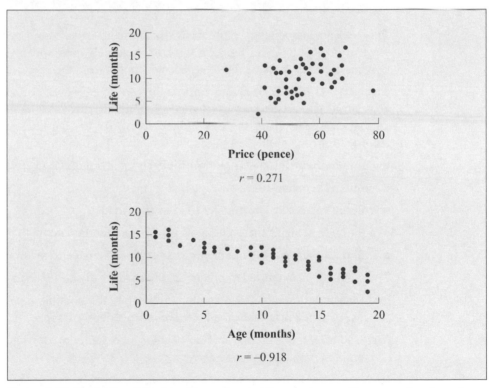

Figure 4.10 (Top) Life and price of batteries and (bottom) age of battery when bought and life

(a) Referring to the graphs and figures supplied as evidence, discuss which factors seem to affect battery life.

(b) Given the following extra information which has been calculated for you from the original data, find the most appropriate linear regression model which might be used to estimate battery life (i.e., one model only).

For age and battery life:

$$\sum x = 508 \qquad \sum y = 499.3 \qquad \sum xy = 4256.9 \qquad \sum x^2 = 6682$$

For price and battery life:

$$\sum x = 2783 \qquad \sum y = 499.3 \qquad \sum xy = 28{,}217.2 \qquad \sum x^2 = 159{,}671$$

(c) Comment on what the regression coefficients you have found tell you about battery life.

(d) Using your regression model, produce forecasts of how long the following batteries should last:

    (i) cost 85p, 2 years old;

    (ii) cost 50p, 6 months old.

(e) Comment on how confident you are about the accuracy of these forecasts.

SPREADSHEET EXERCISE

This exercise introduces the use of the Excel functions used in linear regression and correlation. As no Excel function is available to calculate Spearman's rank correlation coefficient automatically it has been excluded from the exercise.

The file SALES.XLS contains information about employees of a computer supply company. Data relating to mileage covered, number of sales made, period of time employed by the company and number of visits to customers made have been recorded for each of the 150 sales representatives for one month.

● column A contains an ID number for each sales representative;

● column B contains their mileage in a particular month;

● column C contains the number of sales they made;

● column D contains their length of service, recorded in months;

● column E contains the number of customer visits made in the month.

The company is interested in predicting the number of sales made.

(a) Construct three scatter diagrams to illustrate the possible relationships between the dependent variable and the three independent variables.

(b) Use an Excel function to find Pearson's correlation coefficients for the three pairs of variables graphed above.

(c) Make brief comments on the three relationships by referring to both the scatter diagrams and correlation coefficients. Which pair of variables exhibits the strongest relationship?

(d) Using this pair of variables and the relevant Excel functions, find the values of a and b which could be used to make up a linear regression equation to forecast sales. Write out the linear regression model and briefly interpret the values of a and b in this context.

(e) Construct an additional column of figures containing estimated sales figures, basing these on your linear regression equation from part (d) above. Add this set of estimated figures to your original scatter graph of the variables in your model to form a line through the data points.

Hints for completion

In Excel the three functions used in regression and correlation are:

=INTERCEPT(y-data range, x-data range)	Calculates the value of a in the linear regression model (i.e., the point at which the regression line crosses the y-axis)
=SLOPE(y-data range, x-data range)	Calculates the value of b in the linear regression equation
=CORREL(y-data range, x-data range)	Used to calculate Pearson's correlation coefficient

or

=PEARSON(y-data range, x-data range)

=RSQ(y-data range, x-data range)   Calculates the coefficient of determination

Figure 4.11 illustrates how these functions are applied in practice as well as giving the formula that would be required to answer part (e).

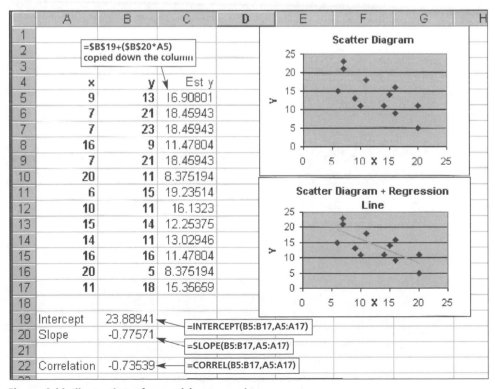

Figure 4.11 Illustration of spreadsheet exercise

CHAPTER 5

Probability and expected value

LEARNING OBJECTIVES

- To explore variability in observed data/outcomes and associated uncertainty in decisions;
- To introduce probability as a measure of likelihood of outcomes and risk in decisions;
- To look at rules of probability in situations where multiple (up to three) events are considered;
- To introduce the idea of expected value and sensitivity analysis as an aid in business decision making.

Introduction

Many quantitative techniques treat situations with certainty, (i.e., they use 'deterministic' models to find 'the' solution). But it is often possible for data to take a range of values. For example,

- consumers are of different sizes, and therefore require clothes, etc., of different sizes;
- bought-in components vary in quality, and can result in faulty products;
- expense claims by company personnel may take a range of values;
- the estimated audience for a 30-second TV advert is not the same for each showing.

So, can confidence be placed in business decisions based on single-point values? In many cases, the answer is *no*! Since there is *variability* in the data used, decisions are made with some degree of uncertainty. It is wise to examine the range of possible values as well as single-point estimates when making a decision.

In this chapter, ways of estimating the effect of such variability will be examined through the development of some simple ideas about probability. Initially, ways of finding the likelihood of various outcomes will be discussed. This will be followed by some consideration of how such estimates might be used to help in making decisions.

5.1 Variability in data

Consider the following data on 900 adult males' shoe sizes:

Shoe size	36	37	38	39	40	41	42	43	44	45	46	47
Number	12	25	90	124	156	185	134	87	56	22	7	2

If this data is presented on a simple bar chart (Figure 5.1) the pattern of variability can be seen. Clearly, the variability from size 36 to size 47 would generate uncertainty as to the sizes of shoe a manufacturer should make and a retail outlet should stock, but also the data shows that some sizes are more likely than others. Thus it is necessary to investigate the *likelihood* of different data values occurring before decisions could be made about stock levels. For example, it might be desirable to know the likelihood of a customer wanting shoes of size 47.

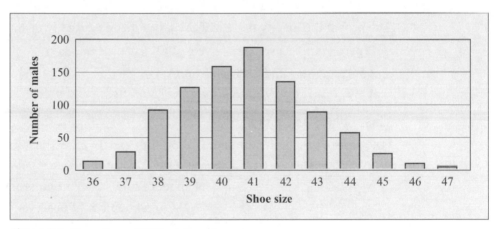

Figure 5.1 Shoe sizes of 900 adult males

Although this size is within the range of the data collected, looking at the bar chart it seems unlikely to occur as only a relatively small number of customers take this size.

Using words (such as unlikely, possible, doubtful, likely, quite certain, etc.) is not a good way of assessing likelihood, particularly as people are not consistent in their use of words. What is needed is a numerical measure for likelihood, and the measure which has developed to do this is **probability**. **Probability distributions** are also often used to help with the calculation of probability – these are simply common patterns of likelihood. Specific examples will be discussed later in this chapter.

5.2 Probability

Probability can be expressed in many ways for example, ratios, odds, percentages, fractions. The mathematical standard is that probability is expressed as a fraction or decimal number between 0 and 1.

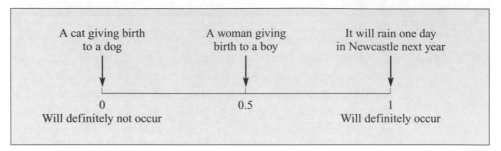

Figure 5.2 The range of probability

The probability of any particular thing occurring is usually denoted by

P(particular occurrence)   e.g., P(3 new orders today)

and must take a value between 0 and 1, i.e.

$0 \leq$ P(particular occurrence) ≤ 1

This is illustrated in Figure 5.2.

One approach to finding the likelihood is to take the observed fraction of occurrences:

$$P(\text{particular occurrence}) = \frac{\text{Number of times the particular thing occurred}}{\text{Total number of observations}}$$

EXAMPLE 5.1

Using the information provided on the shoe sizes of 900 adult males, measure the likelihood of the next male customer at a shoe shop taking (a) size 38 and (b) size 47.

(a)   90 males took size 38 shoes

P(next customer takes size 38) = $^{90}/_{900}$ = 0.1

(b)   2 males took size 47 shoes

P(next customer takes size 47) = $^{2}/_{900}$ = 0.0022 (to 4 d.p.)

It is also very likely that the likelihood of a combination of events occurring may be desired. For example, the probability that the next customer entering the shop takes a size 42 or 43, or the probability that the next two customers entering the shop both take size 40 may be needed. In order to measure these likelihoods, there are a number of probability laws that can be used, and the correct law/s need to be selected and applied to each individual situation to obtain the correct values for the probabilities. These laws and illustrations of situations in which they could be applied will now be considered.

Probability laws and guidelines for their application

Probability that an event does *not* occur

If P(A) is the probability of an event A occurring then

$$P(\text{not } A) = 1 - P(A) \qquad \textit{Note: } P(A) + P(\text{not } A) = 1$$

EXAMPLE 5.2

What is the probability of *not* picking an ace from a pack of cards (excludes jokers)?

There are 4 aces in a pack of 52 cards so $P(\text{Ace}) = \frac{1}{13}$.

By the above rule, the probability of not picking an ace $= 1 - \frac{1}{13} = \frac{12}{13}$.

Probability of one event (A) *or* another event (B) occurring

In this case there are two possible types of situation that must be considered.

If two events are *mutually exclusive* i.e., A and B cannot occur together (for instance, a head and a tail cannot occur together if a coin is tossed once) then:

$$P(A \text{ or } B) = P(A) + P(B)$$

If the two events are not mutually exclusive (for instance, choosing a red card or an ace from a pack of cards) then the formula above would have the effect of double counting (in the case of the cards, the two red aces would be included in each group and hence would be counted twice). In these cases the rule is:

$$P(A \text{ or } B) = P(A) + P(B) - P(A \text{ and } B)$$

The following example illustrates these in practice.

EXAMPLE 5.3

You have been asked to pick one card from a pack. What is the probability that the card is

a diamond or a spade?

a diamond or an ace?

Let A: Picking a diamond {13 diamonds in 52} so $P(A) = \frac{1}{4}$

Let B: Picking a spade {13 spades in 52} so $P(B) = \frac{1}{4}$

A diamond and a spade cannot occur at the same time. The events are therefore mutually exclusive so the rule to apply is:

P(A or B) = P(A) + P(B)

P(A or B) = ¼ + ¼

P(A or B) = ½

Let A: Picking a diamond {13 diamonds in 52} so P(A) = ¼

Let B: Picking an ace {4 aces in 52} so P(B) = $\frac{1}{13}$

but there is one card in the pack which is both a diamond and an ace, meaning A and B are not mutually exclusive. The chances of picking this are $\frac{1}{52}$.

P(A or B) = P(A) + P(B) − P(A and B)

P(A or B) = ¼ + $\frac{1}{13}$ − $\frac{1}{52}$

P(A or B) = $\frac{4}{52}$ + $\frac{13}{52}$ − $\frac{1}{52}$ = $\frac{16}{52}$ = $\frac{4}{13}$

Probability of one event (A) *and* another event (B) occurring

Again, there are two types of situation that must be considered. The first is where the two events are not independent of each other i.e., the result of one affects the subsequent result of the other. For instance, selecting the lottery numbers where (once the first number has been chosen) the second number is chosen from a smaller group of balls and hence the probabilities have altered. Here the formula is:

$$P(A \text{ and } B) = P(A) * P(B|A)$$

where P(B|A) means the probability that B occurs given that A has already occurred.

If the two events are independent of each other (for instance, when choosing two students from different seminar groups the selection of the first has no effect on the composition of the second group and hence no effect on the probability) then the rule is:

$$P(A \text{ and } B) = P(A) * P(B)$$

Again, these differences are illustrated in the example below.

EXAMPLE 5.4

You have been asked to pick two cards from a pack. What is the probability that two diamonds are picked?

Let A: Picking a diamond as the first card, probability is ¼.

Let B: Picking a diamond as second card. There are now only 51 cards in the pack 12 of which are diamonds, so the probability of now picking a diamond is $\frac{12}{51}$ i.e. P(B|A).

$P(A \text{ and } B) = P(A) * P(B|A)$

$P(A \text{ and } B) = \frac{1}{4} * \frac{12}{51}$

$P(A \text{ and } B) = \frac{12}{204} = \frac{3}{51}$

Now you have been asked to pick a card from a pack, replace it and then pick another card. What is the probability that the two cards were both diamonds?

Let A: Picking a diamond for the first card, probability is ¼.

Let B: Picking a diamond for the second card. As the first card has been replaced there are still 52 cards in the pack 13 of which are diamonds.

$P(A \text{ and } B) = P(A) * P(B)$

$P(A \text{ and } B) = \frac{1}{4} * \frac{1}{4} = \frac{1}{16}.$

There are diagrammatic representations (**Tree** and **Venn diagrams**) that can be used to help with the calculation of probabilities. In this book the rules discussed above should be sufficient for the situations considered.

Measuring the likelihood of occurrences does not completely resolve uncertainty for the business decision maker. With a toss of a fair coin it is reasonable to expect the two sides to be equally likely and each to have a probability of ½, yet if the coin were to be thrown a number of times, 60 say, it is unlikely that there would be an exactly equal number of each side. *Variability still exists.*

To the business decision maker, variability and likelihood are just as important as getting an estimate of the most likely or average outcome of an event. Instead of simply having a single-point value for a situation, the business person will have a more complete understanding if the range of variability and the associated probabilities are known.

To conclude, variability is to be expected – it may complicate life but generally it makes things more interesting. Statistics helps us to study and account for variability, and probability gives us a clearer understanding of the effects of variability by measuring the likelihood of occurrence.

REVIEW ACTIVITY 1

A lecturer has bought some sweets to hand round to the conscientious members of her group. There are only 20 sweets in the bag, four are mint humbugs, five are cola cubes, two are pineapple chunks and nine are acid drops (three of which are white in colour and the rest are yellow like the pineapple chunks). What is the probability of the following?

(a) That the first student picks out at random a mint humbug.

(b) That he or she picks out anything other than a pineapple chunk.

(c) That he or she picks out a cola cube or an acid drop.

Review activity 1 *continued*

(d)   That the sweet is yellow or an acid drop.

(e)   That the student picks a cola cube which they don't like so puts it back and picks a mint humbug instead.

(f)   That a greedy student takes two sweets and they are both cola cubes.

Working:

Answers on page 226.

5.3   Simple probability models

Earlier in this chapter it was pointed out that many quantitative techniques treat situations with certainty. The idea of probability and some simple rules for dealing with situations where it is not possible to act with certainty about the outcome have already been explored, and these may be extended to build up simple probability based models which allow the behaviour of a system to be examined in more detail.

Take a very simple deterministic model for the sale and manufacture of an item:

$$\text{Revenue} = \text{Quantity} * \text{Selling price}$$

$$\text{Costs} = \text{Quantity} * \text{Variable cost} + \text{Fixed cost}$$

so,

$$\text{Profit} = \text{Quantity} * (\text{Selling price} - \text{Variable cost}) - \text{Fixed cost}$$

i.e., Profit can be determined exactly for any given quantity sold, so the probability of making various levels of profit can be linked easily to the probability of obtaining the associated levels of demand.

In practice it would not be known in advance what the demand for an item would be. However, the marketing department of an organization should be able to identify the range of possible demands together with their likelihoods.

This would then transform the situation into a **probabilistic model** since a probability distribution (or risk profile) for values in the model would be used. So now there is no single deterministic solution for the profit, instead there will be a distribution of possible profits with their associated probabilities. This model should help the management to decide how much of their product to manufacture by examining the likelihoods of different levels of demand.

Even from the probabilistic model, management will often require a value for the estimated profit, the value used in such situations is known as the **expected value**.

5.4 Expected values

An expected value is simply an average of the possible outcomes weighted according to their probability of occurrence, i.e.:

$$\text{Expected value, } E(x) = x_1\, P(x_1) + x_2\, P(x_2) + \ldots + x_n\, P(x_n)$$
$$= \Sigma x P(x)$$

where $P(x)$ is the probability of event x occurring.

Note: Since the whole (probability) distribution of x values is considered, then (using appropriate notation) $E(x) = \mu$. That is, the expected value of x is equal to the mean of the x values (e.g., taking the roll of a fair die, the mean of the distribution of the scores is $(1+2+3+4+5+6)/6 = 3.5$, which is the same as the expected value).

The expected value does not necessarily take one of the possible values in the distribution e.g., the expected score on the roll of a die is 3.5; and the expected number of children in a family is 2.4. The temptation (as with the measures of central tendency) is to round the expected value. This should *not* be done because the consequences could be great when the expected value is used subsequently in decisions. For example, if there are 10 million families then there will be 24 million children; note the danger in rounding the expected value to 2 children per family!

The example below illustrates a typical situation where an expected value would be used.

EXAMPLE 5.5

A small bed and breakfast establishment has two identical twin rooms. Daily profit depends on the occupancy, where £5 profit is made with one guest, £10 with two guests, £22 with three guests or £45 with four guests.

The probabilities for the number of guests requiring rooms each night are:

P(1 guest) = 0.15   P(2 guests) = 0.45   P(3 guests) = 0.3   P(4 guests) = 0.1.

Find the expected daily profit.

If x = profit on an occupied room,

$$E(x) = £5\,(0.15) + £15\,(0.45) + £22\,(0.3) + £45\,(0.1) = £18.60$$

i.e., the average daily profit for the bed and breakfast will be £18.60.

Notice that the actual daily profit will not be £18.60: rather, this is the average amount that will be made per day over a long period of time.

Expected values have many uses in business situations. Two further examples follow. The first illustrates how expected values are used in decision making and the second shows how expected values can be used in data analysis.

EXAMPLE 5.6

A company has to choose between two alternative products: product A is estimated to have a 0.45 likelihood of success while product B is thought to have a 0.6 probability of success. If product A is sucessful, it will make a profit of £9000 for the company. If it is a failure, it will make a loss of £2100. Product B will give profits of £7500 if it is successful and losses of £1500 if not. By calculating the expected value of each product, suggest which product the company should launch.

E(product A) = 0.45 * 9000 + (1 − 0.45) * (−2100) = £2895

E(product B) = 0.6 * 7500 + (1 − 0.6) * (−1500) = £3900

So it seems that product B would be preferable (since it has the higher expected value).

Note that the expected values themselves are very unlikely to occur, again they represent a long-term average if the products could be launched a number of times. However, they do give a single measure for comparing the two alternatives.

EXAMPLE 5.7

A company buys parts from various suppliers. Each has different guaranteed quality levels. Supplier A says his parts contain no more than 5% defectives, while suppliers B and C say they have no more than 7% defectives. The latest batches received from these suppliers have been tested and there were five defectives out of 160 parts supplied by A, 32 defectives out of 300 parts supplied by B, and 17 defectives out of 250 parts supplied by C. Have the suppliers' claims about the number of defectives been met?

For supplier A we would expect to have received 5% defectives. In a batch of 160 this means:

E(defectives) = 0.05 × 160 = 8

We actually received 5, a percentage difference of

$$\frac{(5-8)}{8} * 100 = -37.5\%$$

For supplier B we would expect to have received 7% defectives. In a batch of 300 this means:

E(defectives) $= 0.07 \times 300 = 21$

We actually received 32, a percentage difference of

$$\frac{(32-21)}{21} * 100 = 52.4\%$$

For supplier C we would expect to have received 7% defectives. In a batch of 250 this means:

E(defectives) $= 0.07 \times 250 = 17.5$

We actually received 17, a percentage difference of

$$\frac{(17-17.5)}{17.5} * 100 = -2.9\%$$

So the figures suggest that supplier A gives fewer defectives than they claim to, supplier B gives more and supplier C is just about as expected.

Note that it is necessary to calculate the percentage change from the expected value in order to make a useful comparison, because a simple difference would be affected by the total number involved.

An expected value represents a 'best' single estimate of an uncertain situation, but it must be remembered that variability exists and that in other situations a range of values might be more appropriate. In these cases, a confidence interval that gives a range in the centre of the distribution of the variable of interest can be calculated. Confidence intervals are discussed in more detail in Chapter 6.

REVIEW ACTIVITY 2

From past experience, a tutor believes that the time spent on completing the additional exercises in Chapter 5 follows the probability distribution given below:

Time(mins)	25	30	35	40	45	50	55
Probability	0.05	0.05	0.2	0.15	0.3	0.15	0.1

Use this information to find the expected time it would take someone to complete the exercises in Chapter 5.

Working:

Answers on pages 226–7.

5.5 Sensitivity analysis

Another way of assessing the impact of variability in data is through the use of **sensitivity analysis**. This area is also explored in the spreadsheet exercise at the end of this chapter. The key idea behind the process is to see whether changes in the probabilities of events would cause the decision made to change. Clearly, this can be useful in the business world where the likelihood of something occurring would probably be estimated, perhaps through market research or using some-one's experience and knowledge about a situation, rather than known exactly. The following example explores this in more detail.

EXAMPLE 5.8

A company has decided to launch a new product. Based on previous experience, they know that there might be high or low levels of demand for it. They estimate the probability of high demand to be 0.4, and if there is high demand they will make a profit of £2.1m in the first year. If there is low demand, they will make a loss of £1.2m.

Find the expected value of the new product.

Market research could be arranged at further cost to the company. This would give more accurate estimates of the probabilities of high and low demand. By investigating the effect of changes in the probabilities, decide whether this infor-mation is likely to be worth purchasing.

Expected value = 0.4 * 2.1 + 0.6 * (−1.2) = 0.84 − 0.72 = £0.12m

So, based purely on this measure, it seems like a good idea to launch the prod-uct: they can expect it to make a profit. However, looking at other slightly lower values for the probability of high demand:

P(high demand)	P(low demand)	Expected value
0.30	0.70	−0.210
0.32	0.68	−0.144
0.34	0.66	−0.078
0.36	0.64	−0.012
0.38	0.62	0.054
0.40	0.60	0.120

(notice that P(high demand) + P(low demand) = 1 always because these are assumed to be the only two possibilities).

The table shows that the probability of high demand would not have to change by much before the expected value would become negative, showing that the product launch could be much riskier. In this case, it would seem to be worthwhile to refine the estimated probabilities by paying for the market research.

REVIEW
ACTIVITY 3

An investor has to choose between two different schemes. Each will return different amounts depending on market conditions. An independent financial adviser estimates that there is a 0.6 chance that interest rates will rise in the next year and a 0.4 chance that they will fall. This would affect the returns from the two schemes as follows:

	Return (£000s) if:	
	Rates rise	Rates fall
Scheme A	54	11
Scheme B	35	23

Find the expected value of each scheme and hence say which offers the better deal for the investor. What might be the potential problems with using expected values to make such a decision?

By experimenting with P(interest rates rise) between 0.4 and 0.7, say whether this seems like a safe decision.

Working:

Answers on page 227.

Key points to remember

1. Probability and probability distributions help to deal with uncertainty in data.

2. Probability is expressed as a value on a scale between 0 and 1.

3. If an event has a probability of 1, it is sure to happen. If it has a probability of 0, it is sure never to happen.

4. There are various rules that can be used to calculate probability:

   $P(\text{not } A) = 1 - P(A)$

   $P(A \text{ or } B) = P(A) + P(B)$ if A and B are mutually exclusive

   $P(A \text{ or } B) = P(A) + P(B) - P(A \text{ and } B)$ otherwise

   $P(A \text{ and } B) = P(A) * P(B)$ if A and B are independent

   $P(A \text{ and } B) = P(A) * P(B|A)$ otherwise

5. The expected value, calculated as

   $E(x) = \sum x P(x)$

   can be used to compare different schemes or to compare what has happened in practice to what might be expected in theory.

6. Sensitivity analysis can be used to assess the effect of changes in estimated probabilities on decisions made.

ADDITIONAL EXERCISES

Question 1   A group of holidaymakers on the same flight to the Greek Islands have been classified according to destination and the cost of their holiday.

Destination	Less than £250	£250–£350	Over £350	Total
Crete	21	24	18	63
Rhodes	30	27	15	72
Kos	6	33	9	48
Total	57	84	42	183

What is the probability that a person chosen at random:

(a) Is going to Rhodes?

(b) Paid less than £250 for their holiday?

(c) Paid over £350 and is going to Kos?

(d) Is going to either Crete or Rhodes?

Question 2   A survey has been conducted into people's attitudes to city centre parking and some of the results are cross-tabulated below. Respondents could choose only one option.

	Sex of respondent	
	Male	Female
Wants more free parking	23	10
Wants less free parking	12	16
Wants paid permit scheme	7	5
Wants more bus/cycle lanes	18	9

Based on these survey results, find the probability that someone chosen at random:

(a) Wants more bus/cycle lanes?

(b) Is female and wants more free parking?

(c) Wants less free parking *or* a paid permit scheme, given that they are male?

(d) Treating the males and females as two separate groups, calculate the percentage who fall into each of the responses. Use your results to comment on whether there seem to be differences in attitude between the males and females in the sample.

Question 3 A sock drawer contains 20 loose socks: four are blue, eight are red, two are white, three are green and the remainder are odd socks. Any two socks the same colour may be worn as a pair, and the odd ones do not match any of the other socks in the drawer.

What is the probability that, when two socks are chosen at random:

(a) A pair of red socks is chosen?

(b) A pair of red or blue socks is chosen?

(c) Any pair of socks is chosen?

(d) An odd sock is chosen so it is put back and a green one picked to replace it?

Question 4 A university has bought 500 computers from three different manufacturers. Twenty per cent of them came from company A, 35% from company B and 45% from company C. From previous experience the university knows that the probability of a computer needing repairs within the first two years of use is 0.1.

Find the probability that a computer chosen at random:

(a) Came from company A and developed no problems.

(b) Came from company A or company B and developed a fault within the first two years.

Question 5 I have the choice of whether or not to play a game. It will cost me 50p to play, and my return depends on the throw of a die with the following outcomes:

throw 1 = lose £1   throw 4 = win £1

throw 2 = lose 25p   throw 5 = win £2

throw 3 = lose 75p   throw 6 = win £3

Assuming that a fair die is used, should I play the game?

Question 6 The marketing department of a company has provided the following information about the possible outcomes were each of two new products to be launched on the market.

Demand	Product A		Product B	
	Probability	Payoff	Probability	Payoff
Low	0.2	−200,000	0.1	−250,000
Medium	0.3	250,000	0.3	320,000
High	0.5	600,000	0.6	710,000

Find the expected value for the payoff if product A is launched.

Find the expected value for the payoff if product B is launched.

If only one product is to be launched, which do you recommend?

Question 7 Drivers' weekly wages at a courier company are distributed according to the following probability distribution. Calculate the expected weekly wage.

Wages (£)	Probability
250 to < 300	0.2
300 to < 350	0.3
350 to < 400	0.4
400 to < 450	0.1

Question 8 The probability that a European farmer keeps cows is 0.3, the probability of him keeping sheep is 0.6 and the probability he keeps both is 0.2. Find:

(a) The probability that a farmer keeps cows *or* sheep.

(b) The probability that neither is kept.

SPREADSHEET EXERCISE

This exercise is intended to introduce more Excel features and to use the package to work with some of the ideas associated with probability. The file RENTALS.XLS will be used: this contains data collected for a company which rents televisions and videos to the public. The information supplied is for 150 customers, and the columns contained in the spreadsheet are:

Column A   An id number for the customer;

Column B   Details of the equipment rented (either a TV, video or joint package);

Column C   The delivery area where the customer lives (coded A to D);

Column D   The type of customer – classified into student, employed and unemployed/retired;

Column E   The payment method chosen – either by direct debit or using a payment book.

(a) Explore the Data, PivotTable (see Chapter 2 spreadsheet exercise) commands on the main menu and use them to create simple cross-tabulations of:

    (i)   order type and customer type;

    (ii)   customer type and payment type;

    (iii)   delivery area and customer type.

(b) Using the tables prepared in part (a), find the probabilities that:

    (i)   each type of order (TV, video or joint package) is made;

    (ii)   an order is to be delivered to a customer in area B;

    (iii)   a student rents a joint package;

    (iv)   an employed customer chooses to pay by direct debit.

The same company is considering branching out into the rental of other products: profits will depend on the level of demand. Market research suggests that the proposed schemes would have the following profit levels at high and low levels of demand (profits are per unit rented).

	High	Low
Scheme A: kitchen appliances	£5.00	£4.00
Scheme B: furniture	£8.00	£2.00
Scheme C: satellite/digital TV systems	£7.50	£3.00

The probability of high demand is currently thought to be 0.7.

(c) Use the information given above to calculate the expected profit for each scheme.

(d) Build a simple model on Excel which would show the scheme that should be chosen when the the probability of a high demand is input.

Hence find the ranges of probabilities for which each scheme would be most profitable.

CHAPTER 6

The normal distribution and confidence intervals

- To introduce the normal distribution as the most common distribution of data;
- To make calculations using standard normal probability tables;
- To introduce the idea of confidence intervals as an aid in business decision making.

Introduction

The idea of a probability distribution was introduced in Chapter 5. This is simply a way of describing how likely the various outcomes from a process are, and is often presented as a graph. In this chapter, one specific (and very commonly used) probability distribution will be discussed: the normal distribution. To illustrate where it comes from, consider the following data relating to heights of a group of 500 eight year old children.

Height (cm)	Frequency
100 to less than 110	20
110 to less than 120	48
120 to less than 130	100
130 to less than 140	170
140 to less than 150	98
150 to less than 160	44
160 to less than 170	20

Source: School survey

Plotting this information on a histogram (as shown in Figure 6.1) gives some idea of the distribution of heights amongst the eight year olds.

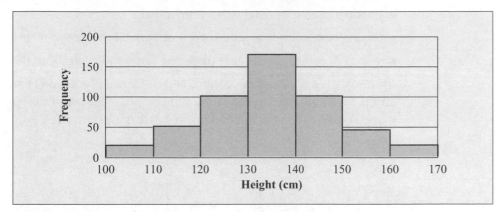

Figure 6.1 Histogram illustrating normal distribution, showing heights of 500 eight year old children

This information can be used to answer simple queries such as 'What is the probability that an eight year old selected at random is over 160 cm in height?'

From the graph it can be seen that 20 children out of the 500 were over 160 cm tall. This gives a probability of $^{20}\!/_{500} = 0.04$.

However, answering a question such as 'What is the probability that an eight year old picked at random is over 163 cm tall?' would be more difficult.

If the group widths were to be made smaller then the histogram would change slightly, as shown in Figure 6.2. This could then help answer more probability related questions.

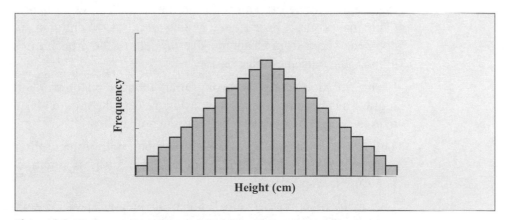

Figure 6.2 Histogram (small categories) illustrating normal distribution

More interestingly, if the general shape of the two histograms is examined, it can be seen that:

- the distribution of heights is symmetrical;
- the majority of the values are grouped around the centre (the mean);
- values become less and less likely the further they are from the mean.

By measuring the heights of more and more eight year olds and taking smaller group intervals, the histogram would approach a smooth symmetrical bell-shaped curve called the **normal curve** or **distribution**. See Figure 6.3.

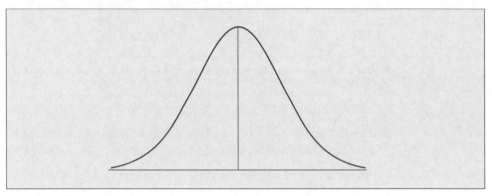

Figure 6.3 Normal curve

Going back to the first histogram (Figure 6.1), if the heights of the bars in the histogram were added together the total would be 500 (the total number of eight year olds measured). To find probabilities, these heights are divided by the total. For example, $^{20}/_{500}$ gave the probability that a child was over 160 cm. Hence if the graph were scaled down by dividing each frequency by the total, the bars would then represent the *probabilities* and the sum of these probabilities would be 1. (This makes sense, because the heights of all of the children surveyed would be counted. Recall from Chapter 5 that the sum of the probabilities associated with all possible outcomes must be 1.)

In the situation where the group intervals have become so small that the histogram has become a curve (as in Figure 6.3) the area under the curve (rather than the height of the bar) represents the probability.

This *normal* distribution of data is common both in naturally occurring things such as heights or IQ, and in many practical business situations such as manufacturing to a specification.

Like many other mathematical/statistical findings standard notation is used as a summary for the normal distribution. In this case the variable X is said to have a normal distribution with mean μ and variance σ^2, and this is often represented using the shorthand notation:

$$X \sim N(\mu, \sigma^2)$$

Clearly, there is a whole family of normal curves, one for each value of μ, σ and n, so to get around this the **standard normal distribution** is used for calculation. This is the distribution to which all other normal curves can be transformed.

6.1 The standard normal distribution

The standard normal distribution has a mean of 0 and a standard deviation of 1 (so the variance is also 1). In order to distinguish it from a typical normal distribution the letter Z is used to represent the standard normal variable.

Using the shorthand notation we have:

$$Z \sim N(0, 1^2)$$

This is shown on the typical bell-shaped curve in Figure 6.4.

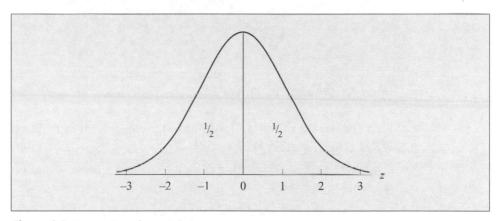

Figure 6.4 Symmetry of normal curve

The total area beneath the curve equals 1, i.e., it is a probability distribution.

Since it is symmetrical, the area on either side of $z = 0$ is equal to ½.

Unfortunately there is no easy formula for calculating other areas beneath the normal distribution so, instead, normal probability tables are used. These are widely available in various formats; two tables are provided in Appendix A.

In one of these tables, less than half the curve is shaded (this will be referred to as the 'tail' table). In the other, the majority of the curve is shaded (and this will be referred to as the 'body' table). The body and tail tables complement each other i.e.,

Body area = 1 – Tail area

Tail area = 1 – Body area

Therefore, only one table is really necessary although two are given here for simplicity.

The following examples illustrate how to use the standard normal tables to find areas for values of Z between –4 and 4. (For areas between –3 and +3 this can be done to two decimal places.)

Note how a small diagram helps to identify the area required in all cases.

EXAMPLE 6.1

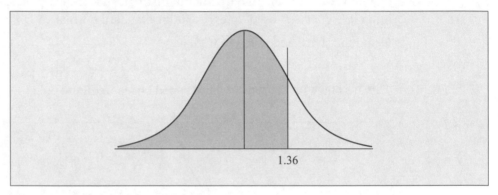

Figure 6.5 Diagram for Example 6.1

Find the area on the standard normal tables which is to the left of 1.36, i.e., $P(Z < 1.36)$ (Figure 6.5).

Choose the appropriate table (i.e., the one with most of the body of the graph shaded – body table).

Look down the left-hand side for row labelled 1.3 and then along the top for the column labelled 0.06.

The value in that row and column gives the area to be 0.9131, which is the probability required.

EXAMPLE 6.2

Find the area from the standard normal table to the right of 2.1, i.e., $P(Z > 2.1)$ (Figure 6.6).

Choose the appropriate table (i.e., the one with the tail of the graph shaded – tail tables).

Look down the left-hand side for row labelled 2.1 and then along the top for the column labelled 0.00.

The value in that row and column gives the area to be 0.0179, which is the probability required.

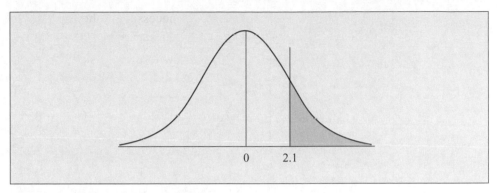

Figure 6.6 Diagram for Example 6.2

Both of these simply required the appropriate choice of table and you may have noticed that no negative values of Z are provided. The next example illustrates how such a situation would be dealt with.

EXAMPLE 6.3

Find the area from the standard normal tables to the left of -0.56, i.e., $P(Z < -0.56)$ (Figure 6.7).

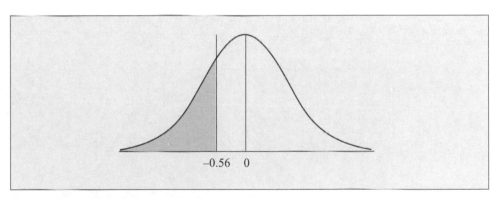

Figure 6.7 Diagram for Example 6.3

To find this area it is necessary to make use of the symmetry of the distribution.

Choose the appropriate table (i.e., tail table).

Due to symmetry the area to the left of -0.56 is the same as the area to the right of $+0.56$ (Figure 6.8). Therefore, look down the first column for the row labelled 0.5 and then along the top for the column labelled 0.06.

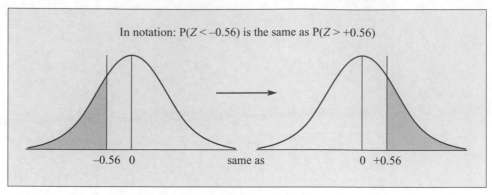

In notation: P(Z < −0.56) is the same as P(Z > +0.56)

−0.56   0   same as   0 +0.56

Figure 6.8 Second diagram for Example 6.3

The value in that row and column is 0.2877, the probability required.

Note: The same principle applies when more than half of the curve has been shaded, i.e., P(Z > −0.56) is the same as P(Z < +0.56).

The next example moves on to look at how the tables can be manipulated together to find areas which are neither just the body nor just the tail.

EXAMPLE 6.4

From the standard normal tables find the area between −0.56 and 1.36, i.e., P(−0.56 < Z < 1.36).

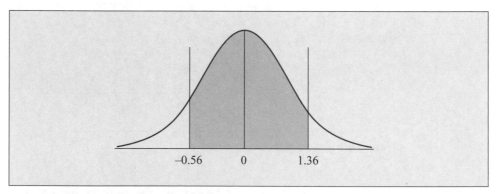

−0.56   0   1.36

Figure 6.9 Diagram for Example 6.4

Here areas found from the two different tables need to be manipulated in order to find the required probability.

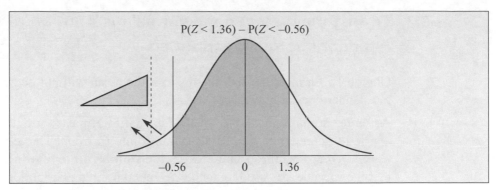

Figure 6.10 Second diagram for Example 6.4

The shaded area in Figure 6.9 is the same as that in figure 6.10. This requires using the body table to find the area to the left of 1.36 and the tail table in conjunction with symmetry to find the area to the left of –0.56.

Fortunately, in this case, these probabilities have already been found in two of the previous examples:

$P(Z < 1.36) = 0.9131$ and $P(Z < –0.56) = 0.2877$

So,

$P(–0.56 < Z < 1.36) = 0.9131 – 0.2877 = 0.6254$

Note: There are other ways in which the areas could be manipulated to yield the same answers. All are acceptable, and the important thing is to visualize the problem and hence the areas required to solve it.

REVIEW ACTIVITY 1

Use the standard normal tables to find the area between the z values of –0.37 and 1.52, i.e., $P(–0.37 < Z < 1.52)$.

Working:

Answer on page 227

6.2 Transforming a general normal distribution to the standard normal distribution

Obviously, for most normal distributions the mean will not be zero and likewise the standard deviation will not be 1.

As tables are only available for this standard normal distribution a formula is applied to convert any other distribution into this one. The tables can then be used to find the appropriate area on the **standard normal tables**. Remember that the variable X is used to denote a general normal distribution while Z is used for the standard normal distribution.

The following equation is used to achieve this transformation:

$$z = \frac{x - \mu}{\sigma}$$

(Note that lower-case characters (x and z) are usually used to denote numbers involved in problem solving whereas upper-case X and Z are saved for describing the overall distribution.) The process of transforming a general normal distribution $X \sim N(\mu, \sigma^2)$ to the standard normal distribution $Z \sim N(0, 1^2)$ using the above equation is called **standardizing**. The example below illustrates how this is applied in practice.

EXAMPLE 6.5

A large store knows that the number of days between sending out a monthly bill and receiving payment from its customers is approximately a normal distribution with a mean of 18 days and standard deviation four days.

(a) Find the probability that a bill will not be paid until after 21 days.

(b) Find the percentage of bills which are paid in less than 12 days.

(c) From 200 bills how many would be expected to be paid between 16 and 20 days?

As with all problems involving the normal distribution, diagrams illustrating the situations are very useful. See Figure 6.11.

(a) Firstly, 21 days must be transformed from $X \sim N(18, 4^2)$ to the standard normal value $Z \sim N(0, 1^2)$.

Using the transformation formula

$$z = \frac{x - \mu}{\sigma} = \frac{21 - 18}{4} = 0.75$$

then looking up this z value in the tail tables gives 0.2266.

So the probability that a bill will not be paid until after 21 days is 0.2266.

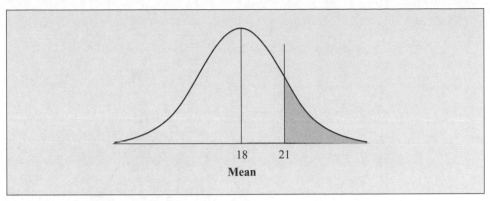

Figure 6.11 Diagram for Example 6.5 part (a)

(b) Again, convert the x value of 12 days to a z value (See Figure 6.12).

Using the transformation formula.

$$z = \frac{x - \mu}{\sigma} = \frac{12 - 18}{4} = -1.5$$

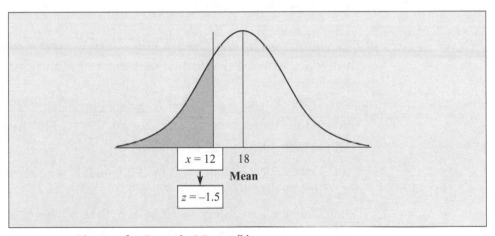

Figure 6.12 Diagram for Example 6.5 part (b)

Using symmetry $P(Z < -1.5)$ is the same as $P(Z > 1.5)$ so looking up $z = 1.5$ on the tail tables gives an area of 0.0668.

To convert this into a percentage simply multiply by 100.

Therefore, 6.68% of bills are paid within 12 days.

(c) To answer this, first find the probability that any bill takes between 16 and 20 days to be paid.

Transform both 16 and 20 into z values using the formula (see Figure 6.13)

$$z = \frac{x - \mu}{\sigma} = \frac{16 - 18}{4} = -0.5$$

$$z = \frac{x - \mu}{\sigma} = \frac{20 - 18}{4} = 0.5$$

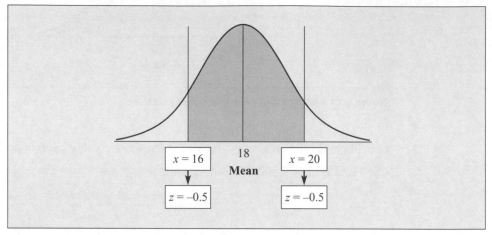

Figure 6.13 Diagram for Example 6.5 part (c)

To find the required shaded area we can take the area under –0.5 from the area under +0.5.

From the body tables we find that the area under +0.5 is 0.6915. The area under –0.5 is the same as the area above 0.5, or –0.3085 from the tail tables.

0.6915 – 0.3085 = 0.3830

To find the expected number from 200, multiply the probability of one bill i.e., 0.383 by the 200 giving 76.6.

Therefore, approximately 77 bills from 200 can be expected to be paid between 16 and 20 days.

Using the standard normal tables in reverse

Standard normal probability tables can also be used in reverse when the area under part of the curve is known and the question requires either a value for z or x to be found.

In this case it is necessary to look in the main part of the table for the known area (probability) or as near as possible to it and then trace back to the row and column headings to read off the resulting value of z. This can then be subsequently used to find an x value, the mean or standard deviation (assuming two of the three are previously known) from any other normal distribution.

Again, when attempting any questions of this type, a diagram helps because the tables only account for positive values for z – it is up to the user to decide whether the actual value required is positive (+) or negative (–).

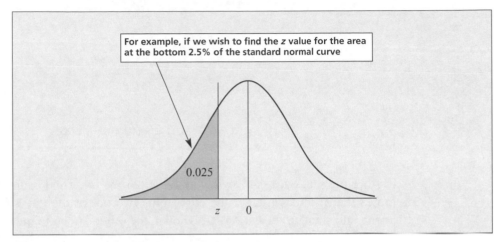

Figure 6.14 Normal tables in reverse

Looking in the body of the tail tables for 0.0250 gives a value of $z = 1.96$ in the corresponding row and column headings.

However, the diagram at the top of the tail tables shows a shaded area to the right, so for an area on the left we require the symmetric negative value of $z = -1.96$.

The next example illustrates how this would work in practice.

EXAMPLE 6.6

Weights of people in a certain age group are normally distributed with a mean of 72 kg and standard deviation 6 kg. Find the weight below which the lightest 10% of the people lie. See Figure 6.15. For a diagrammatic representation.

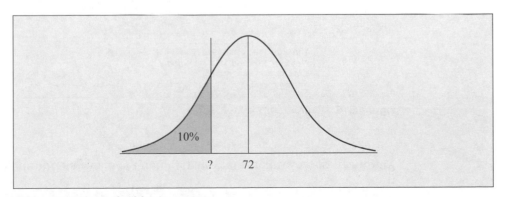

Figure 6.15 Normal tables in reverse

The probability to the left of z is 0.10 (i.e., 10%). Looking in the body of the appropriate table gives $z = 1.28$ for a shaded area on the right of the curve, so $z = -1.28$ as an area on the left of the curve is required. But,

$$z = \frac{x - \mu}{\sigma}$$

so

$$-1.28 = \frac{x - 72}{6}$$

or

$$x = 72 + (-1.28)(6) = 64.32 \text{ kg}$$

Before moving onto the Review activity, here is one final example which illustrates that if an area under the curve plus two out of the three factors (x value, mean and standard deviation) are known, the other can be found.

EXAMPLE 6.7

A builders' merchant wishes to ensure that only 5% of any orders of 3 mm gravel exceed the standard order weight of 1000 kg. If the automatic weighing machine that makes up these orders weighs with a standard deviation of 10 kg, what should the machine's average be set to?

First, gather together the information given in the question – see Figure 6.16.

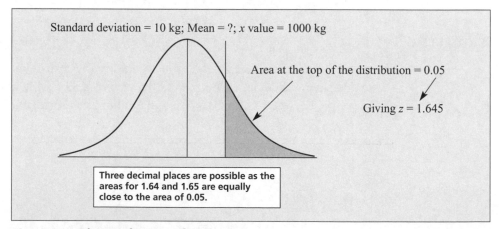

Figure 6.16 Diagram for Example 6.7

Putting all of the available information into the conversion formula we have:

$$z = \frac{x - \mu}{\sigma}$$

$$1.645 = \frac{1000 - \mu}{10}$$

Rearranging the equation to find μ:

$\mu = 1000 - 1.645 * 10$

$\mu = 983.55$ kg

Therefore, to ensure that only 5% of the standard orders are overweight the machine should be set to an average of 983.55 kg.

REVIEW ACTIVITY 2

The reading time for a business mathematics examination paper has been found to be normally distributed with a mean of 7 minutes and a standard deviation of 2.5 minutes.

(a)   What percentage of students take less than 5 minutes to read the examination paper?

(b)   How long does it take the slowest 10% of students to read the examination paper?

(c)   Examiners have taken into account 10 minutes of reading time, assuming that 95% of the candidates will have read the paper in that time. Is this the case? If not, what time allowance (to the nearest minute) should be made?

(*Note*: you may find this a little tricky at first but with careful consideration you should be able to see a solution. Remember to use a diagram to clarify what you are being asked to do!)

Working:

Answers on pages 227–8.

6.3   Confidence intervals

The previous discussion of the normal distribution has centred on the use of point estimates of the mean and standard deviation to assess how likely something is. It is also possible to use the normal distribution to put limits on a range within which the mean value of a distribution will lie. These are called confidence intervals and are particularly useful when a sample of data has been taken.

Rather than using a single-point estimate of the mean (which is very unlikely to coincide with the true population mean) limits for the mean can be calculated to a known degree of accuracy.

When calculating a confidence interval it is usual to specify the percentage of confidence which is acceptable – the higher the percentage specified the wider the range (to be sure that the mean lies within it). One hundred per cent confidence would not be specified because that would produce such a broad range as to include all extreme values and would be of no use in any form of decision making.

A 95% level of confidence is the most commonly used range, this removes the 'worst' 2.5% of values at each end of the distribution of a variable.

Engineers frequently choose 99.8% confidence, allowing only 1 in 1000 items to fail each time; medical researchers usually work to even greater levels of confidence before treatments or drugs are accepted (but this requires more and more data and time).

This links to the normal distribution, because mathematicians in the past found that 68.3% of observations will lie within one standard deviation either side of the mean, with a corresponding figure of 95.4% within two standard deviations.

To find out more useful figures such as how many standard deviations should be taken to include 95% of observations, it is once again necessary to work backwards with the normal tables.

Starting with the standard normal distribution, it is necessary to find z such that 2.5% (0.025) of observations lie above and below it. (This is illustrated in Figure 6.17.) This gives $z = +1.96$ and $z = -1.96$ (refer to Example 6.6 if a reminder is needed on how this is found).

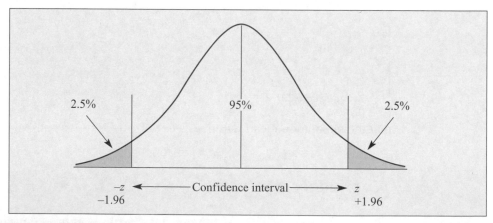

Figure 6.17 Confidence intervals

So, in simplistic terms, a 95% confidence interval (an interval within which 95% of values from a distribution would lie) can be found by taking 1.96 standard deviations from either side of the mean.

When dealing with populations and samples both the way in which a confidence interval is formulated and the way in which it is interpreted vary slightly.

Confidence intervals for populations

For population data a 95% confidence interval is formulated as:

$$\mu - 1.96 * \sigma < x < \mu + 1.96 * \sigma$$

where x represents the variable of interest.

Putting this in words – there is 95% confidence that a value from a normal distribution will lie within 1.96 standard deviations of the mean value (as found above).

EXAMPLE 6.8

IQ for the population is normally distributed with mean 100 and standard deviation 15. Find a 95% confidence interval for the IQ of an 'average' person.

A 95% confidence interval for a population is given by:

$$\mu - 1.96 * \sigma < x < \mu + 1.96 * \sigma$$

$$100 - 1.96 \, (15) < x < 100 + 1.96 \, (15)$$

i.e.,

$$70.6 < x < 129.4$$

The way in which this is then interpreted is:

95% of the population have an IQ of between 70.6 and 129.4.

Confidence intervals for samples

More often than not, sample data are used to represent a population. Here confidence intervals are used in a slightly different way. The aim is to provide limits within which we can be sure (to a predefined level of accuracy: 95%, 99% etc.) that the population mean will lie.

The formula is amended to account for this, and for a 95% confidence interval becomes:

$$\bar{x} - 1.96 * \frac{s}{\sqrt{n}} < \mu < \bar{x} + 1.96 * \frac{s}{\sqrt{n}}$$

where n = number in the sample.

Note: This formula is based around a piece of statistical theory known as the **central limit theorem**. Given the introductory nature of this book details of this theory are not provided.

There are slight variations to this formula, often connected to the size of the sample involved, which may be cited in other texts. For the purpose of this book the formula above will be sufficient.

EXAMPLE 6.9

A survey of the amount spent whilst on a package holiday to Turkey by a random sample of 64 people showed that the mean expenditure was £390, with a standard deviation of £96. Estimate the mean amount spent by 'all' of the holidaymakers to Turkey with 95% confidence.

Here the data are from a sample so a 95% confidence interval is found by:

$$\bar{x} - 1.96 * \frac{s}{\sqrt{n}} < \mu < \bar{x} + 1.96 * \frac{s}{\sqrt{n}}$$

In this example $n = 64$, $\bar{x} = £390$ and $s = £96$.

$$390 - \frac{1.96 * 96}{\sqrt{64}} < \mu < 390 + \frac{1.96 * 96}{\sqrt{64}}$$

$$390 - 23.52 < \mu < 390 + 23.52$$

$$£366.48 < \mu < £413.52$$

Therefore, we can be 95% confident that the mean amount spent by holidaymakers in Turkey is between £366.48 and £413.52.

Calculating intervals for other degrees of confidence

As mentioned earlier, it may be desirable to have an even higher level of accuracy in a confidence interval: 99% or 99.8% are commonly used.

To calculate these intervals, the only difference is in the z value used – they are:

Confidence interval required	z value used
95%	$z = \pm 1.96$
99%	$z = \pm 2.58$
99.8%	$z = \pm 3.10$

REVIEW ACTIVITY 3

Investigations by tutors taking a business mathematics course, based on this book, have revealed that the time taken to complete the exercises in Chapter 5 follow a normal distribution with a mean time of 42 minutes and a standard deviation of 27 minutes. These results were based on a sample of 100 students. Use this information to construct a 95% confidence interval for the mean time spent to complete the exercises in Chapter 5.

Working:

Answer on page 228.

Key points to remember:

1. The normal distribution is one of the most commonly occurring probability distributions.

2. The standard normal distribution has a mean of zero and a standard deviation of 1. Values in this distribution are represented by Z/z. Tables used to perform various calculations on this distribution are provided in Appendix A. In one of these, less than half of the curve is shaded, and this is referred to as the tail table. The other is referred to as the body table. The body and tail tables complement each other i.e., Body area = 1 − Tail area and vice versa.

3. All other normal distributions can be converted to the standard normal distribution by the following formula: $z = (x − \mu)/\sigma$.

4. The standard normal tables can be used in many ways to answer questions involving the normal distribution. Therefore it is imperative that the reader is familiar with their use.

5. Confidence intervals use the normality of a distribution to provide limits on a range within which a mean value for the distribution will lie (mostly used with data originating from a sample).

6. The most common confidence interval used in business is the 95% confidence interval.

7. The 95% confidence interval for a population is formulated as:

$$\mu − 1.96 * \sigma < x < \mu + 1.96 * \sigma$$

where x represents the variable of interest, μ is the population mean and σ is the population standard deviation. This is interpreted by saying that 95% of the values in the population will be between the two values of x found by the formula.

8. The 95% confidence interval for a sample is formulated as:

$$\bar{x} - 1.96 * \frac{s}{\sqrt{n}} < \mu < \bar{x} + 1.96 * \frac{s}{\sqrt{n}}$$

where $\bar{x}$ (bar) is sample mean, s is sample standard deviation and n is sample size.

This is interpreted by saying we are 95% confident that the true population mean lies between the two calculated values. *Note*: Other texts may provide formulae which differ according to sample size.

ADDITIONAL EXERCISES

Question 1   Use Z-tables to find the following probabilities:

(a) $P(Z > 0.34)$

(b) $P(Z < 1.85)$

(c) $P(Z < -1.24)$

(d) $P(1.56 < Z < 2.37)$

(e) $P(-0.37 < Z < 3.4)$

(f) $P(Z < -2.30 \quad \text{or} \quad Z > 1.29)$

Question 2   IQ scores follow a normal distribution with a mean score of 100 and standard deviation of 15 i.e., $X \sim N(100,225)$. Find the percentage of people expected to have an IQ score of:

(a)   Below 70;

(b)   Between 80 and 120;

(c)   Above 50.

Question 3   A university has decided to introduce a new system for grading results: students who achieve a mark below 40 will 'fail', 40–60 will 'pass' and more than 60 will be graded as 'pass with distinction'. All marks are out of 100.

Given that the mean student mark on a particular unit in the past is known to have been 54 with a standard deviation of 8, find:

(a)   The proportion of students who might be expected to achieve each of the possible grades.

(b) The mark which the lowest 5% of students might be expected to achieve.

The university authorities would like the system to work so that no more than 10% of students fail, 60% achieve a 'pass' and 30% a 'pass with distinction'. Calculate the mark boundaries required for these percentages to occur.

Question 4   The lifetime of garden flares are normally distributed with a mean of 240 minutes and it is known that 90% of the flares last at least 200 minutes.

(a) What is the standard deviation for the lifetime of the garden flares?

(b) What percentage of flares will last for more than five hours?

(c) In a consignment of 650 garden flares, how many would be expected to burn out in less than 150 minutes?

Question 5   The average height of a British dairy cow is 140 cm with a standard deviation of 8 cm, while the average height of beef cattle is 147 cm with a standard deviation of 9 cm.

Construct a 95% confidence interval for the height of a dairy cow and a 99% confidence interval for the height of beef cattle.

Question 6   Service costs for a sample of 45 small hatchback cars were found to be normally distributed, with a mean of £59.80 and a standard deviation of £32.50.

(a) Construct a 95% confidence interval for the mean service cost for a small hatchback.

Service costs for a sample of 150 medium sized cars are also normally distributed with a mean of £69.75 and a variance of £676.00.

(b) Construct a 99% confidence interval for the mean service cost of a medium sized car.

Question 7   A department store has analysed the records of a sample of 40 customers who hold charge cards and has found that the mean age is 42.2 years with a standard deviation of 15.046 years. Estimate the percentage of customers aged 65 or above.

A previous study conducted by the marketing manager found that on average a customer spends £85.70 with a variance of £225. Using these figures estimate the minimum amount spent by the bottom 15% of customers.

Given that a sample of 30 female storecard customers made an average of 51.7 purchases in a year, with a standard deviation of 22.7, calculate a 95% confidence interval for the average number of purchases made by all female customers to the nearest integer.

(Assume all data is normally distributed.)

SPREADSHEET EXERCISE

This exercise is designed to consolidate learning in the construction of tables and graphs along with the calculation of summary measures using Excel. The exercise will also introduce the normal distribution functions available in the package.

The file ORDERS.XLS contains data on the number of orders processed by the 'Mullen's Electrics' warehouse on a *sample* of 180 days over the past two years. Use these data to complete the following tasks.

(a) Create a frequency distribution of the number of orders received per day, using 10 groups. From this, calculate the probability that an order falls into each of the groups.

(b) Graph the probabilities against the mid-point of the order groups on a frequency polygon. What does this tell you about the data?

(c) Find the mean and standard deviation of the *sample* of orders.

(d) Using your knowledge relating to the distribution of the data and appropriate Excel commands calculate:

   (i)   the probability that more than 37 orders are placed on any day;

   (ii) the probability that fewer than 14 orders are placed;

   (iii) the probability that between 20 and 35 orders are placed;

   (iv) the minimum number of orders which would be placed on the busiest 5% of days.

   (v)   Compute a 95% confidence interval for the true population mean number of orders processed.

Hints for completion

Excel has a selection of functions relating to the normal distribution and confidence intervals. For normal distribution questions, in a similar manner to using the printed tables, a little thought has to go into the manipulation of the functions to reach the desired outcome. The different commands and examples of how these can be manipulated are given below.

Please note that due to the greater accuracy of Excel some answers gained by use of the tables may differ from those found on the spreadsheet.

Standard normal distribution i.e., $Z \sim N(0, 1^2)$

=NORMSDIST(Z): returns the probability for P($Z <= z$)

i.e., the area below *any* (positive or negative) value of z.

Examples

To find P($Z < 1.68$) the function used is =NORMSDIST(1.68).

To find an area above z remember that the area under the whole curve is 1 and therefore the area above a value of z is (1 – Area below z).

So to find $P(Z > 2.1)$ the formula to enter is =1–NORMSDIST(2.1).

=NORMSINV(p): gives the Z value found when using tables backwards

Example

To find the value ? such that $P(X < ?) = 0.1$ the function is =NORMSINV(0.1)

i.e., the z value corresponding to the bottom 10% of the curve.

=STANDARDIZE(Value, Mean, Std Dev.): converts values from any normal distribution to the standard normal distribution i.e., $x \rightarrow z$

Example

If X is normally distributed with a mean of 50 and a standard deviation of 10, find the value of z when $x = 45$.

The function required is = STANDARDIZE(45,50,10).

Normal distributions i.e., $X \sim N(\mu, \sigma^2)$

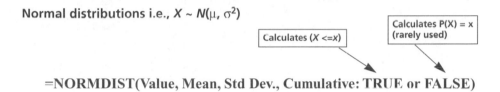

Calculates $(X <= x)$

Calculates $P(X) = x$ (rarely used)

=NORMDIST(Value, Mean, Std Dev., Cumulative: TRUE or FALSE)

Example

The lengths of printer cable from a production line are normally distributed with a mean of 2 m and a standard deviation of 0.05 m. Find the probability that a length of printer cable picked at random is less than 1.9 m long.

The required function is =NORMDIST(1.9,2,0.05,TRUE).

Watch out! There is very little difference between the function wording NORMDIST and NORMSDIST (standard normal) and this can cause frustration when errors occur.

=NORMINV(area, mean, Std Dev.): this function is used for problems where the probability is known and the X value for a normal distribution is required

Example

A group of students scored an average of 57 on an exam with a standard deviation of 9. If the bottom 10% of the group failed what was the pass mark for the exam?

The function required is =NORMINV(0.1,57,9).

Confidence intervals for samples

=CONFIDENCE(interval proportion, standard deviation, sample size)

Note this formula represents the range either side of the sample mean. It does not give the final confidence interval range.

Example

If the sample mean is 45 based on a sample of 50 items and the standard deviation is 4, find a 95% confidence interval for the true mean (μ).

The required upper and lower limits of the interval would be given by

= 45 – CONFIDENCE(0.05,4,50)   (lower limit)

= 45 + CONFIDENCE(0.05,4,50)   (upper limit)

Here 0.05 represents the area in both tails i.e., 5%.

Population confidence intervals

In this case there is no specific function and the lower and upper limits are simply constructed from first principles.

CHAPTER 7

Financial models

LEARNING OBJECTIVES

- To consider different types of interest;
- To discuss calculation of interest;
- To discuss uses of discounting;
- To discuss the meaning and calculation of net present value and internal rate of return.

Introduction

Interest is simply the amount of money that an investment makes over time. In this chapter, some simple mathematical models for calculating interest and comparing the values of investments over time will be considered.

Terminology used

Before we can consider in detail the equations and models in common use, it is important to be familiar with the terminology used to describe the variables involved:

- P is the principal – the amount of money initially invested or borrowed;
- n is the number of time periods which the investment runs for (usually years);
- S_n is the sum accrued – the amount of money obtained after n time periods;
- r is the interest rate expressed as a proportion (i.e., 10% = 0.1).

7.1 Types of interest

There are two main ways of adding interest to a sum of money: simple interest and compound interest.

Simple interest

Here it is assumed that the interest accrues only on the principal – i.e., if £100 is invested at 10% per annum (p.a.) then £10 (10% of £100) is received in the first year, £10 in the second year, £10 in the third year etc.

Using the terminology laid out above, and given that an amount P is invested initially, we have the following table:

Time	Interest received	Amount accrued
1	$r * P$	$S_1 = P + rP$
2	$r * P$	$S_2 = P + rP + rP = P + 2rP$
3	$r * P$	$S_3 = P + 2rP + rP = P + 3rP$
⋮		
⋮		
⋮		
n	$r * P$	$S_n = P + nrP = P + rnP$

Thus the general formula for calculation of the sum received under a simple interest system is:

$$S_n = P + rnP$$

which is equivalent to

$$S_n = P(1 + rn)$$

Note: the total interest received is simply $r * n * P$.

EXAMPLE 7.1

£1200 is invested at 5.2% p.a. simple interest. What is the amount accrued after 15 years?

$n\ = 15$

$r\ = 0.052$

$P\ = £1200$

$S_{15} = 1200 * (1 + 0.052 * 15) = £2136$

The amount accrued after 15 years is £2136.

Alternatively, it may be necessary to 'work backwards'.

EXAMPLE 7.2

Someone borrowed a sum at 4% p.a. simple interest six years ago. They now owe £4960. How much did they borrow?

$n \quad = 6$

$r \quad = 0.04$

$P \quad = ?$

$S_6 \quad = £4960$

$S_n \quad = P(1+rn)$

$4960 = P * (1 + 0.04 * 6)$

$4960 = 1.24P$

Rearranging the equation gives:

$$P = \frac{4960}{1.24} = £4000$$

They borrowed £4000 six years ago.

Compound interest

This is the 'normal' way to calculate interest. Interest payments are based on the total sum accrued, rather than just the principal. For example,

£100 invested at 10% per annum compound interest

after 1 year would yield £110 (£100 + 10% of £100)

after 2 years would yield £121 (£110 + 10% of £110)

after 3 years would yield £133.10 (£121 + 10% of £121)

etc.

The derivation of a formula for calculating compound interest involves slightly more complex algebra than that for simple interest, but is included here for information. Again, considering the situation in terms of the general variables used where P is the initial amount invested:

After 1 time period the amount accrued is

$S_1 = P + rP = P(1 + r)$

S_1 becomes the new investment, so after the next time period the amount accrued will have increased again to:

$S_2 = S_1 + rS_1 = S_1(1 + r)$

but, from above, $S_1 = P(1 + r)$ so substituting this gives

$S_2 = P(1 + r)(1 + r) = P(1 + r)^2$

Continuing in the same way

$$S_3 = S_2 + rS_2 = S_2(1 + r)$$

so

$$S_3 = P(1 + r)^2(1 + r) = P(1 + r)^3$$

So the general formula for calculation of compound interest is

$$S_n = P(1 + r)^n$$

EXAMPLE 7.3

£1200 is invested at 5.2% p.a. compound interest. What is the amount accrued after 15 years?

$P = £1200$

$r = 0.052$

$n = 15$

$S_{15} = 1200 * (1 + 0.052)^{15} = 1200 * 2.1391 = 2566.92$

(Powers like this can be found easily on a scientific calculator – usually the key is marked x^y or y^x.)

After 15 years the investment returns £2566.92.

Working backwards this time:

EXAMPLE 7.4

(a) Someone borrowed a sum at 4% p.a. compound interest six years ago. They now owe £4960. How much did they borrow?

$n = 6$

$r = 0.04$

$P = ?$

$S_6 = £4960$

$S_n = P(1+r)^n$

$4960 = P * (1+0.04)^6$

$4960 = 1.2653P$

$$P = \frac{4960}{1.2653} = £3920.02 \text{ (to 2 d.p.)}$$

They borrowed £3920.02 six years ago.

(b) A clerk's wages have been increased in line with inflation each year for the last 10 years. His initial wage was £4500 p.a. and this has risen to £11,250 p.a. What has the average rate of inflation been over the period?

P = 4500
n = 10
r = ?
S_{10} = 11,250

$S_n = P(1 + r)^n$
$11{,}250 = 4500 \,(1 + r)^{10}$
$(1 + r)^{10} = \dfrac{11{,}250}{4500} = 2.5$

$1 + r = {}^{10}\!\sqrt{2.5} = 1.095958$

(Again, a scientific calculator should be used to calculate the tenth root of 2.5 – usually the key is marked $x^{1/y}$.)

$r = 1.095958 - 1 = 0.095958 = 9.60\%$ (to 2 d.p.)

The average rate of inflation has been 9.60% over the 10 year period.

(c) If inflation had been only 5%, how long would it have taken for his wages to reach the same level?

P = 4500
n – ?
r – 0.05
S_n = 11250

$S_n = P(1 + r)^n$
$11{,}250 = 4500 * (1 + 0.05)^n$

$(1.05)^n = \dfrac{11{,}250}{4500} = 2.5$

To solve this further involves a much more difficult mathematical procedure and logarithms (logs) must be used to isolate the power.

This is the only place that log conversions will be used in this book. Readers are not expected to know anything about the technicalities of how they are calculated, just how to find them on a calculator and apply them in this type of problem. The level of knowledge required is illustrated below:

$\log (1.05)^n = \log 2.5$ (taking logs of both sides)

Magically, this becomes

$n \log (1.05) = \log 2.5$ (which is a special property of logs)

$n = \dfrac{\log 2.5}{\log 1.05} = \dfrac{0.39794}{0.02119} = 18.78$ (to 2 d.p.)

It would have taken approximately 19 years.

Note that there are two forms of logarithm given on scientific calculators: generally the keys are marked LOG and LN. Either may be used in the calculations and the final result will be the same: here LOG has been used.

Sometimes it is necessary to use common sense to answer more complex questions by breaking them down into stages.

EXAMPLE 7.5

(a) £1000 is invested at 4% per annum for five years. If the investor chooses to leave her money in the scheme the interest rate then changes to 7% for a further four years. What would be the total value of the investment after the whole period?

$P = £1000$
$r = 0.04$
$n = 5$
$S_5 = 1000 (1.04)^5 = £1216.6529$

This amount is then reinvested:

$S_9 = 1216.6529 (1.07)^4 = £1594.78$ (to 2 d.p.)

After the total investment period of nine years, the sum accrued would be £1594.78.

(b) What would be the final value if £500 were withdrawn after the initial 5 year period?

Here $S_9 = 716.6529 (1.07)^4 = £939.39$ (to 2 d.p.)

So the final value would be £939.39.

7.2 Effective and nominal interest rates

If interest is not compounded (added to the account) annually then it may be important to calculate an effective annual rate (EAR). For instance, credit cards usually calculate interest on a monthly basis, but must quote an annual percentage rate (APR) by law to give the consumer enough information to make valid comparisons. However, if two different non-annual rates were quoted in different circumstances the EAR would be required in order to make a valid comparison. The formula for this is:

$$\text{EAR} = (1 + r)^m - 1$$

(where m is the number of times interest is calculated annually – 12 if monthly, 4 if quarterly, 52 if weekly etc.)

EXAMPLE 7.6

A local store offers credit at a rate of 2.75% per month. What is the effective annual rate?

$r = 0.0275$

$m = 12$

$EAR = (1+0.0275)^{12} - 1 = 0.38478 = 38.5\%$ (to 1 d.p.)

The effective annual rate is 38.5%.

Nominal rates are sometimes quoted. These are simply the monthly/quarterly/weekly percentages multiplied by the number of time periods e.g., in the above example the nominal rate of interest would be 2.75% * 12 = 33%.

EXAMPLE 7.7

A bank pays a nominal rate of 10%, with interest added to accounts quarterly. What is the effective annual rate?

A nominal rate of 10% paid 4 times a year means 2.5% is paid each quarter so:

$m = 4$

$r = 0.025$

$EAR = (1+0.025)^4 - 1 = 0.103812 = 10.38\%$ (to 2 d.p.)

The effective annual rate is 10.38%.

REVIEW ACTIVITY 1

A department store charges users of its storecard interest at a rate of 2% per month.

Alternatively a customer could choose to take out a loan from the company at a quarterly rate of 6.5%.

(a) By considering the increase in an amount of £1000 borrowed over a year under both schemes (assuming that interest is compounded monthly or quarterly as appropriate), say which is the better option for a customer.

(b) Calculate the effective annual rate which customers pay under each system.

Working:

Answers on page 229.

| 7.3 | Discounting |

Cashflow projections are often made in business situations. When comparing two sets of such cashflows, adjustments are required to take account of the fact that some of the value of money is 'lost' over time.

Common sense dictates that if someone offered £100 now or £100 in six months' time you would take the money now – it is 'worth more' now than in the future because of the effects of inflation on the buying power of money.

There are two methods commonly used to compare money at different points in time: **Net present value (NPV)** and **Internal rate of return (IRR)**.

The NPV technique relies on calculating the **current** value of future payments. It could be thought of as calculating the amount that would need to be invested now to get a particular amount in the future.

The IRR is dependent on calculating the rate of interest at which a project would break even i.e., make no profit or loss overall. Hence it is the maximum rate of interest that should be paid if a project is not to make a loss.

Calculating present values

To calculate the present value of a single sum the formula for compound interest is used again in a slightly different format:

$$S_n = P(1 + r)^n$$

(remembering S is the sum accrued, P is the initial investment, i.e., present value r is the interest rate and n is the number of time periods).

Rearranging this formula slightly gives:

$$P = S_n * \frac{1}{(1 + r)^n}$$

P is also sometimes written as PV for present value.

| EXAMPLE 7.8 |

An investment offers a payment of £1000 now or £1150 in five years' time. If interest rates are 4% p.a., which is the better option?

First work out the present values of the two options:

PV of £1000 now is £1000

£1150 in 5 years must be discounted using the formula:

$$P = S_n * \frac{1}{(1 + r)^n} = \frac{1150}{1.04^5} = £945.22 \text{ (to 2 d.p.)}$$

i.e., £1150 in 5 years is equivalent to only £945.22 now so £1000 now gives the better option.

Net present value

When a series of cashflows (rather than just single figures) are involved, the idea of present value is extended to become net present value (NPV). This involves discounting individual figures and totalling the resulting present values to give NPV for the particular project or investment. If the NPV is positive, the project or investment makes a net profit over time. If the NPV is negative, the project or investment makes a loss.

As this is a commonly used technique, common values of, $\frac{1}{(1+r)^n}$ required in the calculation of present values are readily available (copies are supplied in Appendix B).

EXAMPLE 7.9

An investment is offered on the basis that £1000 would be invested now, and £700 would be paid out at the end of the next two years. A further payment of £1500 would then be made and £800 per year returned for another two years. What is the net present value of the investment if the interest rate is 6%?

A table is often useful to illustrate the information given in the question and to assist in calculations:

End of Year:	Money In:	Money Out:	Net Cashflow (in – out)	PV factor 6%*	PV of cashflows
0 (i.e., now)		1000	(1000)	1.000	1 * (1000) = (1000)
1	700		700	0.943	0.943 * 700 = 660.1
2	700	1500	(800)	0.890	0.890 * (800) − (712)
3	800		800	0.840	0.840 * 800 = 672
4	800		800	0.792	0.792 * 800 = 633.6
Total					NPV = 253.7

* Taken from tables supplied in Appendix B.

(In financial mathematics brackets are often used to denote negative values: hence (800) is the same as −800.)

Hence the NPV of the investment is £253.70.

Internal rate of return

In some cases it is helpful to know the interest rate where a scheme breaks even i.e., makes neither a profit nor a loss and hence has an NPV of 0. This interest rate is called the internal rate of return (IRR). Clearly, the higher the value of the IRR the 'safer' the investment is, as it is less likely to make a loss.

There are several methods for estimating the IRR. Each requires at least two NPVs (usually one positive and one negative) with their interest rates. Two methods will be illustrated here: one graphical and one using a formula.

EXAMPLE 7.10

In Example 7.9, if the interest rate were 20%, the value of the investment would be a loss of £123.30. What is the IRR?

This can be done by graph, plotting the interest rates on the x-axis against the NPV on the y-axis (see Figure 7.1).

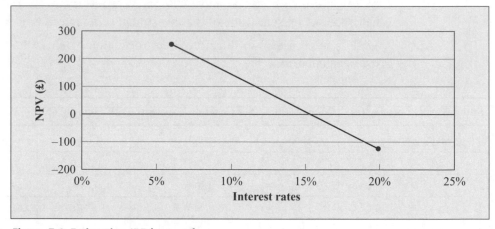

Figure 7.1 Estimating IRR by graph

The IRR is the interest rate at the point where the line crosses the x-axis i.e., approximately 15.5% here.

If three or more points were available it might be better to join them with a curve rather than a straight line. The IRR would still be the point where the line met the x-axis.

Alternatively, a formula can be used:

$$\text{IRR} = \frac{N_1 I_2 - N_2 I_1}{N_1 - N_2}$$

where discount rate I_1 gives NPV N_2, and discount rate I_2 gives NPV N_2.

Note that in this particular formula I is used instead of r to represent the interest rates. Repeating the solution to Example 7.10 using the formula method:

EXAMPLE 7.11

$$I_1 = 6\%$$
$$I_2 = 20\%$$
$$N_1 = £253.70$$
$$N_2 = -£123.30$$

$$\text{IRR} = \frac{(253.7 * 0.20) - (-123.30 * 0.06)}{253.70 - (-123.30)}$$

$$= \frac{50.74 + 7.398}{376.83}$$

$$= \frac{58.138}{376.83} = 0.1542817$$

i.e., the IRR is 15.4% (to 1 d.p.)

As both methods only *estimate* the IRR it would normally be quoted to just one decimal place.

An investment consultant is considering two alternative plans. Project A would involve an investment of £5000 now and would return £7650 in five years' time. Project B requires four yearly investments of £1230 starting immediately and returns £7000 in five years' time.

(a) By using the present value factors for an interest rate of 6% (supplied in Appendix B) calculate the net present value for each project.

(b) Which is the better option for an investor?

If interest rates were 10%, the NPV of Project A above would be approximately a loss of £250.

(c) Use these figures with the NPV of the project, calculated in (a), to determine the internal rate of return for the investment strategy.

Working:

Answers on pages 229–30.

Key points to remember

1. The terminology used in the calculation of interest and present values is that:

    P is the principal, the initial amount;

    n is the number of time periods;

    S (or S_n) is the sum accrued;

    r is the interest rate.

2. Simple interest is calculated by the formula:

    $$S_n = P(1 + rn)$$

3. Compound interest is calculated by the formula:

    $$S_n = P(1 + r)^n$$

4. An effective annual rate of interest can be found using the formula:

    $$\text{EAR} = (1 + r)^m - 1$$

    where m is the number of times per year that interest is paid.

5. The net present value (NPV) of a set of cashflows is the current value of money to be received in the future.

6. A present value for a single cashflow can be calculated using the formula for compound interest.

7. Present values for a series of cashflows over time can be calculated using sets of present value factors (which are supplied for you in Appendix B). The NPV is the sum of the present values for the individual cashflows.

8. The NPV of a project can be used to judge its worth over time or to compare alternative projects. The internal rate of return (IRR) can also be used to do this.

9. The IRR is the interest rate which gives a set of cashflows an NPV of zero i.e., it is the interest rate at the break-even point.

10. The IRR can be calculated by graph or from the formula:

    $$\text{IRR} = \frac{N_1 I_2 - N_2 I_1}{N_1 - N_2} \qquad \begin{aligned} &N = \text{NPV}, \\ &I = \text{interest rate}. \end{aligned}$$

ADDITIONAL EXERCISES

Question 1   An investment which would cost £1000 now would return £1150 in two years' time. What is the rate paid if interest is compounded annually?

Question 2   An individual is reviewing some investments which were made with a view to providing a lump sum on retirement at age 60, which will be in 10 years' time. £7500 is currently invested.

(a) If the predicted growth rate for the investment is 6% p.a. compound, how much might he expect to receive on retirement?

(b) An alternative scheme promises to deliver £17,500 if the money is not withdrawn until age 65. By calculating the compound interest rate for this investment, say whether it is a better scheme than the current one.

(c) There is also an option to invest further in the current scheme. Ideally, the investor would like to receive £18,000 at age 60. How much extra should be invested now?

Question 3   A bank loan is offered at a flat rate of 7% (this is equivalent to simple interest). If £10,000 is borrowed to buy a car, calculate the total amount that will be repaid to the bank over a four year term and the monthly repayments that would be required.

Question 4   What is the present value of £3500 to be received in seven years' time, at an interest rate of 3%?

Question 5   A project has an NPV of £3472 at an interest rate of 5% and an NPV of –£1198 at a rate of 10%. Estimate the IRR for the project using a graph.

A second project has an NPV of £4100 at an interest rate of 6% and an NPV of –£1542 at a rate of 14%. Estimate the IRR for this project using the formula supplied.

Hence say which of the two projects seems like the safer investment.

Question 6   A company plans to launch a new product. Sales are expected to be 4000 items in the first year, rising to 5000 in years 2–4 then dropping back to 2800 in year 5.

Each item sold has a contribution of £185. The company has initial fixed costs of £725,000 per year which are expected to rise by 3% per year over the lifetime of the product. It will cost £180,000 to buy equipment needed before manufacturing can begin.

(a) Find the average cashflow over the lifetime of the product. (*Hint*: first calculate the yearly total contributions, fixed costs and net cashflows).

(b) Find the net present value of the cashflows at a discount rate of 10%.

(c) Given that the NPV of the project at a discount rate of 18% is –£6191.24, find the internal rate of return and explain clearly what this represents.

One of the shareholders of the company has a sum of £125,000 to invest. He could loan this money to the company to finance their new product, in which case they have agreed to return £160,000 to him in five years' time. Alternatively, he could invest in a bond which returns a guaranteed 5% p.a.

(d) Work out the interest rate for the first option, giving your answer to two decimal places, and hence advise him which investment to choose.

(e) How long would his money need to remain in the bond to secure the same return he is offered by the company?

(f) How much would the bond return after five years?

Question 7 Given the following set of cashflows over the lifetime of a project, what is the net present value (to the nearest £) at a discount rate of 8%?

Year	Cashflow (£)
0	−200
1	50
2	150
3	75

Question 8 A company offers cheap loans to its staff to assist with the purchase of annual travel tickets. Interest is charged at 0.5% per month. Calculate the effective annual rate of interest which is being charged to employees.

SPREADSHEET EXERCISE

This exercise is in two parts. The first covers some calculations related to the theory of simple and compound interest and the second introduces some commonly used financial functions on Excel. There is no data file to load, instead a basic model is built up from a blank spreadsheet.

You have £1000 to invest over a 15 year period and are given two options:

A. To invest in an account that pays 20% interest per year but only on the initial capital and not the additional interest accrued.

B. To invest in an account that pays 10% interest per year but this is payable on the cumulative capital accrued, i.e., including the interest generated in the previous year.

(a) Using the spreadsheet, calculate the amount saved in each scheme for years 0 to 15 inclusive by building up a table of values.

(b) Plot a single graph showing the values of these two investments (i.e., year on the *x*-axis and value on the *y*-axis).

(c) In what year are they equal in value?

Now move on to a fresh page on your spreadsheet. This second section covers some calculations related to the theory of net present value and internal rate of return.

A company has to make a choice between two alternative projects which have the following cashflows:

	Project A		Project B	
Year	**Cash inflow**	**Cash outflow**	**Cash inflow**	**Cash outflow**
0		1500		1800
1	250	700	600	500
2	700	0	600	325
3	700	0	600	0
4	700	0	600	0
5	570	250	600	0

(d) By using a built-in function, calculate the NPV for each project with discount factors of 4% and 9% (you will first need to find the net cashflow for each project).

(e) By comparing the NPVs at the rate of 4%, say which project gives the better return to the company.

(f) Construct a table to show the NPV for this project for a range of discount rates between 3% and 12%.

(g) Construct a graph to estimate the IRR using your table.

(h) Confirm the estimate made in Question 7 using the built-in IRR function.

Hints for completion

In Excel, the NPV function will only discount the cashflows beginning from period (year) 1. So to determine the NPV of an investment, the NPV function must be used to discount the cash flows for year 1 onwards, then the initial investments taken into account, i.e., here the function should be of the form:

=NPV(cashflows for year 1 onwards) + cashflow for year 0

The IRR function is easier to understand and simply takes the form:

=IRR(all cashflows)

CHAPTER 8

Linear programming

LEARNING OBJECTIVES

- To review the meaning and uses of linear equations;
- To discuss methods of representing constraints graphically;
- To combine these areas in a discussion of graphical linear programming, a commonly used technique;
- To discuss ways of finding the 'optimal solution' to this type of problem.

Introduction

In this chapter, another widely used modelling technique – linear programming – will be introduced. This draws heavily on the ideas associated with the use and solution of linear equations and, as in Chapter 4, you may find it necessary to revise your knowledge of this area to assist your understanding of some of the principles used here.

In general, linear programming can be thought of as a method for finding the 'best' solution to a problem – the one which maximizes profit made or minimizes costs incurred by making the most efficient use of resources available. This best solution is usually referred to as the **optimal solution**, and the conditions affecting it (such as the amount of materials or manpower available or production requirements) are called the **constraints**.

8.1 Formulating the linear program

The first stage in constructing a linear programming model would be to look at the situation and to construct a set of equations that might be used to describe it. The following example should help to illustrate how this is achieved.

EXAMPLE 8.1

A shopkeeper stocks two types of milk: semi-skimmed and full fat and is trying to decide how many of each to order. He needs to order the milk for delivery one day in advance. He knows he will sell at least 75 pints altogether in a day, so he will not order less than this amount. His contract with his wholesaler says he must take at least 30 pints of semi-skimmed, and he does not have fridge space for more than 100 pints in total.

Represent this problem on a graph by converting the constraints on his order size into equations or inequalities as required.

At first glance this may appear somewhat daunting, as there seems to be a lot of information to process: however, if the solution is tackled stage by stage it is very straightforward.

First, try to *identify the variables* in the problem – what should the answer be? Here, he wants to know how many pints of milk to order, so there must be two variables: number of pints of semi-skimmed to order and number of pints of full fat to order (in all the problems dealt with in this unit only two variables will be considered).

These will be represented by:

- s: number of pints of semi-skimmed;
- f: number of pints of full fat.

(They could have been called x and y or x_1 and x_2 according to personal preference.)

Second, *write the information about the variables* as equations or inequalities. For inequalities simply use ≥ (greater than or equal to) or ≤ (less than or equal to) instead of $=$ signs.

The order size must be at least 75 pints, so this means:

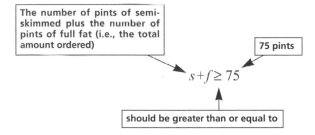

He must take at least 30 pints of semi-skimmed so:

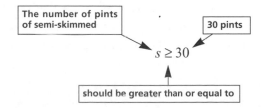

Example 8.1
continued

And he cannot order more than 100 pints in total so:

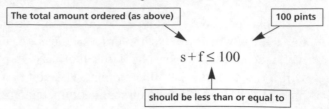

So the three constraints (factors affecting how much milk he should order) could be expressed as:

$$s+f \geq 75$$

$$s \geq 30$$

$$s+f \leq 100$$

It is also necessary (for completeness) to add some non-negativity constraints:

$$s \geq 0$$

$$f \geq 0$$

to indicate that negative solutions are not possible (he cannot buy negative amounts of milk!).

The **third stage** in this solution is to graph the constraints, as requested in the question.

To do this, the inequalities are treated just like straightforward equations i.e., treat $s+f \geq 75$ as $s+f = 75$. Two points satisfying the equation are needed to form the straight line and it is convenient to choose:

$s = 0, f = 75$

$s = 75, f = 0$

(although any two points could be chosen).

When graphed, this gives Figure 8.1. The line represents all of the points where exactly 75 pints are ordered. We are only interested in the area where more than this amount is ordered, so to represent $s + f \geq 75$ the area to the left of the line can be discarded, as illustrated in Figure 8.2.

Adding the other constraints to the same graph in a similar manner:

$s = 30$ is a vertical line through (30, 0)

$s + f = 100$ is graphed using $s = 0, f = 100$; $s = 100, f = 0$

These are shown in Figure 8.3. Notice that the non-negativity constraints are represented by shading below the x-axis and to the left of the y-axis. Also the constraint $s + f \leq 100$ has been shaded on the opposite side to $s + f \geq 75$ because the value must be *less than* 100.

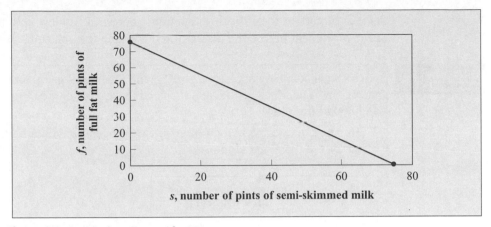

Figure 8.1 Graph showing $s + f = 75$

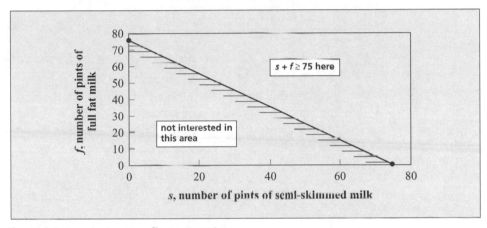

Figure 8.2 Graph showing first constraint

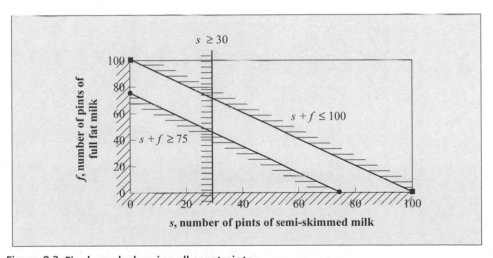

Figure 8.3 Final graph showing all constraints

As it is important to grasp this technique, here is a Review activity to try formulating a problem before the discussion of finding the solution.

A chemical company operates a small plant. Operating the plant requires two raw materials, A and B. The maximum available supply per week is 2700 litres of A and 2000 litres of B.

The plant can operate using either of two processes which have differing raw materials requirements as follows:

Process	Raw materials consumed (litres per hour)	
	A	B
1	20	10
2	30	25

The plant can run for 120 hours per week in total, but for safety reasons Process 1 cannot be operated for more than 100 hours per week.

(a) Formulate this problem as a linear program with the aim of deciding how many hours each process should run for.

(b) Display your linear program on a graph.

Working:

Answers on pages 230–1.

8.2 Finding the solution

Once the constraints have been graphed, the set of possible solutions to the problem can be identified. In the case above, there is an area in the middle of the graph where any point would satisfy all of the constraints (i.e., the points are on the 'correct' side of every line). This is called the **feasible region** because it is the area where any point will give a valid solution (this is shown more clearly in Figure 8.4).

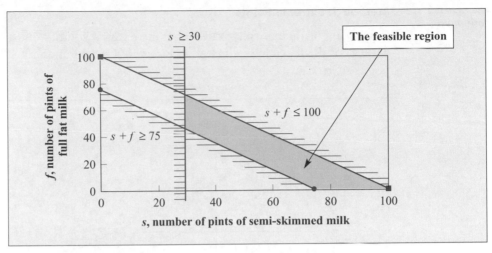

Figure 8.4 **The feasible area**

In the example above, the shopkeeper could choose to stock 40 pints of semi-skimmed and 60 full fat, 70 semi-skimmed and 20 full fat, 30 semi-skimmed and 45 full fat ... there are hundreds of possible combinations, and the problem is now how to find the best one of these – the optimal solution. Before doing this, it is necessary to have some criteria for judging the possible solutions. The objective is usually to maximize profit or minimise cost and the solution that gives lowest cost or highest profit would therefore be the best. In the following example, the solution that would get maximum profit for the shopkeeper is found.

EXAMPLE 8.2

If the shopkeeper makes 15p profit on a pint of semi-skimmed milk and 17p profit on a pint of full fat milk, what should he stock to maximize profit?

Following on from the previous steps in the solution:

Step 4 would be to *find the 'objective function'* – the equation that describes the profit (or loss) which is to be maximized (or minimized).

Here we are asked to maximize profit so we need to know:

$$\text{Profit} = 15s + 17f$$

Notice that the same variables (s and f) have been used as in the constraints.

There are then two ways of completing **the fifth and final step** – *finding the solution* to the problem.

▶

165

Example 8.2
continued

Method 1: Extreme Points

It has been mathematically proven that the optimal solution must lie at one of the corners of the feasible region i.e., in Figure 8.5 the solution must be at one of the points A, B, C or D.

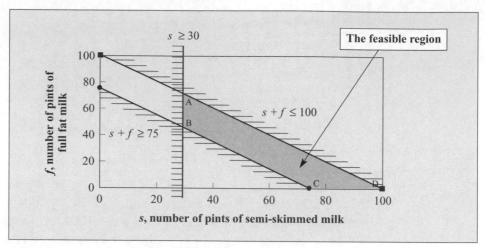

Figure 8.5 Graphical solution method: extreme points

These points can be found by solving the simultaneous equations which cross at each corner (again, this is a basic skill and some of you may find it helpful to refer to other textbooks or notes to remind yourselves of the procedures).

A lies on the lines $s = 30$ and $s + f = 100$

Hence $s = 30$ and $f = 70$

B lies on the lines $s = 30$ and $s + f = 75$

Hence $s = 30$ and $f = 45$

C lies on the lines $s + f = 75$ and $f = 0$

Hence $s = 75$ and $f = 0$

D lies on the lines $s + f = 100$ and $f = 0$

Hence $s = 100$ and $f = 0$

Working out the profit at each of these points:

Corner	s value	f value	Profit = $15s + 17f$
A	30	70	1640p = £16.40
B	30	45	1215p = £12.15
C	75	0	1125p = £11.25
D	100	0	1500p = £15

Hence the best solution is to order 30 pints of semi-skimmed milk and 70 pints of full fat milk.

Method 2: Profit line

The second method involves the use of the graph again. Once the objective function has been found, this can be added to the graph.

From step 4, the objective function is:

profit $= 15s + 17f$

To do this, an arbitrary value for the right-hand side of the equation must be chosen. In this case, a value of 1275 has been picked.

This was achieved by first taking $15 * 17$ (the two coefficients multiplied together to give a number that will divide easily) giving:

255 – too small to graph easily so try doubling it;

510 – still too small so multiply by 5 instead;

1275 – a right-hand side for the equation that can be worked with easily.

$15s + 17f = 1275$ when $s = 0, f = 75$;   when $s = 85, f = 0$

These points are added to the graph and joined with a short line (Figure 8.6). Imagine the line moving upwards and to the right as far as possible to maximize profit – the last point it touches within the feasible region will be the optimal solution. In this case, it would be point A (30, 70) as before.

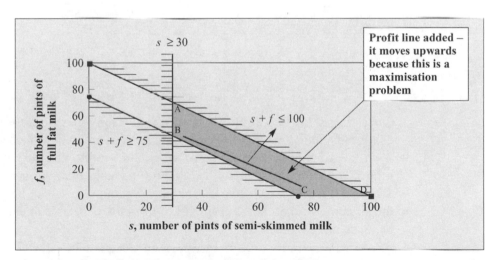

Figure 8.6 Graphical solution method: adding the profit line

If the objective were to minimize costs, the line would be imagined moving downwards and left but the last point it touched inside the feasible region would still be the solution.

The exact coordinates for point A would normally have to be found using simultaneous equations (although here this was not necessary as they had already been found).

REVIEW ACTIVITY 2

Given that the processes described in Review activity 1 make the following contributions to profit:

    Process 1: £50 per hour

    Process 2: £60 per hour

use the graph prepared in Review activity 1 and:

(a) identify the point where the optimal solution lies.

(b) find the *exact* optimal running times for Processes 1 and 2 and the maximum contribution available.

Working:

Answers on pages 231–2.

8.3   Sensitivity analysis

Once the optimal solution has been found it may be desirable to look at how changes would affect it. For example, in the situation above the shopkeeper may wish to know by how much the profit would need to change before a different mix of milk should be bought. Computer packages can be used to assist with this, but it is also worth considering how common sense can be used to analyse the situation further. Some examples of the sorts of simple amendments that can be made are given below.

Adding further constraints

Sometimes a new constraint is discovered once the linear program has been solved. For the simple problems examined in this book, the easiest way to determine whether the solution will change is often to add a new line to the graph so that its effect can be seen. The following example illustrates how this can be done.

EXAMPLE 8.3

The shopkeeper has just discovered that the pints of full fat milk come in wider cartons which take up more space in his fridge. He has a total of 100 units of storage space available. The semi-skimmed milk will take up 1 unit of space per pint and the full fat will take up 1.25 units of space. Will this affect the solution? If so, suggest what the new solution should be and determine what effect the change would have on the profit made.

Expressing the new constraint as an equation in the same format as before gives:

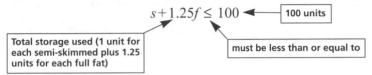

$$s + 1.25f \leq 100$$

Total storage used (1 unit for each semi-skimmed plus 1.25 units for each full fat)

100 units

must be less than or equal to

Adding this to the graph using the points $s = 0, f = 80$; $s = 100, f = 0$ gives us Figure 8.7. From this, it can be seen that the feasible region has changed shape because the new constraint cuts through it. The solution point has also changed – this time it will be at corner D since that is the last point the profit line will touch before leaving the feasible region.

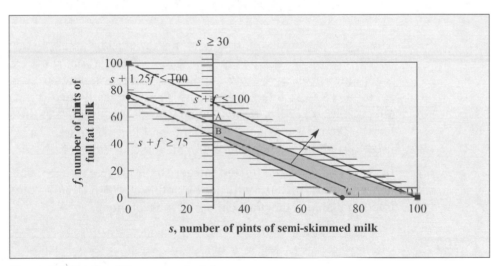

Figure 8.7 Graph with new constraint

At D, $s = 100$ and $f = 0$

Hence

Profit $= 15s + 17f = (15 * 100) + (17 * 0) = 1500$

i.e., profit reduces from £16.40 to £15.00 with the addition of the new constraint.

Slack

If the optimal solution is implemented it is likely that there will be 'spare' capacity under some of the constraints (typically all of the raw materials will not be used up or there may be excess manpower available).

To see whether there is spare capacity, the amount of each resource used in the optimal solution can be calculated and compared to that available. This excess capacity is often referred to as 'slack'.

EXAMPLE 8.4

The shopkeeper has rethought the situation and decided that his minimum order of 75 pints of milk per day may be too low. How much more milk could he sell per day under the optimal solution?

He is currently ordering 100 pints per day under the optimal solution. Hence there is slack of 25 pints per day in this constraint and he will have 25 extra pints per day available for sale.

8.4 Real life linear programming

The problems tackled in this book may seem fairly simplistic in nature, using only two variables and a graphical method for solution. However, in practice, the techniques discussed can be applied – using computer packages to help with solutions – to much larger problems. These typically involve many variables and a large number of constraints. In the spreadsheet exercise at the end of this chapter, the theory is expanded to cover a problem with three variables and Excel is used to find the solution, since graphical means cannot be used.

In this book, the need to find integer solutions (e.g., a whole number of components to make or buy) will not be addressed specifically, but again this is an important area in the practical use of the technique.

REVIEW ACTIVITY 3

Referring back to Review activity 1,

(a) If the quantity of material A available increased to 3500 litres would the solution change? Explain the reason for your answer.

(b) If the company wished to save money by ordering less of material B could they do so? By how much could the order be reduced?

Working:

Answers on page 232.

Key points to remember

1. Linear programming is a modelling technique used to find the optimal solution to a problem (usually production levels which give maximum profit or minimum cost).

2. The problem is first *formulated* – turned into a set of linear equalities and inequalities.

3. A graph may be used to solve two variable problems.

4. The optimal solution can be found by one of two methods in these problems: the method of extreme points or by adding the profit line to the graph.

5. Slack is the amount of spare capacity in constraints that do not directly constrain the optimal solution.

ADDITIONAL EXERCISES

Question 1   A local road transport company is considering investing in specialized lorries for the carriage of chilled and frozen foods.

Type A carries $10m^3$ of chilled food and $15m^3$ of frozen food, while type B can carry $15m^3$ of chilled food and $12m^3$ of frozen food.

They have a minimum weekly load of $1000m^3$ of chilled food and $1200m^3$ of frozen food. In addition, the supplier of the lorries has stipulated that at least 40 type A and 15 type B must be ordered at a time. Given that it costs £17,000 for a type A lorry and £15,000 for type B:

(a) Formulate this situation as a linear program with the objective to minimize costs. Clearly identify the variables in the problem.

(b) Graph the problem and hence identify the optimal solution point on the graph.

(c) Advise the company on the best strategy to minimize costs whilst still meeting the constraints identified.

Question 2   A car manufacturer produces two versions of its popular medium sized model: a hatchback aimed at the family market and a coupé designed to appeal to affluent single customers.

Both are based on the same chassis and differ only in the body kit used to make up the cars. They are both produced at the same factory.

There are 100,000 hours of manpower and 13,250 basic chassis units available each week. The hatchback takes six hours of assembly time while a coupé takes nine hours.

At least 4000 hatchback models should be produced per week.

Production is also constrained by the fact that owing to problems with a supplier only 60,000 door handles are available per week. A hatchback uses five of these door handles while a coupé uses three.

The profit to the factory on a hatchback model is estimated to be £1500 while the profit on a coupé is £2000.

The market demand for the cars is high. It is known that demand will exceed production for some time to come so they should be able to sell whatever mix of cars is produced.

(a) Formulate this problem as a linear program, and hence find the number of each model which the company should be trying to make and sell per week in order to maximize profit in the factory.

(b) If a further requirement were added such that the number of hatchbacks produced must make up at least 60% of the total output, how would this be expressed as a constraint?

(c) If the factory could obtain *one* of the following, which would allow them to produce more cars?

    (i)   More chassis units.   (iii) Increased profit margin on each car.

    (ii) More door handles.   (iv) Constraint removed on hatchback production.

(d) How many excess door handles would be received by the factory each week if the recommended production mix was followed?

Question 3   A small local bakery has won an order to supply two types of bread – cheese flat-bread and poppy seed rolls – to a sandwich delivery service. They will receive 5p for every poppy seed roll and 8p for every cheese flatbread they supply.

Initially, the sandwich delivery company is happy to buy as much as the bakery can produce of these two types of bread. The bakery already has weekly orders for 100 kg of flour and 1 kg of yeast, and would like to be able to meet their new contract without increasing these amounts.

Each poppy seed roll takes 30 g of flour and 0.5 g of yeast while each cheese flat-bread takes 125 g of flour and 1 g of yeast.

The agreement says that they must supply at least 1000 poppy seed rolls and between 300 and 500 cheese flatbreads each week.

(a) Formulate and graph this problem as a linear program.

(b) Hence say how many of each type of bread the bakery should aim to supply each week to maximize profit. What is this maximum profit?

(c) If the bakery wished to reduce their flour order could they do so? By how much?

Question 4   A computer manufacturer produces its best selling PC in two versions: both use the same production line and staff for manufacture. The two types differ only in the type of processor installed. There are 5500 of the basic shell units available to the production line each week. The type A computer takes 40 minutes of assembly time while the type B takes 30 minutes. There are 3250 hours of assembly time available each week. At least 2000 type A computers must be made per week to meet existing orders. The company makes £100 profit on a type A computer and £80 profit on a type B.

(a) Formulate this problem as a linear program with the aim of maximizing profit.

(b) Graph the problem and clearly identify the feasible region. Explain what this area of the graph represents.

(c) Identify the optimal solution point on your graph. Hence use simultaneous equations to find the exact production mix which would give maximum profit to the manufacturer.

(d) What is the maximum profit that could be made?

(e) If the factory wished to reduce the number of basic units ordered each week could they do so? By how much?

SPREADSHEET EXERCISE

This exercise is designed to illustrate how more complex linear programming problems can be solved using a computer package – Microsoft Excel in this case. To start with, an extensive worked example is presented to show how linear programs can be laid out and solved in Excel. This is followed by another (slightly more complex) example.

Referring back to the Review activity used in this chapter, recall that the formulation of the problem was:

Maximize:

$$50x_1 + 60x_2$$

Subject to the constraints:

$$20x_1 + 30x_2 \leq 2700$$
$$10x_1 + 25x_2 < 2000$$
$$x_1 + x_2 \leq 120$$
$$x_1 \leq 100$$
$$x_1, x_2 \geq 0$$

where x_1 = number of hours that Process 1 should run and x_2 = number of hours that Process 2 should run.

The graphical solution was found to be that $x_1 = 90$ and $x_2 = 30$ for maximum profit.

Using Excel to find the same solution requires the use of the Solver add-in. Figure 8.8 gives a suggested layout for the spreadsheet and details of how to use this part of the package.

Once the spreadsheet has been set up in this way the Solver add-in (found under Tools on the main menu in Excel) can be used to enter the problem, as Figure 8.9 shows.

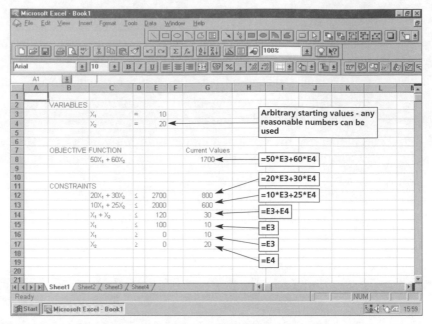

Figure 8.8 Example of linear program set up in Excel

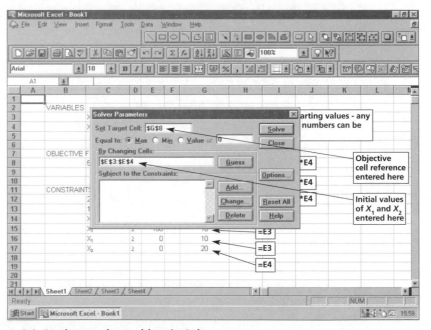

Figure 8.9 Setting up the problem in Solver

The constraints can then be added by clicking the Add button. See Figure 8.10 for instruction.

When all the constraints have been added, click on OK to go back to the previous screen. All of the information you have input will be displayed. When you are happy that it is correct, click Solve to find the solution (see Figure 8.11).

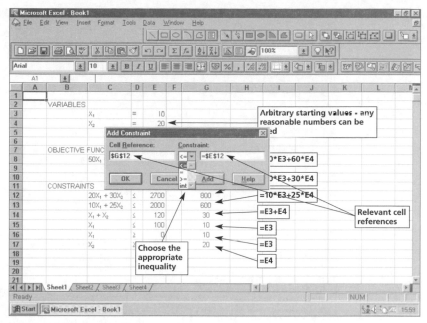

Figure 8.10 **Adding constraints**

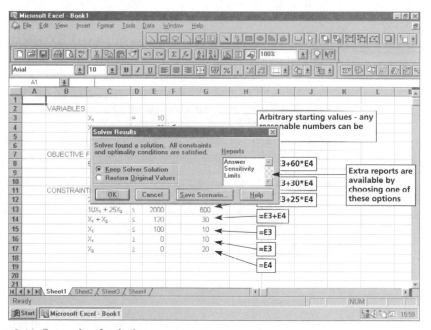

Figure 8.11 **Example of solution screen**

Simply clicking on OK will display the solution (Figure 8.12): note that there are other reports here which give extra information (although their meaning will not be discussed in detail here).

Notice that the values displayed for the constraints show how much of each is being used: these could be helpful in the sort of simple sensitivity analysis discussed in the solutions to Review activity 3 parts (a) and (b).

175

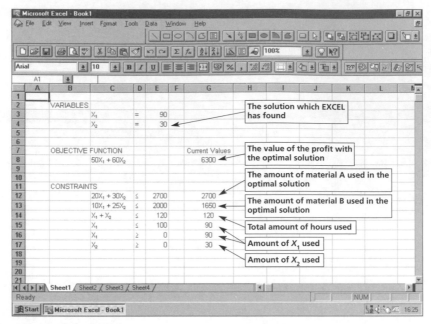

Figure 8.12 The solution

Scenario

The bakery discussed in Question 3 of the Additional exercises has decided to expand its product range, and will now be producing a second type of bread (sun-dried tomato). They have changed their orders of flour and yeast to meet increased demand and now have 250 kg of flour and 3 kg of yeast delivered each month. Requirements for each product are as follows:.

Bread type	Yeast requirement (g)	Flour requirement (g)	Profit (pence per item)
Poppy roll	0.5	30	5
Sun-dried tomato bread	1.2	140	10
Cheese flatbread	1.0	125	8

In addition, existing orders mean that they must produce at least 1500 rolls and 800 loaves of bread each week.

What amount of each product should the bakery make and sell to maximize profit?

If they wanted to reduce the amount of yeast ordered could they do so? By how much?

CHAPTER 9

Index numbers

LEARNING
OBJECTIVES

- To illustrate how the two most common forms of index number (i.e. simple and chain base) are calculated and interpreted;
- To discuss the appropriate selection of a base period;
- To show how simple index numbers can be compared across a change of base period;
- To introduce weighting and its role in a commonly used index number.

Introduction

In this short chapter, the calculation and use of index numbers will be discussed: they are commonly used as a way of describing and comparing series of figures that have been collected over several years. Many of the sources of secondary information discussed in Chapter 1 make extensive use of index numbers to present time series of data (time series will be discussed more specifically in the following chapter).

9.1 Simple index numbers

The **simple index** is probably the most frequently applied index number. It measures the percentage change in value of an item relative to its value at a predefined historical point known as the **base period**. At this base period the index number is equal to 100 and all subsequent index numbers are calculated as percentages of that base period value.

This can be represented by the general formula:

$$\text{Simple index} = \frac{\text{Value at period } n}{\text{Value at base period}} * 100$$

EXAMPLE 9.1

The yearly profit of Robson's Manufacturing for four successive years is given as:

Year	Profit (£)
1995	20,000
1996	24,000
1997	19,500
1998	34,000

For the purpose of confidentiality, construct a simple index for the profits using 1995 as a base year.

To find the index number for 1996 divide the 1996 price by the 1995 price and multiply by 100:

(24,000 / 20,000) * 100 = 120

Similarly, for 1997,

(19,500 / 20,000) * 100 = 97.5

and 1998,

(34,000 / 20,000) * 100 = 170

Hence, the completed table of simple index numbers is:

Year	Index (1995 = 100)
1995	100
1996	120
1997	97.5
1998	170

Note: The notation 1995 = 100 is used to denote the base, since all comparisons are made with this particular year.

Interpretation of the index numbers

The interpretation of an index number is based on the following criteria.

Value of index	Interpretation
> 100	Value has increased relative to the base year
= 100	Value has remained the same
< 100	Value has decreased relative to the base year

In Example 9.1, the index number for profit in 1996 was 120. This indicates that Robson's Manufacturing's profit has increased since 1995. This can be interpreted further by saying that the company's profit has increased by 20% from 1995 to 1996.

However, in 1997 the simple index number was 97.5. This indicates a decrease in profit of 2.5% from 1995.

9.2 Selecting the base period

In Example 9.1, the base period (1995) was selected in an arbitrary manner. In a business application the choice of base period is very important. The base year should be a 'normal' representative period when no abnormal changes have occurred. If the period is 'abnormal', then future periods of relatively minor changes in price or quantity will be very difficult to reflect in the index number – they then cover up any significant change in the value of the business variable being considered.

For example, it would be inappropriate to measure the change in house prices in the UK if the base year was selected in the late 1980s, as the end of this decade represented a time of boom for this sector of the economy. All subsequent (smaller) increases in prices will yield a set of index numbers that are similar in value and hence will be difficult to interpret adequately.

9.3 Accounting for change of base period

When making comparisons over long periods of time index numbers can become too large, too small or too similar to be meaningful. Therefore, it is appropriate at times to 'reset' the base period. If a comparison of index numbers is required over a period of time where there has been a change of base, appropriate calculations are made. These are illustrated in Example 9.2.

EXAMPLE 9.2

The owner of Delaney's record shop wishes to compare unit sales between 1970 and 1994. Up to 1983 unit sales were recorded in index form, using 1970 as the base year. In 1983 the index had the value 295, but was re-based to 100.

Year	Index (1970 = 100)	Index (1983 = 100)
1970	100	–
1971	115	–
⋮	⋮	⋮
1983	295	100
1984	–	98
⋮	⋮	⋮
1994	–	104

In order to compare 1994 directly with 1970 it is necessary to calculate either an index number for 1970 using 1983 as the base, or an index number for 1994 with 1970 as the base. Here the latter option has been taken.

From the table above it can be seen that from 1983 to 1994 the index increased from 100 to 104 (4%); therefore the 'old' index number in 1983 (295) needs to be increased by the same proportion.

Thus

$$\frac{1994 \text{ Index } (1970 = 100)}{295} = \frac{104}{100}$$

$$1994 \text{ Index } (1970 = 100) = \frac{104 * 295}{100} = 306.8$$

Readers confident in carrying out percentage calculations will also see that to find this value we are simply increasing 295 by 4%, i.e., 295 + 295 * 0.04 = 306.8 results in the same answer.

So between 1970 and 1994 the index of unit sales had increased from 100 to 306.8 – an increase in sales by a factor of 3.

Before moving on to the next type of index number – the chain base index – check out your knowledge on simple index numbers by completing the following activity.

REVIEW ACTIVITY 1

The price of a litre of petrol was recorded over a six month period:

Month	Jan.	Feb.	Mar.	Apr.	May	June
Price (p)	50	48	45	49	52	60

(a) Using January as the base period, complete a simple index for February to June inclusive.

(b) A large tax increase on petrol was announced in June, therefore it was decided to 'reset' the base at that period. In October the 'new' index was 110. What would have been the index number if January had been the base?

Working:

Answer on page 233.

9.4 Chain base index numbers

With a chain base index the base year progresses by one time period each calculation so that each index is measured relative to the previous period.

In the same way as for simple index numbers a base period (start of the chain) is selected and the index number for that period equals 100. The subsequent index numbers are then calculated as follows:

$$\frac{\text{Price/Quantity at time } n}{\text{Price/Quantity at time } n-1} * 100$$

EXAMPLE 9.3

The table below shows the week-ending share price on the stock exchange over a period of four weeks for a local company's shares:

Week	1	2	3	4
Price (p)	28	32	34	25

Calculate and interpret a chain base index using week 1 as the base.

Index (wk 1) = 100

Index (wk 2) = $\dfrac{\text{Price wk 2}}{\text{Price wk 1}} * 100 = \dfrac{32}{28} * 100 = 114.29$ (to 2 d.p.)

Index (wk 3) = $\dfrac{\text{Price wk 3}}{\text{Price wk 2}} * 100 = \dfrac{34}{32} * 100 = 106.25$ (to 2 d.p.)

Index (wk 4) = $\dfrac{25}{34} * 100 = 73.53$ (to 2 d.p.)

At the end of the second week the share price had increased by 14% from the end of the first week. By the end of the third week the share price had increased again but at a slower rate (6% when compared with week 2). In week 4 the price had dipped with a 26% decrease from week 3.

One advantage of using chain base index numbers as opposed to simple index numbers is that it is not as important to ensure that a 'normal' time period is selected to represent the base year.

9.5   Presenting index numbers graphically

As already discussed in Chapter 2, it is normal to use a line graph to present time based data, where the *x*-axis carries the time periods and the *y*-axis the variable of interest. This is illustrated in the following example.

EXAMPLE 9.4

Present the following set of chain base indices on a suitable graph.

Week	1	2	3	4	5
Index (wk 1 = base)	100	114	106	74	101
Week	6	7	8	9	10
Index (wk 2 = base)	85	110	120	98	105

The 10 indices are simply shown on a line graph with the week labels on the *x*-axis. See Figure 9.1.

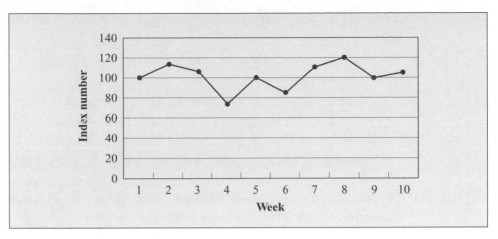

Figure 9.1 Chain base index

9.6 A commonly used index number

The retail prices index

The retail prices index (RPI) is used to measure the change in the cost of living for a 'typical' UK household. It is compiled and published monthly by the UK government. The RPI measures the monthly change in the cost of a group of items and is used by the government as a measure of inflation.

The index is constructed from the prices of a representative basket of goods. This basket of goods contains items that are bought each month by a 'typical' UK household, and are assumed to reflect the general attributes of households with respect to income and expenditure. This is continually reviewed: for example, in March 1999 the Office for National Statistics announced that items such as exercise bikes, dried cat food and electric keyboards were now popular enough to be included in the retail price index, whereas packet soup and malt vinegar were no longer to be considered.

Using the information collected by the government, the representative basket of goods is usually divided into the following groups:

- alcohol and tobacco;
- food and catering;
- housing and housing expenditure;
- motoring;
- personal expenditure;
- travel and leisure.

The RPI for any particular month is then calculated as follows:

1. The average price of each of the items covered by the index is calculated for that month using data from the prices survey (carried out by the Department of Employment).

2. The average price is divided by the average price for the same item in the previous January. This gives the price ratio for that item relative to the previous January.

3. These price ratios are then combined; first, into *section* price ratios; secondly into *sub-group* ratios; thirdly into the *group* ratios mentioned above; and finally into an *all-item* price ratio (still relative to the previous January). At each stage in this combination process weighted means are used, where the weights are derived from the expenditure patterns observed in *The Family Expenditure Survey*. The same weights are used throughout the year.

These steps can be summarized by the following formula:

$$\frac{\sum w(p_n/p_0)}{\sum w} * 100$$

where w = weight; p_n = price now; and p_0 = price at base period.

This is the general formula for a **base weighted index** of which the RPI is an example.

A major problem encountered when constructing this index is collecting information that is typical of most households. Obviously, some households will spend more on certain items than other households. Nevertheless, the basket consists of many items and therefore should be able to provide an accurate measurement of the rate of increase in family expenditure.

Other weighted index numbers

As mentioned above, weights are used to label the importance of a particular item. There are also many other forms of index numbers that include some method of weighting in their calculation. Laspeyres and Paasche, for instance, are common forms of weighted index numbers mentioned in many quantitative techniques texts. As this book is mainly concerned with making the reader aware of the existence of index numbers and their appropriate interpretation, details of the calculation of these index numbers are not included here.

REVIEW ACTIVITY 2

Using the same figures as given in Review activity 1 for the price of a litre of petrol over a six month period:

Month	Jan.	Feb.	Mar.	Apr.	May	June
Price (p)	50	48	45	49	52	60

Calculate the chain base index for each month by first comparing the percentage change in price between January and February.

Working:

Answers on page 233.

Key points to remember

1. A simple index measures the percentage change in the value of an item relative to its value at a predefined point known as the base period. The formula for its calculation is:

$$\text{Simple index} = \frac{\text{Value at period } n}{\text{Value at base period}} * 100$$

2. For a simple index a value of 100 is given to the base period and all comparisons are made with that point. Care must be taken in the selection of that base period.

3. It may be required to compare simple index numbers over a change in base period. In order to do this all the index numbers need to be converted onto one base.

4. In a chain base index the base period progresses by one time period each time, therefore each index number is interpreted relative to the previous period.

$$\text{Chain index} = \frac{\text{Price/Quantity at time } n}{\text{Price/Quantity at time } n-1} * 100$$

5. To present index numbers graphically use a line graph.

ADDITIONAL EXERCISES

Question 1   An index of sales for airline tickets sold by the Pan Ting airline on their Far Eastern routes is required. Annual sales (in £000s) are as follows:

Year	1988	1989	1990	1991	1992	1993	1994	1995	1996	1997
Sales	6.4	4.7	5.4	6.9	7.8	6.8	6.5	7.3	8.8	9.1

(a) Using 1991 as the base year (=100), find the index numbers for sales of airline tickets over the whole period. Display the indices on an appropriate graph.

(b) If the base year was changed to 1994, what would the indices for 1988 and 1995 be?

(c) Calculate the chain base index for each year by first comparing the percentage change in sales between 1988 and 1989.

Question 2   A wage index for the staff of the Lyster and Gale Engineering works in the late 1990s is given below:

Year	1994	1995	1996	1997	1998
Index	97	99	100	106	114

(a) Change the base year from 1996 to 1994 and calculate the new indices (to the nearest integer) for each year. Display these indices on a graph and make appropriate comments.

(b) If the wage in 1998 was £270 per week, what was the weekly wage in 1994?

Question 3   The share price of the Scoobie Dog Food company is monitored on a monthly basis. The table below shows the average share price over the three month period leading up to Christmas. Given that at the base period (April of the year shown) the share price was £1.45, calculate the corresponding simple index numbers for the three months shown. (Give your answers to one decimal place.)

Month	Price
October	£ 1.60
November	£ 1.35
December	£ 2.50

Ms Phillips, the managing director of the company, wishes to compare December's figure with the same month in the previous year. The recorded simple index number at that time point was 350.2. As stated above, the index numbers were re-based in April of the year shown. Given that at that time the simple index value based on the old base period was 410.0 calculate a suitable comparative index number and comment on changes in the share price.

Question 4 Figures for milk production throughout Europe between 1986 and 1993 are given below:

Year	1986	1987	1988	1989	1990	1991	1992	1993
Total whole milk production (million tonnes)	133	127	124	122	122	126	124	123

Adapted from: EUROSTAT Agriculture Statistical Yearbook

(a) Calculate a chain base index for these numbers, giving your answers to one decimal place.

(b) Draw a suitable graph to represent the indices calculated above. Comment on the salient features of the graph.

SPREADSHEET EXERCISE

This exercise will provide an opportunity to revise some of the basic spreadsheet techniques such as formula creation, copying, fixing cell references and creating graphs. Emphasis is placed on the interpretation of results.

The community charges on households worth £40,001 to £50,000 in the town of Hampson over the last 10 years are as follows:

Year	1	2	3	4	5	6	7	8	9	10
Charge (£)	510	561	688	724	745	760	800	750	800	810

The equivalent community charges in Ashville over the same time period are:

Year	1	2	3	4	5	6	7	8	9	10
Charge (£)	565	627	763	808	808	810	820	825	825	840

Enter these figures onto a spreadsheet and perform the following tasks:

(a) Create a simple index for the town of Hampson using year 1 as the base.

(b) Display these indices on a suitable graph. Comment on the main features of the graph.

(c) Create a comparative simple index for the town of Ashville and add these indices to the graph created in task (b).

(d) Comment on the similarities and/or differences in the fluctuations in community charges for the two towns.

(e) For the town of Ashville create a chain base index starting at year 1. From these indices identify the two years over which the largest increase in community charge was incurred. What was the percentage increase in community charge over these two years?

CHAPTER 10

Time based forecasting models

- To introduce the idea of time based models and their uses in forecasting;
- To discuss the meaning of 'trends' in data and the use of linear regression to estimate them;
- To develop the ideas of forecasting time series, discussing the components involved.

Introduction

The idea of time series data – information measured or collected over time, such as weekly sales figures or monthly enquiry levels – has already been introduced in Chapters 3 and 9 of this book. Here, the use of **time based models** for such data will be developed, the aim being to forecast future behaviour of a time dependent variable whose past behaviour shows a predictable pattern.

Initially, the application of regression models to this area will be discussed, so you may find it helpful to review Chapter 4 before progressing.

10.1 Linear time based models

In many business situations where variables are involved, the values of linear time based models show some form of marked pattern over time. Data collected over a period of time is usually called a *time series*. As discussed previously, this type of data is normally displayed on a line graph with *time periods* forming the *x*-axis and *data values* shown on the *y*-axis.

Consider the following example.

EXAMPLE 10.1

Graph the data in the table below which shows the number of colour television licences held at the end of each year from 1991 to 1998.

Year	1991	1992	1993	1994	1995	1996	1997	1998
No. of colour TV licences (millions)	18.4	18.9	20.1	20.4	21.0	21.4	21.9	22.7

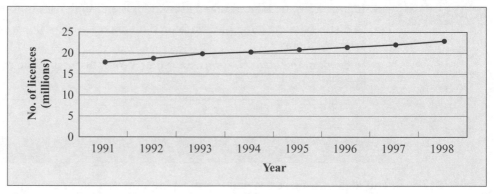

Figure 10.1 Number of colour TV licences held

As the pattern in Figure 10.1 shows, the number of licences has risen steadily between 1991 and 1998.

Trends in time series

The word **trend** is usually used to describe the underlying direction of a time series. In Example 10.1 above, the data has an *upward* trend as it clearly increases over time. Furthermore, the trend is reasonably *linear* in this case. The estimation of straight lines through data with a linear pattern using linear regression has already been discussed in detail in Chapter 4, and the following example will show how the same technique may be applied to time series data.

EXAMPLE 10.2

Fit a linear regression model to the data in Example 10.1 and add it to the graph.

It is usual when modelling time series data to use an ordered series to replace the years, days of the week etc., in the calculations – this avoids problems with making days of the week or quarters fit into the model structure. As with all regression models x is the independent variable and y is the dependent variable. Obviously here the time period is the x variable and the number of colour TV licences is the y variable. The linear regression coefficients can then be calculated as usual:

Year	Time period (x)	No. of licences (y)	xy	x^2
1991	1	18.4	18.4	1
1992	2	18.9	37.8	4
1993	3	20.1	60.3	9
1994	4	20.4	81.6	16
1995	5	21.0	105	25
1996	6	21.4	128.4	36
1997	7	21.9	153.3	49
1998	8	22.7	181.6	64
	$\Sigma x = 36$	$\Sigma y = 164.8$	$\Sigma xy = 766.4$	$\Sigma x^2 = 204$

Then (using formulae from Chapter 4):

$$b = \frac{n\Sigma xy - \Sigma x \Sigma y}{n\Sigma x^2 - (\Sigma x)^2} = \frac{(8 * 766.4) - (36 * 164.8)}{(8 * 204) - (36)^2} = \frac{198.4}{336} = 0.590476$$

$$a = \frac{\Sigma y}{n} - b * \frac{\Sigma x}{n} = \frac{164.8}{8} - 0.590476 * \frac{36}{8} = 17.942858$$

Note: even though the full calculation of a and b has been shown here, in practice a spreadsheet or calculator functions could be used to find the same values more easily.

So the linear regression equation is

$$y = 17.94 + 0.59x$$

This might also be expressed as:

No. of licences held $= 17.94 + 0.59 *$ Time period

(with the final values rounded to two decimal places in each case) and where 'time period' simply represents the ordered variable used in the construction of the model.

Adding this to the graph using techniques also discussed in Chapter 4 results in Figure 10.2. It can be seen that the forecasts produced by the linear regression model (represented by the dotted line in the figure) relate closely to the actual figures.

▶

Example 10.2
continued

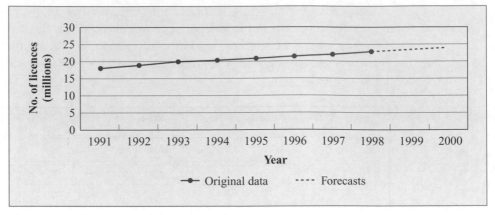

Figure 10.2 Forecast of colour TV licences

10.2 Forecasting using simple linear models

Once the linear model has been estimated, the production of forecasts is relatively straightforward. However, it should be remembered that in forecasting into the future **extrapolation** is used – there is an assumption that the pattern seen in the past will continue into the future. For time series models this is usually reasonable.

EXAMPLE 10.3

Use the model prepared in Example 10.2 to forecast colour TV licences held in the next three years.

The model produced was:

No. of licences held = 17.94 + 0.59 * Time period

Since the time periods considered in the original data went up to 8, the next three will be 9, 10 and 11. Substituting these into the equation gives:

Year	Time period	Forecast licences held (millions)
1999	9	17.94 + 0.59 * 9 = 23.25
2000	10	17.94 + 0.59 * 10 = 23.84
2001	11	17.94 + 0.59 * 11 = 24.43

**REVIEW
ACTIVITY 1**

The following data have been collected. They show sales of a particular product over a series of 20 months since its launch.

Month	Sales	Month	Sales
August	1362	June	4836
September	1623	July	4901
October	2117	August	5052
November	2253	September	6606
December	2910	October	6085
January	3125	November	6536
February	3262	December	7540
March	4026	January	6675
April	3971	February	7688
May	4618	March	7698

(a) Graph these data and comment on the pattern that is present.

(b) Construct a linear regression model to explain sales in terms of time.

(c) Forecast sales of the product for the next three months. Comment on any potential problems with your forecasts.

Working:

Answers on pages 233–5.

10.3 Components of a time series

The simple linear model considered previously is suitable for forecasting time series data show a strong linear pattern over time.

What if the time series does not show this sort of growth or decline, but instead shows some kind of repeated pattern? For example, it is easy to imagine a situation where the value of a variable systematically changes over the course of a year, like that illustrated in Figure 10.3.

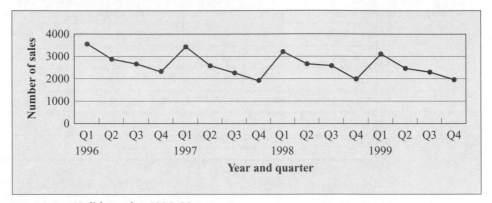

Figure 10.3 Holiday sales 1996–99

In this situation, the type of linear models discussed previously would clearly not be appropriate. Instead, the time series is split into various components, and these are each forecast separately. Two such models are discussed in this text: in one, the elements are added together to form the data series (and it is therefore referred to as an **additive** model). In the other they are multiplied together (and it is called a **multiplicative** model). The additive model is generally considered more suitable for data where the seasonal fluctuations remain roughly the same size over time (illustrated in Figure 10.4), while the multiplicative model is usually applied to data where the size of the seasonal effects increase (as in Figure 10.5).

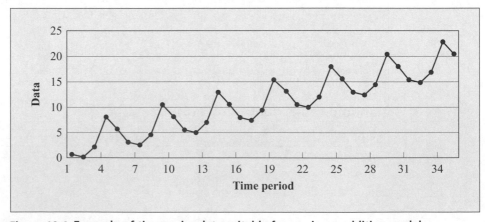

Figure 10.4 Example of time series data suitable for use in an additive model

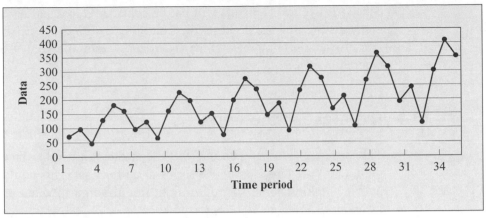

Figure 10.5 Example of time series data suitable for use in a multiplicative model

The components used to make up these models are usually referred to as trend, seasonal factors, cyclical factors and random or residual factors.

Trend (*T*)

As already discussed for the simple linear models, the trend is the underlying movement in the data — it may be upward, downward or stationary.

Seasonal factors (*S*)

These are regular fluctuations within a complete time period (a day, a week, a month etc.). The important thing about seasonal factors is that they represent some sort of repeating pattern e.g., in Figure 10.3 the peaks and troughs are associated with each quarter and repeat once a year.

Cyclical factors (*C*)

These are longer-term fluctuations in the data and are similar to seasonal factors. They can be difficult to identify unless a long series of data is available. They may be related to economic factors e.g., holiday sales may reduce during periods of recession. Given this, the estimation of cyclical effects will not be considered in this book, but you should be aware that they exist in many sets of time series data.

Random or residual factors (*E*)

As in any statistical analysis, there will be some unpredictable element to the data. In the data shown in Figure 10.3 this could be owing to something like unusual weather conditions affecting holiday sales. Since, by their nature, the effects cannot be forecast they will be present in the models developed here but not predicted in any way.

Since the cyclical elements will not be considered in detail here and the random elements are impossible to predict, building the model consists of isolating the two predictable components: the **trend** and **seasonal** effects. These will be considered in turn.

10.4 Forecasting the trend

The aim here is to 'smooth out' the effects due to the other factors, leaving only the underlying direction of the series to be forecast. This could be done simply by eye – taking some sort of straight line through the data and attempting to extend it. See Figure 10.6 for example.

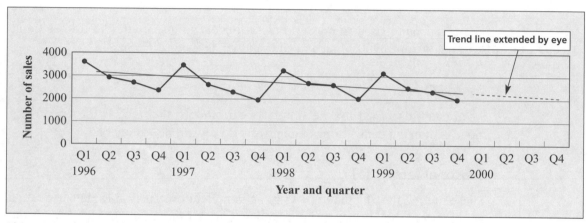

Figure 10.6 Holiday sales, including trend estimated by eye

A more reliable/scientific way of doing this is by the use of **moving averages**.

Moving averages

Moving averages are often used to smooth out variations in a data set with the aim of isolating the trend part of the data so that forecasts of future values of this trend can be made. Averages are generally taken over the natural *period* of the data (the amount of time over which the seasonal pattern repeats). For quarterly data this is usually 4, for daily data 5 or 7 depending on the number of days being considered etc. The moving average is said to be an *n*-point moving average with *n* being the number of values that go to make up the average e.g., a 4-point moving average for quarterly data. Generally, it is found by taking the average of each successive *n* observations in turn formed by 'dropping' the first point in the sequence and 'picking up' the next one each time.

Trend is calculated slightly differently depending on whether the data has an odd or even period. The different approaches will be illustrated by example.

Odd-point moving averages

EXAMPLE 10.4

Consider the following data set, which is for number of enquiries received by telephone operators staffing a customer help line:

Week	1					2					3				
Day	M	Tu	W	Th	F	M	Tu	W	Th	F	M	Tu	W	Th	F
No. of enquiries	33	41	77	81	99	39	49	84	90	107	47	55	91	102	113

Use moving averages to produce trend values for these data.

An initial plot of the data is always a good idea, to pick up any clear patterns, to identify the period of the data (if there is one) and generally get a feel for what's going on. This is shown in Figure 10.7.

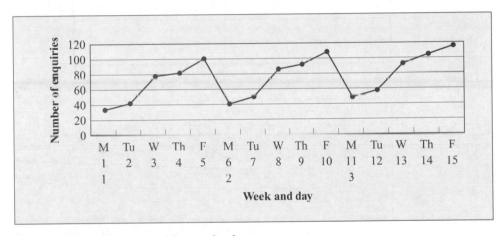

Figure 10.7 Telephone enquiries received

From this, it can be seen that there is a clear pattern repeating every five days confirming that a 5-point moving average should be used.

Notice the position of the results in the table overleaf: as the moving average is a measure of central tendency the results are placed against the *middle* of the set of five values that go to make up each average. Thus spaces must be left at the top and bottom of the column. The moving averages, which represent the trend (T) of the data, can be added to the graph, as shown in Figure 10.8.

The graph shows that the moving averages have an upward linear pattern i.e., the trend in the data is generally upward.

▶

Example 10.4
continued

Day	No. of enquiries	5-point moving average
M	33	
Tu	41	
W	77	66.2
Th	81	67.4
F	99	69.0
M	39	70.4
Tu	49	72.2
W	84	73.8
Th	90	75.4
F	107	76.6
M	47	78.0
Tu	55	80.4
W	91	81.6
Th	102	
F	113	

$= (33+41+77+81+99)/5$

$= (41+77+81+99+39)/5$

$= (77+81+99+39+49)/5$

... etc.

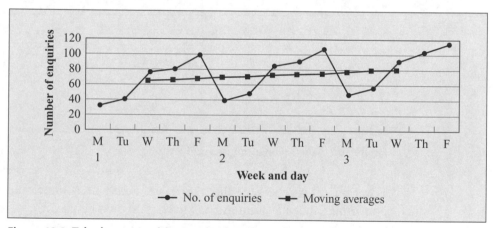

Figure 10.8 Telephone enquiries received, with moving average

Even-point moving averages

EXAMPLE 10.5

Produce estimates of the trend for the following quarterly holiday sales data.

Holiday sales	1996	1997	1998	1999
Q 1	3576	3462	3222	3141
Q 2	2927	2627	2719	2499
Q 3	2710	2315	2614	2347
Q 4	2364	1944	2041	1986

(These data has already been graphed in Figure 10.3.)

In this case it is clear from the graph that the data repeats over four quarters – so a 4-point moving average is needed.

If the period of the data is even, as here, an extra step is required. This is because for four numbers the 'centre' is between two data points and is therefore out of line with the original values – so no direct comparison is possible. To overcome this, the moving average values are still calculated in the same way but are then used to form a further 2-point or **centred moving average** which is then used to represent the trend. This is illustrated in Figure 10.9.

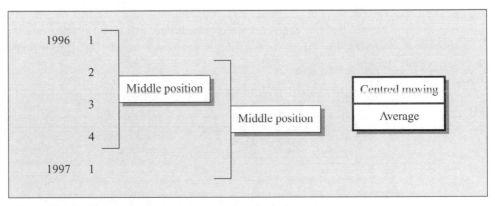

Figure 10.9 Calculation of centred moving averages

For this example the calculations involved in this are as follows:

Year	Quarter	Holiday sales	4-point moving average		Centred moving average	
1996	Q 1	3576				
	Q 2	2927	2894.25	=(3576+2927+2710+2364)/4		
	Q 3	2710	2865.75	=(2927+2710+2364+3462)/4	2880	=(2894.25+2865.75)/2
	Q 4	2364	2790.75		2828.25	=(2865.75+2790.75)/2
1997	Q 1	3462	2692		2741.375	⋮
	Q 2	2627	2587		2639.5	etc.
	Q 3	2315	2527		2557	
	Q 4	1944	2550		2538.5	
1998	Q 1	3222	2624.75		2587.375	
	Q 2	2719	2649		2636.875	
	Q 3	2614	2628.75		2638.875	
	Q 4	2041	2573.75		2601.25	
1999	Q 1	3141	2507		2540.375	
	Q 2	2499	2493.25		2500.125	
	Q 3	2347				
	Q 4	1986				

Again, notice the 'missing' values which have been left blank because of the layout of the data.

As before, the centred values may be added to the graph, this is shown in Figure 10.10. This graph shows that, in this case, there is a slight downward linear trend in the data.

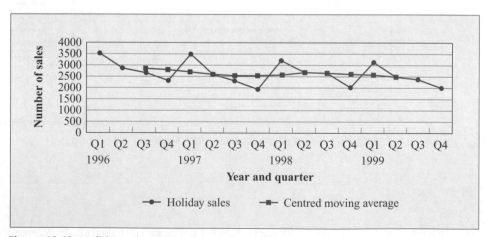

Figure 10.10 Holiday sales data, with centred moving averages

Forecasting the trend from the moving averages

Once the trend has been isolated by use of moving averages, the problem of forecasting this part of the data becomes very straightforward. It can be seen from both sets of moving averages produced in Examples 10.4 and 10.5 that the values are broadly linear.

The use of least squares regression to produce a model of linear time series data has already been discussed in detail earlier in this chapter – using the moving average figures (trend) as the y data and the time period as the x data will produce an equation which can then be used to forecast the trend.

From here onwards, T will be used to represent the trend (found through the use of moving averages) and y will be reserved to represent the original raw data. Hence the regression equation to explain the trend part of the data will have the form:

$$T = a + bx$$

where T is the centred moving average trend and x is the time period.

As the calculation of a and b has already been illustrated (see Example 10.2) from here onwards it will be assumed that a calculator or spreadsheet is used to find them, and they will simply be quoted (the notes accompanying the spreadsheet exercise at the end of the chapter show how the values can be found in Excel).

For Examples 10.4 and 10.5 the trend equations can be found to be:

Example 10.4: Telephone enquiries trend $(T) = 61.25 + 1.56x$
where $x = 1$ is for Monday of week 1.

Example 10.5: Holiday sales trend $(T) = 2862.65 – 26.10x$
where $x = 1$ is for 1996 quarter 1.

REVIEW ACTIVITY 2

The production figures for a fruit dealer (in 000 units) are shown below:

Year	Quarter 1	Quarter 2	Quarter 3	Quarter 4
1997	4.3	9.8	11.1	7.7
1998	5.0	11.0	12.7	8.7
1999	5.9	12.3	13.4	9.7

(a) Plot these figures on a graph and comment on any trend or seasonal effect that seems to be present.

(b) Calculate the trend (using a suitable moving average) and add it to your graph.

(c) Given that a regression of the trend values against time (quarter 1 1997 = 1) gives the equation $T = 7.51 + 0.28x$, calculate forecasts for the trend in the four quarters of 2000 and add these figures to the graph.

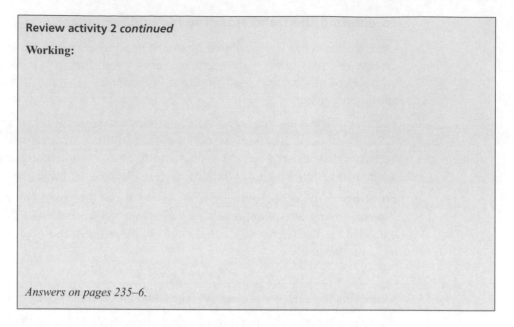

Answers on pages 235–6.

10.5 Forecasting the seasonal effects

Once the trend has been isolated and forecast from a linear regression model based on moving averages, the problem that remains is how to identify and forecast the seasonal effects (the fluctuating part of the data).

As mentioned in Section 10.3, two models which combine the individual components will be considered here: the additive and multiplicative models. Each is considered in turn.

The additive model

In this model, it is assumed that the components of the time series are added together to form the data i.e.,

$$y = T + S + C + E$$

Since (as already discussed) the forecast of the cyclical effects will not be considered here, the model effectively reduces to:

$$y = T + S + E$$

The trend component has already been found through the use of moving averages – so the seasonal (and error) terms can be isolated by subtracting the trend from the original data i.e.,

$$S + E = y - T$$

As previously stated, the error component cannot be directly isolated. However, it can be minimized by averaging out the seasonal effects for each time period to give a set of factors for forecasting. This is illustrated in the following example.

EXAMPLE 10.6

Using the telephone enquiries data and trend calculated in Example 10.4, estimate the seasonal effects. Assume an additive model is appropriate.

Given that the trend equation is $T = 61.25 + 1.56x$ where x is the time period and Monday week 1 = 1, use both trend and seasonal factors to forecast expected enquiry levels for the coming week.

The first step is to subtract the trend (moving average) from the original data. This gives:

Week	Day	No. of enquiries y	5-point moving average T	Additive seasonal Effect y – T (= S +E)
1	M	33		
	Tu	41		
	W	77	66.2	77 – 66.2 = 10.8
	Th	81	67.4	81 – 67.4 = 13.6
	F	99	69.0	30.0
2	M	39	70.4	–31.4
	Tu	49	72.2	–23.2
	W	84	73.8	10.2
	Th	90	75.4	14.6
	F	107	76.6	30.4
3	M	47	78.0	–31.0
	Tu	55	80.4	–25.4
	W	91	81.6	9.4
	Th	102		
	F	113		

Note: the moving averages, rather than trend calculated from the equation, are used to give greater accuracy.

A summary of these seasonal effects is then made. There are three values for Wednesday (10.8, 10.2 and 9.4); two for Thursday (13.6 and 14.6) etc. They are different because of the random effect that is still present. To minimize this, the values for each weekday are averaged.

▶

Example 10.6
continued

Week	M	Tu	W	Th	F	
1			10.8	13.6	30.0	
2	−31.4	−23.2	10.2	14.6	30.4	
3	−31.0	−25.4	9.4			
Average	−31.2	−24.3	10.13333	14.1	30.2	sum = −1.06667

In an additive model, the sum of the final factors should be 0. Here they add to −1.06667 (the total random effect) so it is necessary to adjust each factor slightly by 'sharing' this total among the seasonal effects.

The amount to adjust each factor by is:

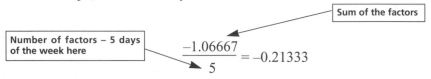

$$\frac{-1.06667}{5} = -0.21333$$

The adjusted averages are then:

Day	Average	Adjustment	Adjusted average
Monday	−31.2	−0.21333	−31.2 − (−0.21333) = −30.99
Tuesday	−24.3	−0.21333	−24.3 − (−0.21333) = −24.09
Wednesday	10.13333	−0.21333	10.35
Thursday	14.1	−0.21333	14.31
Friday	30.2	−0.21333	30.41
Sum			−0.01

The final sum is not quite 0 due to rounding errors (going from four to two decimal places) but −0.01 is acceptable.

To find the final forecasts, the trend (from the regression equation) and the seasonal effects are combined: as the model is additive they are added together. As Monday of week 1 = time period 1, counting down shows that Monday of week 4 = time period 16.

Week	Day	Time period	Trend	Seasonal effect	Forecast (trend + season)
4	M	16	61.25 + (1.56 * 16) = 86.21	−30.99	86.21 − 30.99 = 55.2
	Tu	17	61.25 + (1.56 * 17) = 87.77	−24.09	87.77 − 24.09 = 63.7
	W	18	61.25 + (1.56 * 18) = 89.33	10.35	89.33 + 10.35 = 99.7
	Th	19	61.25 + (1.56 * 19) = 90.89	14.31	90.89 + 14.31 = 105.2
	F	20	61.25 + (1.56 * 20) = 92.45	30.41	92.45 + 30.41 = 122.9

The multiplicative model

Here, the underlying model assumes that the components multiply together to form the overall data:

$$y = T * S * C * E$$

As for the additive model, in the simple situations examined here the cyclical effects will be discarded to give:

$$y = T * S * E$$

Hence, rather than subtracting the trend from the original data to leave the seasonal (and error) terms behind, in this model the original data is divided by the trend:

$$S * E = \frac{y}{T}$$

Again, error terms are minimized in a similar way to that for the additive model and once these seasonal effects have been isolated, they are forecast separately from the trend. The two components are then multiplied together to give a final forecast for the original data. The details of the calculations are shown in the following example.

EXAMPLE 10.7

Find the multiplicative seasonal effects for the holiday sales data used in Example 10.5 and hence produce forecasts of sales for 2000 if the trend equation is $T = 2862.65 - 26.10x$ where 1996 quarter 1 is $x = 1$.

	Year/ quarter	Holiday sales (y)	Centred moving average (T)	Multiplicative seasonal effects (y/T)	
1996	Q 1	3576			
	Q 2	2927			
	Q 3	2710	2880.000	0.9410	=2710/2880.000
	Q 4	2364	2828.250	0.8359	=2364/2828.250
1997	Q 1	3462	2741.375	1.2629	=3462/2741.375
	Q 2	2627	2639.500	0.9953	:
	Q 3	2315	2557.000	0.9054	etc.
	Q 4	1944	2538.500	0.7658	
1998	Q 1	3222	2587.375	1.2453	
	Q 2	2719	2636.875	1.0311	
	Q 3	2614	2638.875	0.9906	
	Q 4	2041	2601.250	0.7846	
1999	Q 1	3141	2540.375	1.2364	
	Q 2	2499	2500.125	0.9996	
	Q 3	2347			
	Q 4	1986			

▶

Example 10.7
continued

As in the additive model it is necessary to obtain an average value for each time period as there will be some random element present (which explains why the factors for each of the four quarters are not identical).

Year	Q1	Q2	Q3	Q4	
1996			0.9410	0.8359	
1997	1.2629	0.9953	0.9054	0.7658	
1998	1.2453	1.0311	0.9906	0.7846	
1999	1.2364	0.9996			
Average	1.2482	1.0087	0.9457	0.7954	Sum: 3.9980

Again, the averages are added together. In the multiplicative model they should add to the number of seasons (four here) and the 'sharing' adjustment is done by multiplying each of the original seasonal averages by:

$$\frac{\text{Number of seasons}}{\text{Sum of }(\Sigma)\text{ original averages}}$$

So here:

Number of seasons = 4

Sum of seasonal effects: 3.9980

Adjustment factor is: $\dfrac{4}{3.9980} = 1.0005$

	Quarter 1	Quarter 2	Quarter 3	Quarter 4
Initial average	1.2482	1.0087	0.9457	0.7954
Adjustment	1.0005	1.0005	1.0005	1.0005
Seasonal effect	1.2482 * 1.0005 = 1.249	1.009	0.946	0.796

Checking the seasonal values do add to 4:

Σ (seasonal effects) = 1.249 + 1.009 + 0.946 + 0.796 = 4.000

Thus, on average, in quarter 1 the data is 1.249 times the trend value, in quarter 2 it is 1.009 times the trend value etc.

The two parts of the data (the trend and seasonal effects) can then be combined in a forecast for the original data. The only difference from the additive model is that the values are multiplied together to give the final forecasts (rather than added). Given that 1996, quarter 1 = time period 1 and counting forwards gives 2000, quarter 1 = time period 17, so:

Quarter	Time period	Forecast trend (T)	Seasonal effect (S)	Final forecast (T * S)
2000 1	17	2862.65 – (26.10 * 17) = 2418.95	1.249	2418.95 * 1.249 = 3021
2	18	2862.65 – (26.10 * 18) = 2392.85	1.009	2392.85 * 1.009 = 2414
3	19	2366.75	0.946	2366.75 * 0.946 = 2239
4	20	2340.65	0.796	2340.65 * 0.796 = 1863

To complete the picture, it is often useful to add the forecasts to a graph of the original data to check that the results look sensible (Figure 10.11). This seems fine as the clear pattern visible in the previous results is continued in the forecasts.

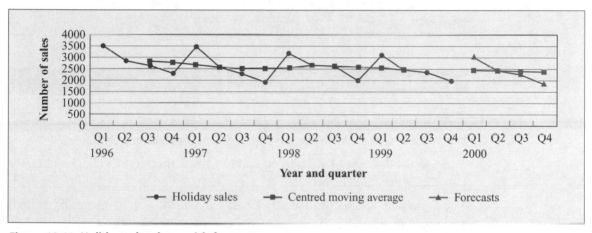

Figure 10.11 Holiday sales data, with forecasts

REVIEW ACTIVITY 3

This exercise continues from the work done in Review activity 2.

(a) Using the table of fruit production and centred moving averages with a multiplicative model, calculate the seasonal effect for each quarter.

(b) Tabulate these seasonal effects and find the average value for each quarter. Adjust these to give estimates of the overall seasonal effects.

(c) Combine the forecasts of the trend in the data (prepared in the previous exercise) with these seasonal effects to give an overall estimate of fruit production in the four quarters of 1998.

(d) Graph the original data, the trend and your forecasts to check the answers you have obtained.

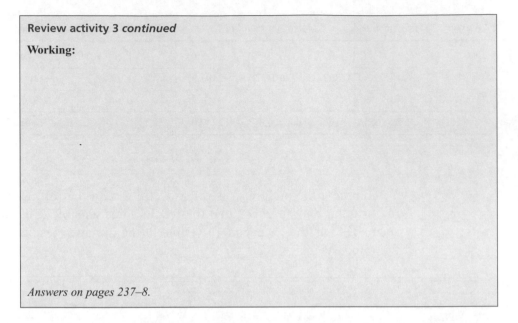

Review activity 3 *continued*

Working:

Answers on pages 237–8.

Key points to remember

1. Time based data is usually presented on a line graph.

2. Linear time series can be forecast using linear regression techniques.

3. Time series data may have a trend and/or seasonal effect. Cyclical and residual effects may also be present.

4. The trend part of a set of time series data can be isolated by the use of centred moving averages.

5. The period of the moving average is chosen to match the repeating pattern in the data.

6. Once the trend has been isolated, the seasonal part of the data can be found from one of two different models:

   an additive model, which assumes that $y = T + S + E$;

   a multiplicative model, which assumes that $y = T * S * E$.

7. Care should be taken when forecasting into the future with these models (since extrapolation is being performed).

ADDITIONAL EXERCISES

Question 1   A cinema has been monitoring its ticket sales over the past 20 weeks and the data collected are shown below.

Week	1	2	3	4	5	6	7	8	9	10	11	12	13	14	15	16	17	18	19	20
No. of tickets	6742	6812	6677	6820	7461	7351	7691	7691	8458	8663	8216	7946	8877	8091	8538	8675	8603	8286	8794	8905

(a) Graph these data and comment on any pattern that seems to be present. Hence choose a suitable forecasting method for predicting future ticket sales.

(b) Use your chosen method to develop a model to describe these data, and hence produce forecasts of sales for the next four weeks.

(c) How good do you expect the forecasts to be? What potential problems are there with the method you have used?

Question 2   The data below have been collected over the past 20 weeks by the new managing director of a chain of supermarkets. As he is concerned about the level of customer complaints received by the organization he has introduced a new staff training policy designed to reduce the numbers of complaints.

He is now interested in forecasting future levels of complaints using the data collected.

Week	1	2	3	4	5	6	7	8	9	10	11	12	13	14	15	16	17	18	19	20
No. of complaints (000)	6.0	4.9	3.8	3.9	2.7	5.6	4.6	4.0	3.4	2.5	5.3	4.3	3.4	3.1	2.1	4.9	3.6	3.4	2.9	2.2

(a) Graph data, and hence comment on any trend or seasonal effect that is present. Does the manager's new training policy seem to be working?

(b) Calculate a suitable moving average to isolate the trend in these data.

(c) Estimate the seasonal effects in this data using a multiplicative model.

(d) Find the regression equation which could be used to estimate the trend, and hence forecast complaint levels for the next four weeks.

(e) Comment on how accurate you expect your forecasts to be.

Question 3   These data, relating to profits (£000s) made by a company over four years, has been collected:

Year	Q1	Q2	Q3	Q4
1996	1.20	1.71	2.30	1.63
1997	1.55	2.18	2.63	1.81
1998	1.76	2.33	2.78	2.16
1999	2.14	2.84	3.36	2.48

(a) Graph the data and hence discuss any pattern present.

(b) What period should be used in a moving average series to isolate the trend in these data? Why use this value?

(c) Calculate a trend equation for the data using a moving average series, and estimate the seasonal effects with an additive model.

(d) Forecast the expected profit for the company in 2001. Discuss any problems you foresee with these forecasts.

Question 4 A call centre has recently been set up to handle enquiries from customers of an insurance company telephoning for help with claims. It is very important for the call centre management to be able to forecast the likely number of calls in advance so that they can plan staff shift patterns.

The (incomplete) analysis shown in Figure 10.12 was produced in Excel and shows the daily calls received over the past six weeks.

You are required to:

(a) Graph the data for the number of calls received and comment on any trend or seasonal effects present.

(b) Explain why a 6-point moving average series was chosen, and why it was also necessary to calculate the column of centred moving averages.

(c) Calculate the 'missing' figures for the 6-point moving average, centred moving average and seasonal effects.

(d) Give the exact wording of two different formulae which could be used in cells K17 and K18 to reproduce the 'a' and 'b' values shown on the printout and briefly explain what these numbers represent.

(e) Using your answers to part (c), complete the table of seasonal effects and calculate the overall seasonal value for each day of the week.

(f) Hence provide forecasts of the likely level of calls that would be received in the first three days of week 7.

Question 5 The personnel section of a large company suspects that the sickness absence rates of their employees follow a seasonal pattern. They are interested in predicting levels of this type of absence during the coming winter, so that they can set fair targets for the various departments.

They have access to the following data relating to the amount of sickness absence recorded (in hours per person per week) for each quarter over the past five years:

Year	Q1	Q2	Q3	Q4
1995	2.23	1.65	1.50	2.14
1996	2.49	1.75	1.56	2.18
1997	2.41	1.91	1.60	2.29
1998	2.53	1.89	1.70	2.31
1999	2.77	2.13	1.91	2.65

You are required to analyse this data to determine whether there is indeed a seasonal pattern present. Once this is done, prepare a suitable forecasting model to predict sickness absence in the next two quarters. Present your conclusions in the form of a report to the Head of the Personnel Department, including discussion of how the model could be used and the potential problems with the technique.

	A	B	C	D	E	F	G	H	I	J	K	L	M	N	O	P
1											Mon	Tue	Wed	Thu	Fri	Sat
2	Time Period	Week			6pt MA	Cent MA	Seas			Week 1				0.984	1.334	1.327
3	1	1	Monday	117						Week 2	0.629	0.921	0.825	0.984	1.291	1.477
4	2		Tuesday	125						Week 3						
5	3		Wednesday	141						Week 4	0.685	0.730	0.842	1.201	1.116	1.472
6	4		Thursday	185	177.33	177.75	1.041			Week 5	0.637	0.764	0.749	1.288	1.001	1.669
7	5		Friday	244	178.17	182.92	1.334			Week 6	0.583	0.737	0.837			
8	6		Saturday	252	187.67	189.92	1.327									
9	7	2	Monday	122	192.17	193.92	0.629									
10	8		Tuesday	182	195.67	197.67	0.921									
11	9		Wednesday	168	199.67	203.75	0.825									
12	10		Thursday	206	207.83	209.25	0.984									
13	11		Friday	268	210.67	207.67	1.291									
14	12		Saturday	301	204.67	203.84	1.477									
15	13	3	Monday	139												
16	14		Tuesday	146												
17	15		Wednesday	158						a:	188.2					
18	16		Thursday	278						b:	1.804					
19	17		Friday	263												
20	18		Saturday	345												
21	19	4	Monday	164	238.33	239.42	0.685									
22	20		Tuesday	176	240.50	241.09	0.730									
23	21		Wednesday	204	241.67	242.42	0.842									
24	22		Thursday	291	243.17	242.25	1.201									
25	23		Friday	270	241.33	241.92	1.116									
26	24		Saturday	354	242.50	240.50	1.472									
27	25	5	Monday	153	238.50	240.25	0.637									
28	26		Tuesday	183	242.00	239.42	0.764									
29	27		Wednesday	180	236.83	240.33	0.749									
30	28		Thursday	312	243.83	242.17	1.288									
31	29		Friday	239	240.50	238.75	1.001									
32	30		Saturday	396	237.00	237.25	1.669									
33	31	6	Monday	133	237.50	228.25	0.583									
34	32		Tuesday	162	219.00	219.75	0.737									
35	33		Wednesday	183	220.50	218.75	0.837									
36	34		Thursday	201	217.00											
37	35		Friday	248												
38	36		Saturday	375												

Figure 10.12 Data on calls received

SPREADSHEET EXERCISE

This exercise covers the stages in the production of a simple time series forecasting model. The process followed will be exactly as for the completion of the previous examples, but Excel will be used to perform the repetitive calculations of the moving averages and seasonal effects, and to find the 'a' and 'b' coefficients in the calculation of the trend equation. To assist, the data and results used in Examples 10.5 and 10.7 are first reproduced with details of the Excel formulae and calculations used. Figure 10.13 shows the results (notice that the figures are close to those obtained in Examples 10.5 and 10.7: the small differences are due to the increased accuracy obtained when using Excel because there is no need to round the figures).

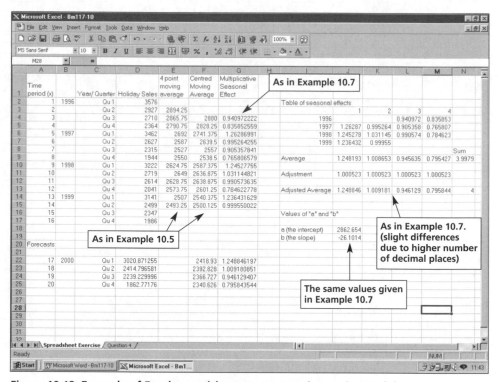

Figure 10.13 Example of Excel spreadsheet to create a time series model

Figures 10.14 and 10.15 show the same spreadsheet, with formulae instead of figures to show how the values are achieved.

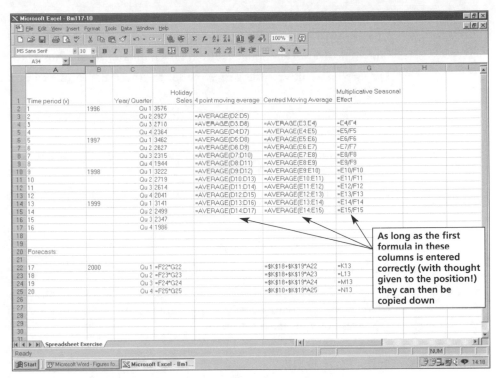

Figure 10.14 Excel spreadsheet showing formulae used

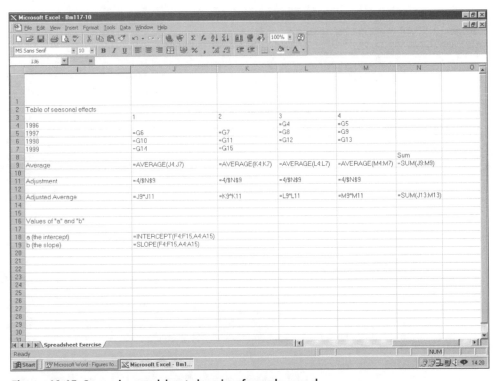

Figure 10.15 Second spreadsheet showing formulae used

Exercise

The file SHOPPING.XLS contains information about the number of visitors to a large out-of-town shopping centre for each quarter from 1995 to 1999.

Prepare an additive time series model for these data, following the steps detailed below.

(a) *Graph* the data and comment on any trend or seasonal effects that seem to be present.

(b) *Determine* a suitable period to use in a moving average series and hence calculate trend values for the data.

(c) *Add* this moving average series to your graph and comment on the direction of any trend in the data.

(d) *Calculate* a regression equation to explain the trend, considering the goodness of fit of the resulting model to the data.

(e) *Estimate* the trend figure for the four quarters of 2000 using your regression equation.

Note: if extra spreadsheet examples are required, the data given in the additional exercises could be used for practice.

WORKED SOLUTIONS TO REVIEW ACTIVITIES

Review activity 1   (a) Temperatures are generally stated to the nearest whole number, so the immediate reaction of most people is to say that these data are discrete. However, temperature can be *measured* very accurately so is therefore continuous.

(b) Nominal – as names are used.

(c) Discrete – the key word is number of products, so counts are dealt with.

(d) Ordinal – chart position is a number which represents the *ranking* of sales.

Review activity 2   *Note: As random numbers are involved there is no one right answer so the working below simply explains the correct methods to be used.*

(a) Simple random sampling

The first column of names are allocated numbers 01 to 10 and the second column are allocated 11 to 20. Then the random number list provided is used starting at the first value (11) with every other number chosen subsequently (so that the random numbers chosen are 11, 05, 18 etc.). Those people whose allocated number matches up with the random number are then identified as the random sample.

(Note that it would be perfectly acceptable to choose numbers from anywhere else in the table given – this is just one way of doing it).

> 11 – John North
>
> 05 – Patrick Dixon
>
> 18 – Angela Stewart
>
> 18 – Ignore as already used
>
> 15 – Karen Morris
>
> 07 – John Murray

(b) Stratified random sampling (based on gender)

There are eight females and 12 males in the group, which means the ratio of male to female students is 3:2. So in a sample of 5 there should be three males and two females. In this particular sample the second row of random numbers is used (beginning at 17) ignoring those which would result in too many of either gender, i.e.,

> 17 – Vicki Plant (F)
>
> 13 – Sue Peters (F – now have two females as required)
>
> 09 – Ivor Thompson (M)
>
> 01 – Lynn Black (F so do not include)

07 – John Murray (M)

13 – Already used so ignore

08 – Alan Smith (M)

(c) Systematic random sampling

There are 20 people and a sample of 5 is required. Therefore pick every 20/5 = 4th person from the list i.e.,

Anne Hobson

Alan Smith

Malcolm Fox

Gail Philipson

Liz Smith

(A random start point could have been chosen – it is not necessary to start with the 4th person.)

Review activity 3   (a) The number of colours given as alternatives is very limited and it would be very likely that the *Other* category would have a high number of responses. In order to improve the questions a much greater variety of choices needs to be provided. However, it must also be recognized that it would be impossible to provide every possible shade.

What is the colour of your new car?

Red	☐	Blue	☐	White	☐
Green	☐	Yellow	☐	Gold	☐
Brown	☐	Black	☐	Silver	☐
Grey	☐	Purple	☐	Other	☐

(b) The two choices may be a bit restrictive – for instance it is possible that a part payment was made in cash (say a deposit). Rather than changing the question into multiple choice format the actual wording of the question can be changed to make it less ambiguous.

Was cash used for payment or part payment of the car ?

Yes   ☐   No   ☐

(c) This is a classic example of a question where the responses are not comprehensive and the categories are not mutually exclusive.

To illustrate these two points ask yourself if the car cost £4900 (or £11,500) which box would you tick? If the car cost exactly £9000 would you tick the second or third box?

The improved question should be:

How much did you pay for the car?

Less than £5000	☐	£5000 to less than £7000	☐
£7000 to less than £9000	☐	£9000 to less than £11,000	☐
£11,000 or over	☐		

(d) In this question there are more choices on the 'for' side than on the 'against' side.

Do you feel that the service you received from our staff was

Excellent   ☐   Satisfactory   ☐   Poor   ☐ ?

CHAPTER 2

Review activity 1   (a) In this case there are a few possible options of suitable class widths for this continuous data. In this solution, the ones used are: Under 5 hours, 5 up to 10 hours, 10 up to 15 hours, 15 up to 20 hours, 20 up to 25 hours.

The result is shown in Table S.2.1.

Table S.2.1 Revision time of 30 students taking a statistics exam

Time in hours	Frequency
under 5	1
5 up to 10	4
10 up to 15	13
15 up to 20	10
20 up to 25	2

Source: Student survey

(b) By using the tally system the resulting cross tabulation is as shown in Table S.2.2.

Table S.2.2 Gender, and number of post-16 qualifications held by students on BA Ceramics

Number of post-16 qualifications	Male	Female	Total
1	3	7	10
2	6	4	10
3	5	6	11
4	1	2	3
5	0	2	2
Total	15	21	36

Source: Student survey

(Remember to include *all* of the points discussed i.e., headings, titles, source etc.)

Review activity 2   As the accommodation data provided is classified as nominal, the two obvious choices for graphical representation are either a bar chart or a pie chart. The question requested that proportion be shown, therefore of these two a pie chart would be the more appropriate.

Review activity 3   All the categories, apart from the last, have a width of 10. Since the last category is open ended (quite common), a width for this category is needed in order to calculate the frequency density. In line with recommendations made within the chapter, here the last category has been taken as twice the width of the others (i.e., 20). This gives a set of uneven categories, therefore to construct the histogram frequency densities are required.

The calculations required to find the frequency density are shown in Table S.2.3.

Table S.2.3 Calculations required to find the frequency density

Monthly rent (£)	Frequency (f)	Class width	Frequency density
100 to less than 110	1	10	$\frac{1}{10} = 0.1$
110 to less than 120	4	10	$\frac{4}{10} = 0.4$
120 to less than 130	7	10	$\frac{7}{10} = 0.7$
130 to less than 140	13	10	$\frac{13}{10} = 1.3$
140 to less than 150	7	10	$\frac{7}{10} = 0.7$
150 to less than 160	3	10	$\frac{3}{10} = 0.3$
160 to less than 180	1	20	$\frac{1}{20} = 0.05$

So the resulting histogram is as shown in Figure S.2.1.

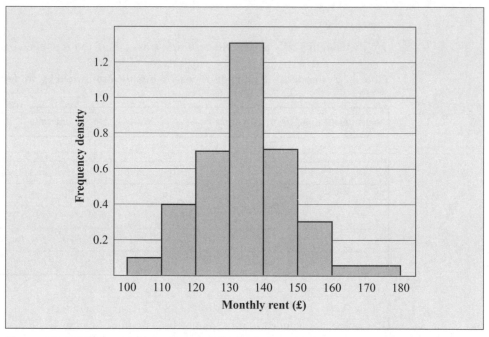

Figure S.2.1 Histogram for Review activity 3, showing students' monthly rent
Source: Student survey

Review activity 4 Given the two groups differ in size and the sub-divisions are small a stacked bar chart (Figure S.2.2) is perhaps the most suitable graphical representation for the data.

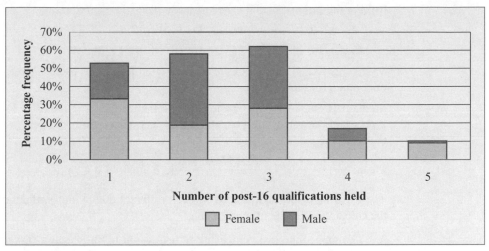

Figure S.2.2 Chart for Review activity 4, showing gender, and number of post-16 qualifications held by BA Ceramics students
Source: Student survey

CHAPTER 3

Review activity 1 (a) First it is necessary to find the mid points for each of the groups. If these cannot be spotted easily, the mid point can be found by adding together the lowest value in each end of the group and dividing by 2. The mid point values are then multiplied by the group's frequency and this produces Table S.3.1.

Table S.3.1

Time (hours)	Frequency (f)	Mid point (x)	fx
Under 5	1	2.5	$1*2.5=2.5$
5 up to 10	4	7.5	30
10 up to 15	13	12.5	162.5
15 up to 20	10	17.5	175
20 up to 25	2	22.5	45
	$\Sigma f = 30$		$\Sigma fx = 415$

To calculate the mean, the frequency (f) column is totalled, then the frequency times the mid point (fx) column is calculated and used in the formula:

$$\bar{x} = \frac{\Sigma fx}{\Sigma f} = \frac{415}{30} = 13.83 \text{ hours (to 2 d.p.)}$$

(b) For the original data it is necessary to place the values in order:

4, 6, 9, 9, 9, 10, 11, 11, 11, 12, 12, 12, 12, 13, 13,

13, 13, 14, 15, 15, 15, 15, 16, 16, 18, 18, 18, 19, 20, 21

Mode: 12, 13 and 15 hours have all been cited four times each. Therefore there is no distinct mode for this data set.

Median: There are 30 values altogether so the median is in the $(30+1)/2$th $= 15\frac{1}{2}$th position when the values are placed in order. The 15th value $= 13$ and the 16th value $= 13$, therefore the median value is 13 hours.

Mean: $\dfrac{4 + 6 + 9 + ... + 19 + 20 + 21}{30} = 13.33$ hours (to 2 d.p.)

The two values for the mean are slightly different due to a loss of detail and accuracy in the calculation for the grouped data.

(c) The most appropriate measure to use would be the mean as the data is fairly symmetrically distributed and there are no extreme values. The mean for the raw data (13.33 hours) would be chosen as it is more accurate than the mean for the tabulated data.

Review activity 2 (a) (i) For the original data (working from the ordered set as before):

4, 6, 9, 9, 9, 10, 11, 11, 11, 12, 12, 12, 12, 13, 13,

13, 13, 14, 15, 15, 15, 15, 16, 16, 18, 18, 18, 19, 20, 21

Since there are an even number of values it is acceptable to use $n/4$ and $3n/4$ values as the quartiles.

There are 30 values, therefore the lower quartile is the

$n/4$th $= 30/4$th $= 7.5$th value

The 7th and 8th observations are 11, therefore the lower quartile is 11, and the upper quartile is the

$3n/4$th $= 90/4$th $= 22.5$th value

The 22nd and 23rd observations are 15 and 16, therefore the upper quartile is 15.5.

So the inter-quartile range is $15.5 - 11 = 4.5$ for the raw data.

For the grouped data it is necessary to construct an ogive (Figure S.3.1), which requires cumulative frequencies:

Time (hours)	Cumulative frequency
Less than 5	1
Less than 10	5
Less than 15	18
Less than 20	28
Less than 25	30

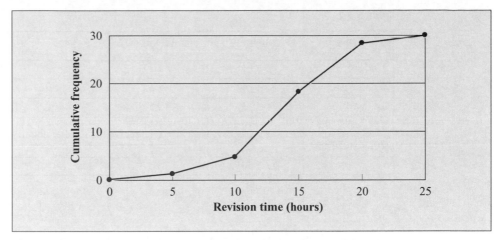

Figure S.3.1 Ogive for Review activity 2, showing student revision times
Source: Student survey

The upper quartile is obtained by taking the $3n/4$th value (22.5th value as above). From the graph this is approximately 16 hours. The lower quartile, the $n/4$th value (7.5th value as above), is approximately 11 hours from the graph.

Hence the inter-quartile range for the tabulated data is $16 - 11 = 5$ hours.

(ii) For the raw data, the following values are needed to calculate the variance:

$$\Sigma x^2 = 4^2 + 6^2 + 9^2 + \ldots + 20^2 + 21^2 = 5792$$

$$\Sigma x = 400$$

Then using the formula:

$$\sigma^2 = \frac{\Sigma x^2}{n} - \frac{(\Sigma x)^2}{n} = \frac{5792}{30} - \frac{(400)^2}{30}$$

$$= 193.066666 - 13.333333^2 = 15.2888888$$

Since the data are taken from a sample it is necessary to adjust the variance:

$$s^2 = \frac{n}{n-1} * \sigma^2 = \frac{30}{29} * 15.288888 = 15.8160919$$

$$s = \sqrt{15.8160919} = 3.98 \text{ (to 2 d.p.)}$$

i.e., the standard deviation for the raw data is 3.98 hours.

When working with the tabulated data it is first necessary to construct the extra columns to find the Σfx and Σfx^2 values (here, the table used to calculate the mean can be amended to give Table S.3.2).

Table S.3.2

Time (hours)	Frequency (f)	Mid point (x)	fx	fx^2
Under 5	1	2.5	2.5	$1*2.5*2.5 = 6.25$
5 up to 10	4	7.5	30	225
10 up to 15	13	12.5	162.5	2031.25
15 up to 20	10	17.5	175	3062.5
20 up to 25	2	22.5	45	1012.5
	$\Sigma f = 30$		$\Sigma fx = 415$	$\Sigma fx^2 = 6337.5$

$$\sigma^2 = \frac{\Sigma fx^2}{n} - \left[\frac{\Sigma fx}{n}\right]^2 \text{ where } n = \Sigma f$$

$$= \frac{6337.5}{30} - \left[\frac{415}{30}\right]^2 = 211.25 - 13.8333333^2$$

$$= 211.25 - 191.36111 = 19.888889$$

Since the data are from a sample, the correction factor is needed:

$$s^2 = \frac{n}{n-1} * \sigma^2 = \frac{30}{29} * 19.888889 = 20.574713$$

$$s = \sqrt{20.574713} = 4.54 \text{ (to 2 d.p.)}$$

So for the tabulated data, the standard deviation is 4.54.

(b) As for the mean, the answers for the raw and tabulated data differ due to the loss of accuracy when the data are tabulated.

(c) Since the mean was chosen as the measure of central tendency, the standard deviation (for the raw data) should be chosen to partner it.

CHAPTER 4

Review activity 1 (a) Let percentage mark given for speed $= x$ and percentage mark given for print quality $= y$. Table S.4.1 is then constructed.

Table S.4.1

x	y	x^2	y^2	xy
20	65	400	4225	1300
45	35	2025	1225	1575
25	55	625	3025	1375
10	85	100	7225	850
30	15	900	225	450
25	25	625	625	625
35	45	1225	2025	1575
30	25	900	625	750
20	55	400	3025	1100
25	35	625	1225	875
$\Sigma x = 265$	$\Sigma y = 440$	$\Sigma x^2 = 7825$	$\Sigma y^2 = 23{,}450$	$\Sigma xy = 10{,}475$

Using the data in the table calculate:

$$r = \frac{n\Sigma xy - \Sigma x\Sigma y}{\sqrt{\{n\Sigma x^2 - (\Sigma x)^2\}\{n\Sigma y^2 - (\Sigma y)^2\}}}$$

$$= \frac{(10*10,475) - (265*440)}{\sqrt{\{(10*7825) - 265^2\}\{(10*23,450) - 440^2\}}}$$

$$= \frac{104,750 - 116,600}{\sqrt{\{78,250 - 70,225\}\{234,500 - 193,600\}}}$$

$$= \frac{-11,850}{\sqrt{8025*40,900}} = \frac{-11,850}{18,116.912}$$

$$= -0.654 \text{ (to 3 d.p.)}$$

This suggests there is a reasonably strong correlation between the speed and the print quality of the machine. As the correlation coefficient is negative this would suggest that as speed increases then print quality decreases.

(b) Before calculating the rank correlation coefficient, the prices of the machines require ranking. The ranks awarded (where 1 = most expensive) are shown in Table S.4.2. It should be noted that the two cheapest printers share the ranks of 9 and 10 giving them each a rank of 9.5.

Table S.4.2

Overall rank	Price (£)	Price rank	d	d^2
5	410	3	2	4
3	396	6	−3	9
8	350	9.5	−1.5	2.25
7	530	1	6	36
4	399	5	−1	1
10	353	8	2	4
1	430	2	−1	1
2	404	4	−2	4
9	350	9.5	−0.5	0.25
6	375	7	−1	1
				$\Sigma d^2 = 62.5$

Then calculate:

$$r = 1 - \frac{6\Sigma d^2}{n(n^2-1)}$$

$$= 1 - \frac{6*62.5}{10*99} = 1 - \frac{375}{990}$$

$$= 1 - 0.3787878 = 0.621 \text{ (to 3 d.p.)}$$

The correlation coefficient of 0.621 suggests there is a reasonable level of agreement between the overall rank awarded to the printer and its price.

Review activity 2   (a) Phoneyvode:

$y = 15 + 0.5x$ *or*   charges $= 15 + 0.5 *$ minutes of calls

Purplecom:

$y = 17.25 + 0.35x$ *or*   charges $= 17.25 + 0.35 *$ minutes of calls

In each case $y =$ charges, $x =$ number of minutes of calls made.

(b) Calculations required:

Minutes of calls (x)	0	20	40
Phoneyvode charge	15	25	35
Purplecom charge	17.25	24.25	31.25

This gives a graph as shown in Figure S.4.1.

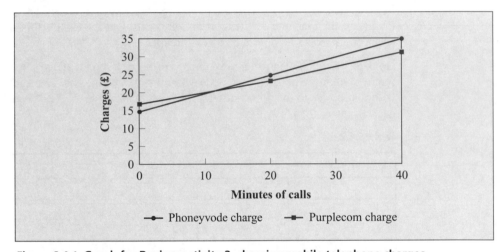

Figure S.4.1 Graph for Review activity 2, showing mobile telephone charges

(c) Purplecom becomes cheaper where the two lines cross. To find this point exactly:

$15 + 0.5x = 17.25 + 0.35x$

$0.15\,x = 2.25$

$$x = \frac{2.25}{0.15} = 15$$

i.e., if less than 15 minutes of calls per month are to be made, Phoneyvode should be chosen. If the anticipated call level is higher, Purplecom is the cheaper option.

(d) Either equation can be used:

$x = 15$ gives $y = 15 + 0.5 * 15 = 15 + 7.5 = 22.5$

or

$x = 15$ gives $y = 17.25 + 0.35 * 15 = 17.25 + 5.25 = 22.5$

The overall charge for 15 minutes of calls (on either scheme) is £22.50 per month.

Review activity 3   (a) Takings $= y$ and Number of coaches $= x$.

(b) The calculations needed are shown in Table S.4.3.

Table S.4.3

Day number	No. of coaches	Takings (£)		
	x	y	xy	x^2
1	24	962	23088	576
2	30	1181	35430	900
3	9	578	5202	81
4	48	1429	68592	2304
5	38	1324	50312	1444
6	15	752	11280	225
7	5	542	2710	25
8	38	1355	51490	1444
9	15	788	11820	225
10	24	998	23952	576
11	49	1462	71638	2401
12	10	650	6500	100
13	17	862	14654	289
14	11	719	7909	121
15	16	828	13248	256
	$\Sigma x - 349$	$\Sigma y = 14430$	$\Sigma xy = 397825$	$\Sigma x^2 = 10967$

The data from the table gives:

$$b = \frac{n\Sigma xy - \Sigma x \Sigma y}{[n\Sigma x^2 - (\Sigma x)^2]} = \frac{15 * 397825 - 349 * 14430}{(15 * 10967 - 349^2)} = \frac{931305}{42704} = 21.80837$$

$$a = \frac{\Sigma y}{n} - \frac{b\Sigma x}{n} = \frac{14430}{15} - 21.80837 * \frac{349}{15} = 962 - 507.40807 = 454.5919$$

Hence the regression equation is:

$y = 454.59 + 21.81x$

or

Takings $= 454.59 + 21.81 *$ No. of coaches

(Notice that calculations have been done using a number of decimal places, with rounding only carried out at the very end to avoid errors.)

(c) (i) If $x = 27$, $y = 454.59 + 21.81 * 27 = £1043.46$

(ii) If $x = 55$, $y = 454.59 + 21.81 * 55 = £1654.15$

(d) Answer (i) above is likely to be reliable because the forecast has been made using data inside the range used to make up the regression equation (interpolation).

Answer (ii) may be less reliable. The value of 55 coaches is outside the range used to make up the equation, and it is not known whether the model is still valid. For example, there may be limited parking in the town which would lead to problems if larger numbers of coaches arrive.

CHAPTER 5

Review activity 1   (a)   There are four mint humbugs in 20 sweets so P(humbug) = $\frac{4}{20}$ = $\frac{1}{5}$

(b)   There are two pineapple chunks so P(pineapple) = $\frac{2}{20}$
Therefore P(not pineapple) = $1 - \frac{2}{20} = \frac{18}{20} = \frac{9}{10} = 0.9$

(c)   Picking a cola cube and picking an acid drop are mutually exclusive events.
P(cola cube) = $\frac{5}{20}$ P(acid drop) = $\frac{9}{20}$
So P(cola cube or acid drop) = $\frac{5}{20} + \frac{9}{20} = \frac{14}{20} = \frac{7}{10} = 0.7$

(d)   P(acid drop) = $\frac{9}{20}$ P(yellow) = $\frac{8}{20}$
So P(acid drop or yellow) = $\frac{9}{20} + \frac{8}{20}$

But the events are not mutually exclusive as the pineapple chunks are also yellow,
so P(acid drop or yellow) = $\frac{9}{20} + \frac{8}{20} - \frac{6}{20} = \frac{11}{20} = 0.55$

(e)   Picking a cola cube then putting it back before picking a mint humbug makes the two events independent of each other.
P(cola cube) = $\frac{5}{20}$ P(mint humbug) = $\frac{4}{20}$
P(cola cube and mint humbug) = $\frac{5}{20} * \frac{4}{20} = 0.05$

(f)   Taking two sweets at once means the events are not independent.
P(first sweet cola cube) = $\frac{5}{20}$
P(second sweet is cola cube given first is cola cube) = $\frac{4}{19}$
P(both cola cubes) = $\frac{5}{20} * \frac{4}{19} = 0.0526$ (to 4 d.p.)

Review activity 2   Let x = number of minutes

P(x) = probability of spending x minutes on the exercise

Then construct a table (Table S.5.1) which calculates xP(x). To find the expected value add up the xP(x) values i.e., find ΣxP(x).

Table S.5.1

x	P(x)	xP(x)
25	0.05	25 * 0.05 = 1.25
30	0.05	30 * 0.05 = 1.5
35	0.2	35 * 0.2 = 7
40	0.15	40 * 0.15 = 6
45	0.3	45 * 0.3 = 13.5
50	0.15	50 * 0.15 = 7.5
55	0.1	55 * 0.1 = 5.5

$$\Sigma x P(x) = 1.25 + 1.5 + 7 + 6 + 13.5 + 7.5 + 5.5 = 42.25$$

Therefore the expected completion time for the Chapter 5 seminar exercises is 42.25 minutes.

Review activity 3   P(rates rise) = 0.6

So P(rates fall) = 0.4

Expected value of scheme A = $0.6 * 54 + 0.4 * 11 = 36.8$

Expected value of scheme B = $0.6 * 35 + 0.4 * 23 = 30.2$

So, based on expected value, it would seem that scheme A offers the better deal. However, it should be remembered that the expected value represents a long-term average, i.e., that scheme A will never actually return £36,800. Scheme A also seems to be the riskier investment, with a wider range of possible returns, so a cautious investor might still prefer scheme B.

Taking a few values for P(interest rates rise) and calculating the expected value of each scheme gives:

P(rates rise)	EV(A)	EV(B)
0.4	28.2	27.8
0.5	32.5	29
0.6	36.8	30.2
0.7	41.1	31.4

which suggests that the decision is fairly safe: the probability could change quite a bit before a different decision would be suggested by the expected value approach.

CHAPTER 6

Review activity 1 $P(-0.37 < Z < 1.52)$

This area is also the same as $P(Z < 1.52) - P(Z < -0.37)$

$P(Z < 1.52) = 0.9357$, $P(Z < -0.37)$ is same as $P(Z > 0.37) = 0.3557$

So

$P(-0.37 < Z < 1.52) = 0.9357 - 0.3557 = 0.58$

Review activity 2   (a) $P(x < 5 \text{ mins})$

First transform $x = 5$ to a Z value:

$$Z = \frac{5 - 7}{2.5} = -0.8$$

Using symmetry look up +0.8 in tail tables = 0.2119. So the percentage of students taking less than 5 minutes = 21.19%.

(b) Slowest 10%: Area at the top end of the curve = 0.1

From the tail tables find the z value which gives a probability of 0.1.

Nearest $z = 1.28$, therefore

$$1.28 = \frac{x - 7}{2.5} \quad x = 1.28 * 2.5 + 7 = 10.2 \text{ mins}$$

So the slowest 10% of students take over 10.2 minutes to read the paper.

(c) P(X < 10mins)

$$z = \frac{10 - 7}{2.5} = 1.2$$

From body tables P(z < 1.2) = 0.8849

Therefore the percentage of students who take less than 10 minutes to read the paper is 88.49%. This is an under-estimate of the 95% assumed by the examiners.

To rectify this, a z value which would result in the shaded area as found above being 0.95 is required. The value of x can then be calculated.

From body tables the z value giving a probability of 0.95 is equal to +1.645.

So

$$1.645 = \frac{x - 7}{2.5} \quad \text{i.e., } x = 1.645 * 2.5 + 7 = 11.1 \text{ (to 1d.p.)}$$

Therefore, in order to ensure that 95% of the students have read the paper in the time allowance allocated, this time should be set as 12 minutes.

Review activity 3 To find a 95% confidence interval for a sample the formula is:

$$\bar{x} - 1.96 * \frac{s}{\sqrt{n}} < \mu < \bar{x} + 1.96 * \frac{s}{\sqrt{n}}$$

For this example $\bar{x} = 42$, $s = 27$ and $n = 100$.

So

$$42 - 1.96 * \frac{27}{\sqrt{100}} < \mu < 42 + 1.96 * \frac{27}{\sqrt{100}}$$

$$42 - 1.96 * \frac{27}{10} < \mu < 42 + 1.96 * \frac{27}{10}$$

$$42 - 1.96 * 2.7 < \mu < 42 + 1.96 * 2.7$$

$$42 - 5.292 < \mu < 42 + 5.292$$

$$36.708 < \mu < 47.292$$

Therefore we can be 95% confident that a student will spend between 36.708 and 47.292 minutes to complete the exercises in Chapter 5.

CHAPTER 7

Review activity 1   (a) Compound interest, so the formula to use is $S = P(1 + r)^n$

At 2% per month, interest would be charged 12 times per year. Hence:

$P = 1000$ $n = 12$ $r = 0.02$

$S = P(1 + r)^n = 1000 * 1.02^{12} = 1000 * 1.26824 = £1268.24$ owed

At 6.5% per quarter, interest is charged four times per year. Hence:

$P = 1000$ $n = 4$ $r = 0.065$

$S = P(1 + r)^n = 1000 * 1.065^4 = 1000 * 1.28647 = £1286.47$

So the storecard offers the better deal for a customer, as less money is owed at the end of the year.

(b) Storecard: $r = 0.02$; $m = 12$

$EAR = (1 + r)^m - 1 = (1 + 0.02)^{12} - 1 = 0.2682$ i.e., 26.8% p.a.

Loan: $r = 0.065$; $m = 4$

$EAR = (1 + r)^m - 1 = (1 + 0.065)^4 - 1 = 0.2864$ i.e., 28.6% p.a.

confirming that the storecard offers the better deal, as the EAR is lower.

Review activity 2   (a) Table S.7.1 shows that the net present value for Project A is £715.

Table S.7.1

Year	Cash invested	Cash returned	Net cashflow	PV factor	Present value
0	5000		(5000)	1.000	(5000)
1			0	0.943	0
2			0	0.890	0
3			0	0.840	0
4			0	0.792	0
5		7650	7650	0.747	5714.55
					NPV £715

Table S.7.2 shows that for Project B it is £711.

Table S.7.2

Year	Cash invested	Cash returned	Net cashflow	PV factor	Present value
0	1230		−1230	1.000	−1230
1	1230		−1230	0.943	−1159.89
2	1230		−1230	0.890	−1094.7
3	1230		−1230	0.840	−1033.2
4			0	0.792	0
5		7000	7000	0.747	5229
					NPV £711

(b) Option A is better since it has the higher NPV.

(c) Using the formula:

$N_1 = 71$

$I_1 = 0.06$

$N_2 = -249$

$I_2 = 0.10$

$$\text{IRR} = \frac{N_1 I_2 - N_2 I_1}{N_1 - N_2} = \frac{(715 * 0.10) - (-249 * 0.06)}{715 - (-249)} = \frac{71.5 + 14.94}{964} = \frac{86.44}{964} = 0.0896$$

i.e., the IRR is around 9%.

(Alternatively the same answer could be achieved by graph.)

CHAPTER 8

Review activity 1 (a) The constraints are:

$$20x_1 + 30x_2 \leq 2700 \quad \text{(amount of A used)}$$
$$10x_1 + 25x_2 \leq 2000 \quad \text{(amount of B used)}$$
$$x_1 + x_2 \leq 120 \quad \text{(running time)}$$
$$x_1 \leq 100 \quad \text{(time for process 1)}$$
$$x_1, x_2 \geq 0 \quad \text{(non-negativity)}$$

where x_1 = no. of hours of Process 1, x_2 = no. of hours of Process 2.

(b) See Figure S.8.1.

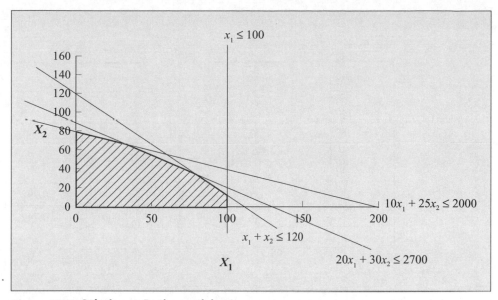

Figure S.8.1 Solution to Review activity 1

Review activity 2 (a) The expression for contribution to profit will be

$$50x_1 + 60x_2$$

ABCDEF in Figure S.8.2 represents the feasible area where a solution will be found.

To add the objective function to this area, a value of 3000 is chosen for the right-hand side ($50*60$ to give an easy number to work with):

$$50x_1 + 60x_2 = 3000$$
$$x_1 = 0, x_2 = 50; x_1 = 60, x_2 = 0$$

Adding this to the graph, we have Figure S.8.2 overleaf.

(b) Using the objective function line, the optimal solution must lie at point C. Point C is where the lines $20x_1 + 30x_2 = 2700$ and $x_1 + x_2 = 120$ cross.

Using simultaneous equations:

$$20x_1 + 30x_2 = 2700 \qquad (1)$$
$$x_1 + x_2 = 120 \qquad (2)$$

Multiplying (2) * 20:

$$20x_1 + 20x_2 = 2400 \qquad (3)$$
$$20x_1 + 30x_2 = 2700 \qquad (1)$$

Subtracting (3) – (1)

$$10x_2 = -300$$
$$x_2 = 30$$

231

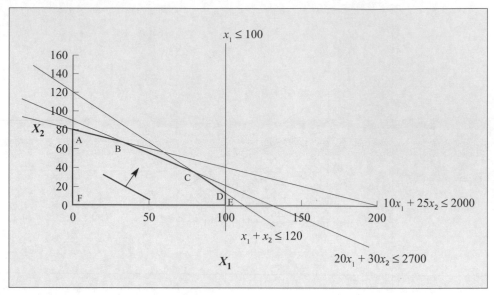

Figure S.8.2 Solution to Review activity 2

Then substituting $x_2 = 30$ in (2):
$$x_1 + x_2 = 120$$
$$x_1 + 30 = 120$$
$$x_1 = 90$$

Checking by substituting in (1):
$$20x_1 + 30x_2 = (20*90) + (30*30) = 1800 + 900 = 2700 \checkmark$$

So the optimal solution is to run Process 1 for 90 hours and Process 2 for 30 hours.

Contribution to profit would then be:
$$50x_1 + 60x_2 = (50*90) + (60*30) = 4500 + 1800 = \pounds6300 \text{ per hour}$$

Review activity 3 (a) Start by asking what is the 'slack' on material A?

The amount of A available is 2700 litres per hour.

The amount of A used is $20x_1 + 30x_2$.

In the optimal solution,
$$\text{Amount of A used} = (20*90) + (30*30) = 1800 + 900$$
$$= 2700 \text{ litres per hour}$$

i.e., all of the available material A is currently being used – so it is likely that increasing the amount available *would* change the solution.

(If you wish to find the new solution for extra practice, the solution is $x_1 = 66.7$ hours and $x_2 = 53.3$ hours.)

(b) Amount of material B available = 2000 litres.

Amount used = $10x_1 + 25x_2$.

In the optimal solution,

$$\text{Amount of B used} = (10 * 90) + (25 * 30) = 900 + 750$$
$$= 1650 \text{ litres per hour}$$

i.e., 350 litres are ordered and not used – so 350 litres less could be ordered without affecting the optimal solution.

CHAPTER 9

Review activity 1

(a) Feb. index $\quad = \dfrac{48}{50} * 100 = 96$

March index $= \dfrac{45}{50} * 100 = 90$

April index $\quad = \dfrac{49}{50} * 100 = 98$

May index $\quad = \dfrac{52}{50} * 100 = 104$

June index $\quad = \dfrac{60}{50} * 100 = 120$

(b) $\dfrac{\text{Index Oct. (Jan.} = 100)}{120} = \dfrac{110}{100} = \dfrac{110 * 120}{100} = 132$

Review activity 2

Chain base index:

Feb. $\quad = \dfrac{48}{50} * 100 = 96$

March $= \dfrac{45}{48} * 100 = 93.8$

April $\quad = \dfrac{49}{45} * 100 = 108.9$

May $\quad = \dfrac{52}{49} * 100 = 106.1$

June $\quad = \dfrac{60}{52} * 100 = 115.4$

Note: Where appropriate, answers have been rounded to one decimal place.

CHAPTER 10

Review activity 1

(a) See Figure S.10.1.

Sales appear to be increasing over time with a linear pattern.

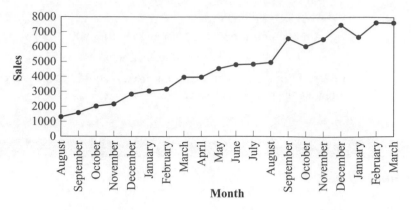

Figure S.10.1 Graph for Review activity 1, showing sales over time

Table S.10.1

Month	Time period (X)	Sales (Y)	XY	X²
August	1	1362	1362	1
September	2	1623	3246	4
October	3	2117	6351	9
November	4	2253	9012	16
December	5	2910	14550	25
January	6	3125	18750	36
February	7	3262	22834	49
March	8	4026	32208	64
April	9	3971	35739	81
May	10	4618	46180	100
June	11	4836	53196	121
July	12	4901	58812	144
August	13	5052	65676	169
September	14	6606	92484	196
October	15	6085	91275	225
November	16	6536	104576	256
December	17	7540	128180	289
January	18	6675	120150	324
February	19	7688	146072	361
March	20	7698	153960	400
	$\sum X = 210$	$\sum Y = 92884$	$\sum XY = 1204613$	$\sum X^2 = 2870$

(b) From the data in Table S.10.1, we calculate:

$$b = \frac{n\Sigma xy - \Sigma x \Sigma y}{n\Sigma x^2 - (\Sigma x)^2} = \frac{20 * 1204613 - 210 * 92884}{20 * 2870 - (210)^2} = 344.85864$$

$$a = \frac{\Sigma y}{n} - \frac{b * \Sigma x}{n} = \frac{92884}{20} - 344.85864 * \frac{210}{20} = 1021.18428$$

i.e., the linear regression equation is:

$$y = 1021 + 344.9x \qquad \text{where } y \text{ is the number of sales and } x \text{ is the time period}$$

(Note that the 'longhand' way of calculating the equation is shown here: it would be more practical to use a scientific calculator or spreadsheet to find the same values.)

(c)

Month	Time period	Forecast
April	21	1021 + 344.9 * 21 = 8264
May	22	1021 + 344.9 * 22 = 8609
June	23	1021 + 344.9 * 23 = 8954

This method of forecasting assumes that the pattern seen previously will continue: in reality, sales will probably level off at some point. It would be wise to check that the model continues to reflect what actually happens in the future, and not to use it to forecast too far ahead.

Review activity 2   (a) Figure S.10.2 shows there is a clear seasonal effect: production is highest in the third quarter and lowest in the first. There is also a trend of generally increasing production levels over time.

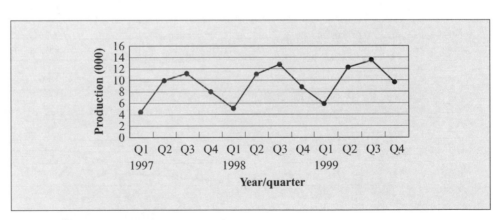

Figure S.10.2 **Graph of fruit production**

(b) See Table S.10.2.

Table S.10.2

Year		Time period	Production	4-pt M.A.	Centred M.A. (trend)
1997	Quarter 1	1	4.3		
	Quarter 2	2	9.8		
	Quarter 3	3	11.1	8.225	8.3125
	Quarter 4	4	7.7	8.4	8.55
1998	Quarter 1	5	5	8.7	8.9
	Quarter 2	6	11	9.1	9.225
	Quarter 3	7	12.7	9.35	9.4625
	Quarter 4	8	8.7	9.575	9.7375
1999	Quarter 1	9	5.9	9.9	9.9875
	Quarter 2	10	12.3	10.075	10.2
	Quarter 3	11	13.4	10.325	
	Quarter 4	12	9.7		

(c) See Table S.10.3. From this we get Figure S.10.3.

Table S.10.3

Quarter	Time period	Trend forecast
1	13	7.51 + 0.28 * 13 = 11.15
2	14	7.51 + 0.28 * 14 = 11.43
3	15	7.51 + 0.28 * 15 = 11.71
4	16	7.51 + 0.28 * 16 = 11.99

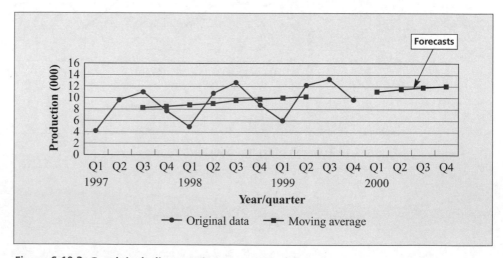

Figure S.10.3 **Graph including moving average and forecasts**

Review activity 3   (a) See Table S.10.4.

Table S.10.4

Year		Time period	Production	4-pt M.A.	Centred M.A.	Seas effect
1995	Quarter 1	1	4.3			
	Quarter 2	2	9.8			
	Quarter 3	3	11.1	8.225	8.3125	1.3353
	Quarter 4	4	7.7	8.4	8.55	0.9006
1996	Quarter 1	5	5	8.7	8.9	0.5618
	Quarter 2	6	11	9.1	9.225	1.1924
	Quarter 3	7	12.7	9.35	9.4625	1.3421
	Quarter 4	8	8.7	9.575	9.7375	0.8935
1997	Quarter 1	9	5.9	9.9	9.9875	0.5907
	Quarter 2	10	12.3	10.075	10.2	1.2059
	Quarter 3	11	13.4	10.325		
	Quarter 4	12	9.7			
1998	Quarter 1	13			11.15	
	Quarter 2	14			11.43	
	Quarter 3	15			11.71	
	Quarter 4	16			11.99	

(b) See Table S.10.5.

Table S.10.5

	Q1	Q2	Q3	Q4	
1995			1.3353	0.9006	
1996	0.5618	1.1924	1.3421	0.8935	
1997	0.5907	1.2059			
Average	0.5763	1.1992	1.3387	0.8971	sum = 4.0113

Adjustment: $\dfrac{4}{4.0113} = 0.9972$

	0.5763 * 0.9972 =	1.1992 * 0.9972 =	1.3387 * 0.9972 =	0.8971 * 0.9972 =	
	0.5747	1.1958	1.3349	0.8946	sum = 4

(c) See Table S.10.6.

Table S.10.6

	Trend	Seas. effect	Forecast of production (000 units)
Quarter 1	11.15	0.5747	= 11.15 * 0.5747 = 6.41
Quarter 2	11.43	1.1958	11.43 * 1.1958 = 13.67
Quarter 3	11.71	1.3349	11.71 * 1.3349 = 15.63
Quarter 4	11.99	0.8946	11.99 * 0.8946 = 10.73

(d) See Figure S.10.4.

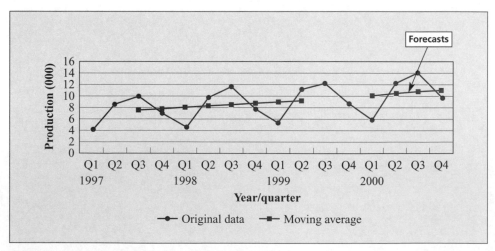

Figure S.10.4 Fruit production, and final forecasts

ANSWERS TO EVEN-NUMBERED ADDITIONAL EXERCISES

1.2 (a) Continuous data

(b) Nominal data

(c) Continuous data

(d) Nominal data

1.4 This answer is indicative of the sorts of issues to be considered: an alternative scheme, if justified, may be equally acceptable.

First consider the population of interest. Presumably the newspaper is not just interested in its own readers' views, but in the views of everyone, so it would not be sufficient to (say) include a questionnaire with the paper and ask people to return it on a voluntary basis.

The sample should include people from a wide range of backgrounds, ages, areas of the country to ensure it is representative.

Cluster sampling: initially parliamentary constituencies could be chosen using stratified sampling based on the political party of the sitting MP to try to ensure a range of political views. Within those constituencies particular areas/streets could then be chosen (perhaps stratified again by council tax band or value of property to ensure a range of income levels/social classes) and door-to-door interviews carried out (consider who should be interviewed. Head of household? Whoever answers the door?). Alternatively, at this second stage voters could be chosen randomly from the electoral roll (resulting in multistage sampling) and contacted by post (although the effects of non-responses and only targeting those registered to vote should be considered).

Again, these answers are indicative of the general method which should be followed.

1.6 (a) Simple random sampling: each person is given a number with those names in the first column numbered 1–10 and those in the second column 11–20.

Random numbers are then taken from the table, starting at the second value and choosing every third number thereafter:

15 – Anne Smith

17 – Stuart Trainer

20 – Zoe Wilkinson

18 – Philip Twist

(b) Stratified random sampling based on sex: the population contains 10 males and 10 females. Hence the sample should contain:

$^{10}/_{20} * 4 = 2$ i.e., choose 2 males

The remaining 2 should obviously be female.

Using the random number tables again, this time starting on the third row and using every number:

15 – Anne Smith

16 – Elizabeth Swift

10 – David Wright

07 – Sarah Gray but already have 2 females so *ignore*

13 – Jacqui Hobson female so *ignore*

16 – already used

01 – Steven Adams

(c) Systematic random sampling: we require 4 people from 20 so we choose every fifth person.

Randomly select a start point – the third person:

3 – Graham Buckley

8 – Joanne Keane

13 – Jacqui Hobson

18 – Philip Twist

1.8 (a) Multistage (or cluster) sampling would seem to be the most appropriate method since the farms are likely to be widely spread. This could start with a sample of countries (chosen randomly), then areas and farms within the areas might be chosen using stratified sampling to give a representative mixture of farm sizes.

(b) A multiple choice question is best, something along the lines of:

How many different breeds of cows do you keep?

1 ☐   2 ☐   3 ☐   More than 3 ☐

Ensure that the usual principles for multiple choice questions are followed i.e., categories are mutually exclusive and cover all possibilities.

CHAPTER 2

2.2 **Regional unemployment (in thousands) for 1985, 1990 and 1993**

	1985	**1990**	**1993**
North	219	123	170
Yorkshire	280	161	244
South-east	729	372	928
South-west	191	97	217

Source: Regional Trends

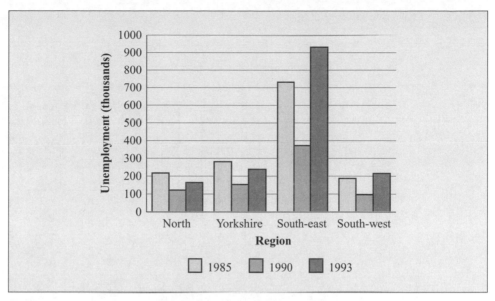

Figure E.2.1 Regional unemployment in 1986, 1990 and 1993

We can see from Figure E.2.1 that in all regions, unemployment decreased between 1985 and 1989 and then increased again in 1993. In the north and Yorkshire levels in 1993 were below those experienced in 1985, while in the south-east and south-west they were higher. The danger in looking at these figures in this way is that it would be easy to say that unemployment in the south-east is much worse than in the other regions. To make these sorts of statements, some account must be taken of relative population sizes. In fact, the unemployment rates for the four regions in 1993 were 12%, 10%, 10.2% and 9.8%.

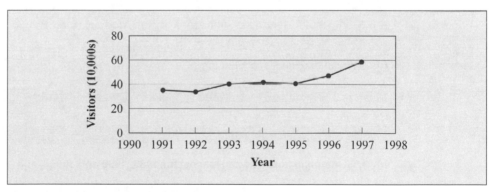

Figure E.2.2 Visitor numbers at local museum 1991–97

2.4. We can see from the Figure E.2.2, that visitor numbers showed a small steady incline between 1991 and 1995. In the following two years the numbers show a somewhat larger increase in numbers.

2.6 See Figure E.2.3.

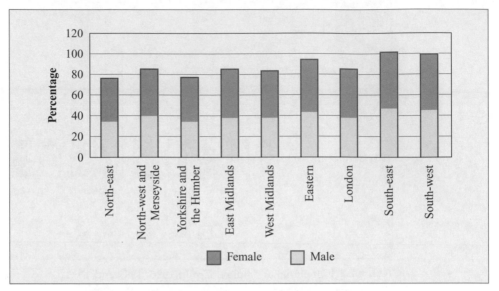

Figure E.2.3 Percentage of pupils with five A*–C grades by region
Source: Department of Education and Employment

CHAPTER 3

3.2 (a) Mode = 4 h; Mean = 6.875 h; Median = 6.5 h

(b) Range = 9 h; IQR = 5 h; Std Dev. = 3.314 h

(c) Mode = 4; Mean = 9.444 (to 3 d.p.); Median = 8; Range = 27; IQR = 7; Std Dev. = 8.308 (to 3 d.p.)

(d) Median and inter-quartile range

3.4 Mean = 2.66; Median = 2; Mode = 2 and 3; Range = 9; IQR = 3; Std Dev. = 2.041 (to 3 d.p.)

Median and inter-quartile range

3.6 (a) The frequency densities which will be required on a histogram are as follows: 21, 23.1, 17.3, 8.5, 2.07

(b) Modal class = 5 up to 15 years

(c) Mean = 15.84 (to 2 d.p.); Std Dev. = 10.48 (to 2 d.p.)

(d) Median = 14; IQR = 16

(e) Median and inter-quartile range as the data distribution is skewed

CHAPTER 4

4.2 (a) Spearman's rank correlation coefficient, $r = 0.8929$ (to 4d.p.)

(b) This indicates a high level of agreement

4.4 Weight loss (lb) $= -0.8111 + 0.0175 *$ minutes of aerobic exercise. When 150 minutes of aerobic exercise is carried out the predicted weight loss is 1.814 lb.

4.6 (a) Age when bought has a strong negative relationship with battery life. In the case of price there is little evidence of a relationship with battery life.

(b) Battery life $= 15.438 - 0.537 *$ Age when bought

(c) When batteries are new they have an expected lifetime of around 15½ months. For every month after this lifetime reduces by one half of a month.

(d) (i) 2.55 months; (ii) 12.216 months

(e) d(i) Extrapolation has occurred so the forecast may be unreliable

CHAPTER 5

5.2 (a) P(wants more bus/cycle lanes) $= 0.27$

(b) P(female and wants more free parking) $= 0.10$

(c) P(wants less free parking|male) $= 0.20$

(d) Table showing percentage in each group:

	Sex of respondent	
	Male	**Female**
Wants more free parking	38%	25%
Wants less free parking	20%	40%
Wants paid permit scheme	12%	13%
Wants more bus/cycle lanes	30%	23%

This suggests that males are more in favour of free parking than females; both groups have a similar proportion of people in favour of permits; more males than females want more bus/cycle lanes.

5.4 (a) P(A AND no problems) $= 0.18$

(b) P(A OR B AND problems) $= 0.055$

5.6 Expected payoff for Product A $= £335,000$

Expected payoff for Product B $= £497,000$

Based on the expected values, Product B should be launched (since it has the higher expected payoff).

5.8 (a) P(cows OR sheep) = 0.7

(b) P(neither) = 0.3

CHAPTER 6

6.2 (a) 2.28%

(b) 81.64%

(c) 99.95%

6.4 (a) sd = 31.25 hours

(b) 2.74%

(c) 1.3 flares

6.6 (a) £50.30 < μ < £69.30

(b) £64.27 < μ < £75.23

CHAPTER 7

7.2 (a) S = £13,431.36

(b) r = 5.81%, hence the initial 10 year investment offers the better deal

(c) P = £10,051.10

£7500 is already invested, so he would need to add around £2551 to ensure he receives £18,000 on retirement.

7.4 P = £2845.82

7.6 (a) Average cashflow = £646.09 per year

(b) NPV is £3540.68

(c) IRR = 12.93%. This is the discount rate at which the project will break even.

(d) r = 5.06%. Hence the investment in the company seems a better deal, however, since the difference is small he may also want to consider the relative safety of the two options before making a final decision.

(e) The money would have to remain in the bond for 5 years and 1 month (5.08 years).

(f) £159,535.20

7.8 The EAR is 6.2%

8.2 (a) h: number of hatchbacks produced

c: number of coupés produced

maximize $1.5h + 2c$

subject to $h + c \leq 13250$

$6h + 9c \leq 100000$

$h \geq 4000$

$5h + 3c \leq 60000$

$h, c \geq 0$

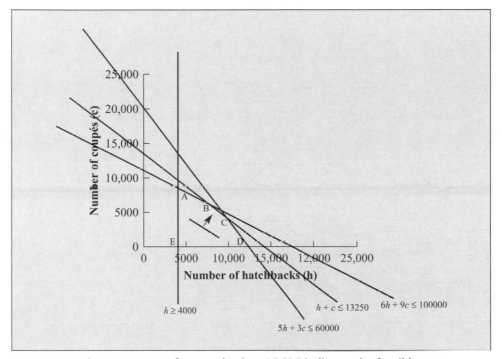

Figure E.8.1 Linear program of car production. ABCDE indicates the feasible area

From Figure E.8.1 we can see that the solution is at point B where

$c = 6833.33$

$h = 6416.67$

Hence the optimal solution is to produce 6417 hatchbacks and 6833 coupés to give profit of £23,291,500.

(b) $0.4h - 0.6c \geq 0$

(c) Of the options given, the only binding constraint in the optimal solution is the one related to the number of chassis units available, hence this is the option which would allow them to produce more cars.

(d) Usage under optimal solution = 52,584

They receive 60,000 per week

Slack is therefore 60,000 − 52,584 = 416 handles

8.4 (a) a: number of type A computers

b: number of type B computers

maximize $100a + 80b$

subject to $a + b \leq 5500$

$0.67a + 0.5b \leq 3250$ (converted to hours)

$a \geq 2000$

$a, b \geq 0$

(b) In Figure E.8.2 the feasible region represents the set of feasible solutions to the problem i.e., all of the possible combinations of production levels of the two computers which would satisfy all of the constraints.

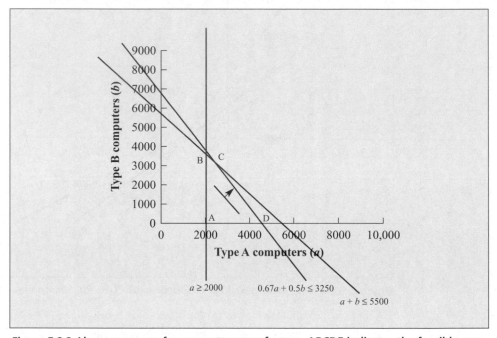

Figure E.8.2 Linear program for computer manufacture. ABCDE indicates the feasible area.

(c) The solution is at point C on Figure E.8.2 where:

$a = 2941.18$

$b = 2558.82$

Hence the best solution is to produce 2941 type A computers and 2559 type B.

(d) Profit = £498,820

(e) Basic units used = 5500

So all of the units are used under the optimal solution: there is no scope for reduction.

CHAPTER 9

9.2 (a) 1994: 100; 1995: 102; 1996: 103; 1997: 109; 1998: 118

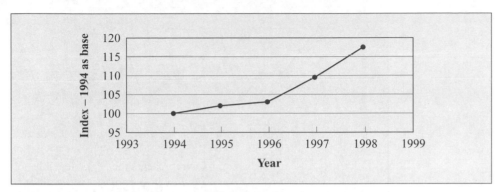

Figure E.9.1 Wage index for Lyster and Gale Engineering

Figure E.9.1 shows that wages remained fairly steady during 1994–96 with two relatively large increases occurring in 1997 and 1998 respectively.

(b) £228.81

9.4 (a) 1986: 100; 1987: 95.5; 1988: 97.6; 1989: 98.4; 1990: 100; 1991: 103.3; 1992: 98.4; 1993: 99.2

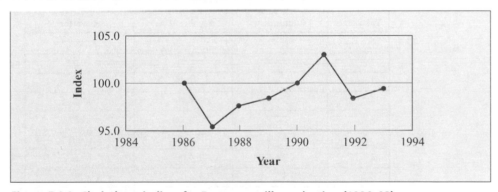

Figure E.9.2 Chain base indices for European milk production (1986–93)

(b) We can see from Figure E.9.2 that 1987 saw a fall in milk production as compared with 1986, with production up until 1990 still being below the previous year's figure but with a decreasing decline. In 1991 there was a sharp upturn with production increasing from 1990. However, in the two subsequent years the decreased production pattern returns.

CHAPTER 10

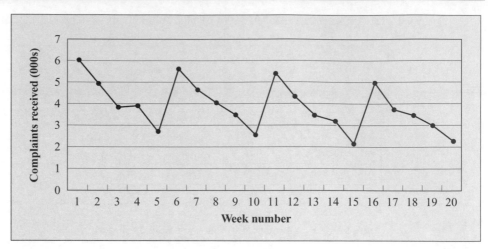

Figure E.10.1 Customer complaints over 20 weeks

10.2 (a) We see from Figure E.10.1 there seems to be a downward trend in the complaints, indicating that the training policy is working. There is also a strong seasonal effect repeating over a five week period. Might it be worth investigating why (e.g., is there any link to staff shift patterns?)?

(b) & (c) A 5-point moving average should be used:

Week	Complaints	5-point M.A.	Seas. effect
1	6		
2	4.9		
3	3.8	4.26	0.892
4	3.9	4.18	0.933
5	2.7	4.12	0.655
6	5.6	4.16	1.346
7	4.6	4.06	1.133
8	4	4.02	0.995
9	3.4	3.96	0.859
10	2.5	3.90	0.641
11	5.3	3.78	1.402
12	4.3	3.72	1.156
13	3.4	3.64	0.934
14	3.1	3.56	0.871
15	2.1	3.42	0.614
16	4.9	3.42	1.433
17	3.6	3.38	1.065
18	3.4	3.40	1.000
19	2.9		
20	2.2		

Overall seasonal effects:

	1	2	3	4	5	
			0.892	0.933	0.655	
	1.346	1.133	0.995	0.859	0.641	
	1.402	1.156	0.934	0.871	0.614	
	1.433	1.065	1.000			
						Sum
Average	1.394	1.118	0.955	0.888	0.637	4.992
Adjustment	1.002	1.002	1.002	1.002	1.002	
Adjusted avg.	1.396	1.12	0.957	0.889	0.638	5

(d) Either longhand, by calculator or Excel, the regression equation is

Trend = 4.489 − 0.065 * Time period   where week 1 = time period 1

Hence:

Week	Trend	Seas. effect	Forecast
21	3.124	1.396	4.4
22	3.059	1.120	3.4
23	2.994	0.957	2.9
24	2.929	0.889	2.6

(e) Care should be taken: these forecasts fit well with the previous pattern and are probably quite accurate as they do not project too far into the future. However, it would be unreasonable to assume that complaints will continue to fall (presumably they will level out at some point).

10.4 (a) From Figure E.10.2 there seems to be a strong upward trend and a seasonal pattern repeating each week, with calls highest on a Saturday and lowest on a Monday.

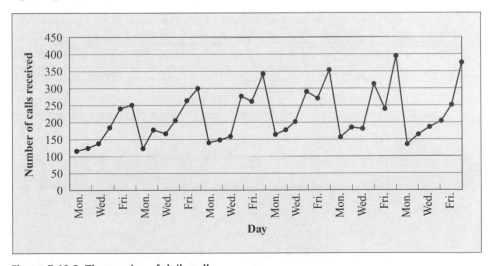

Figure E.10.2 Time series of daily calls

249

(b) 6-point average was chosen because the data repeat over a week (6 days). The column of centred moving average was required because this is an even-point moving average.

(c) The 'missing' figures are:

Week 3	Mon.	139	203.00	209.00	0.665
	Tues.	146	215.00	214.59	0.680
	Wed.	158	214.17	217.84	0.725
	Thurs.	278	221.50	223.59	1.243
	Fri.	263	225.67	228.17	1.153
	Sat.	345	230.67	234.50	1.471

(d) K17: =intercept(F6:F35,A6:A35)

K18: =slope(F6:F35,A6:A35)

These two figures are the coefficients of the regression equation which can be used to estimate the trend (centred moving average) according to the equation

Trend = 188.2 + 1.804 * Time period

(e) Completed table is:

	Mon.	**Tues.**	**Wed.**	**Thurs.**	**Fri.**	**Sat.**	
Week 1				1.041	1.334	1.327	
Week 2	0.629	0.921	0.825	0.984	1.291	1.477	
Week 3	0.665	0.680	0.725	1.243	1.153	1.471	
Week 4	0.685	0.730	0.842	1.201	1.116	1.472	
Week 5	0.637	0.764	0.749	1.288	1.001	1.669	
Week 6	0.583	0.737	0.837				
							Sum
Avg.	0.640	0.766	0.796	1.151	1.179	1.483	6.015
Adjustment	0.9975	0.9975	0.9975	0.9975	0.9975	0.9975	
Adjusted avg.	0.638	0.764	0.794	1.148	1.176	1.479	5.999

(f)

		Time period	Trend	Seas. effect	Forecast
Week 7	Mon.	37	254.948	0.638	163
	Tues.	38	256.752	0.764	196
	Wed.	39	258.556	0.794	205

APPENDIX A
Areas under the standard normal distribution

Table A1 gives the cumulative probability *above* the standardized normal value z, i.e.

$$P[\,Z > z\,] = \int_{-\infty}^{z} \frac{1}{2\pi} \exp(-\tfrac{1}{2}\,Z^2)\,dZ$$

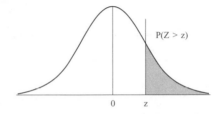

$P(Z > z)$

Table A1

z	0.00	0.01	0.02	0.03	0.04	0.05	0.06	0.07	0.08	0.09
0.0	0.5000	0.4960	0.4920	0.4880	0.4841	0.4801	0.4761	0.4721	0.4681	0.4641
0.1	0.4602	0.4562	0.4522	0.4483	0.4443	0.4404	0.4364	0.4325	0.4286	0.4247
0.2	0.4207	0.4168	0.4129	0.4090	0.4052	0.4013	0.3974	0.3936	0.3897	0.3859
0.3	0.3821	0.3783	0.3745	0.3707	0.3669	0.3632	0.3594	0.3557	0.3520	0.3483
0.4	0.3446	0.3409	0.3372	0.3336	0.3300	0.3264	0.3228	0.3192	0.3156	0.3121
0.5	0.3085	0.3050	0.3015	0.2981	0.2946	0.2912	0.2877	0.2843	0.2810	0.2776
0.6	0.2743	0.2709	0.2676	0.2643	0.2611	0.2578	0.2546	0.2514	0.2483	0.2451
0.7	0.2420	0.2389	0.2358	0.2327	0.2296	0.2266	0.2236	0.2206	0.2177	0.2146
0.8	0.2119	0.2090	0.2061	0.2033	0.2005	0.1977	0.1949	0.1922	0.1894	0.1867
0.9	0.1841	0.1814	0.1788	0.1762	0.1736	0.1711	0.1685	0.1660	0.1635	0.1611
1.0	0.1587	0.1562	0.1539	0.1515	0.1492	0.1469	0.1446	0.1423	0.1401	0.1379
1.1	0.1357	0.1335	0.1314	0.1292	0.1271	0.1251	0.1230	0.1210	0.1196	0.1170
1.2	0.1151	0.1131	0.1112	0.1093	0.1075	0.1056	0.1038	0.1020	0.1003	0.0985
1.3	0.0968	0.0951	0.0934	0.0918	0.0901	0.0885	0.0869	0.0853	0.0838	0.0823
1.4	0.0808	0.0793	0.0778	0.0764	0.0749	0.0735	0.0721	0.0708	0.0694	0.0681
1.5	0.0668	0.0655	0.0643	0.0630	0.0618	0.0606	0.0594	0.0582	0.0571	0.0559
1.6	0.0548	0.0537	0.0526	0.0516	0.0505	0.0495	0.0485	0.0475	0.0465	0.0455
1.7	0.0446	0.0436	0.0427	0.0418	0.0409	0.0401	0.0392	0.0384	0.0375	0.0367
1.8	0.0359	0.0351	0.0344	0.0336	0.0329	0.0322	0.0314	0.0307	0.0301	0.0294
1.9	0.0287	0.0281	0.0274	0.0268	0.0262	0.0256	0.0250	0.0244	0.0239	0.0233
2.0	0.0228	0.0222	0.0217	0.0212	0.0207	0.0202	0.0197	0.0192	0.0188	0.0183
2.1	0.0179	0.0174	0.0170	0.0166	0.0162	0.0158	0.0154	0.0150	0.0146	0.0143
2.2	0.0139	0.0135	0.0132	0.0129	0.0126	0.0122	0.0119	0.0116	0.0113	0.0110
2.3	0.0107	0.0104	0.0102	0.0099	0.0096	0.0094	0.0091	0.0089	0.0087	0.0084
2.4	0.0082	0.0080	0.0078	0.0076	0.0073	0.0071	0.0070	0.0068	0.0066	0.0064
2.5	0.0062	0.0060	0.0059	0.0057	0.0055	0.0054	0.0052	0.0051	0.0049	0.0048
2.6	0.0047	0.0045	0.0044	0.0043	0.0042	0.0040	0.0039	0.0038	0.0037	0.0036
2.7	0.0035	0.0034	0.0033	0.0032	0.0031	0.0030	0.0029	0.0028	0.0027	0.0026
2.8	0.0026	0.0025	0.0024	0.0023	0.0023	0.0022	0.0021	0.0020	0.0020	0.0019
2.9	0.0019	0.0018	0.0018	0.0017	0.0016	0.0016	0.0015	0.0015	0.0014	0.0014

z	3.00	3.10	3.20	3.30	3.40	3.50	3.60	3.70	3.80	3.90
P	0.0014	0.0010	0.0007	0.0005	0.0003	0.0002	0.0002	0.0001	0.0001	0.0000

Table A2 gives the cumulative probability *below* the standardized normal value z, i.e.

$$P[\,Z < z\,] = \int_{-\infty}^{z} \frac{1}{2\pi} \exp(-\tfrac{1}{2}\,Z^2)\,dZ$$

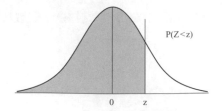

Table A2

z	0.00	0.01	0.02	0.03	0.04	0.05	0.06	0.07	0.08	0.09
0.0	0.5000	0.5040	0.5080	0.5120	0.5159	0.5199	0.5239	0.5279	0.5319	0.5359
0.1	0.5398	0.5438	0.5478	0.5517	0.5557	0.5596	0.5636	0.5675	0.5714	0.5753
0.2	0.5793	0.5832	0.5871	0.5910	0.5948	0.5987	0.6026	0.6064	0.6103	0.6141
0.3	0.6179	0.6217	0.6255	0.6293	0.6331	0.6368	0.6406	0.6443	0.6480	0.6517
0.4	0.6554	0.6591	0.6628	0.6664	0.6700	0.6736	0.6772	0.6808	0.6844	0.6879
0.5	0.6915	0.6950	0.6985	0.7019	0.7054	0.7088	0.7123	0.7157	0.7190	0.7224
0.6	0.7257	0.7291	0.7324	0.7357	0.7389	0.7422	0.7454	0.7486	0.7517	0.7549
0.7	0.7580	0.7611	0.7642	0.7673	0.7704	0.7734	0.7764	0.7794	0.7823	0.7854
0.8	0.7881	0.7910	0.7939	0.7967	0.7995	0.8023	0.8051	0.8078	0.8106	0.8133
0.9	0.8159	0.8186	0.8212	0.8238	0.8264	0.8289	0.8315	0.8340	0.8365	0.8389
1.0	0.8413	0.8438	0.8461	0.8485	0.8508	0.8531	0.8554	0.8577	0.8599	0.8621
1.1	0.8643	0.8665	0.8686	0.8708	0.8729	0.8749	0.8770	0.8790	0.8804	0.8830
1.2	0.8849	0.8869	0.8888	0.8907	0.8925	0.8944	0.8962	0.8980	0.8997	0.9015
1.3	0.9032	0.9049	0.9066	0.9082	0.9099	0.9115	0.9131	0.9147	0.9162	0.9177
1.4	0.9192	0.9207	0.9222	0.9236	0.9251	0.9265	0.9279	0.9292	0.9306	0.9319
1.5	0.9332	0.9345	0.9357	0.9370	0.9382	0.9394	0.9406	0.9418	0.9429	0.9441
1.6	0.9452	0.9463	0.9474	0.9484	0.9495	0.9505	0.9515	0.9525	0.9535	0.9545
1.7	0.9554	0.9564	0.9573	0.9582	0.9591	0.9599	0.9608	0.9616	0.9625	0.9633
1.8	0.9641	0.9649	0.9656	0.9664	0.9671	0.9678	0.9686	0.9693	0.9699	0.9706
1.9	0.9713	0.9719	0.9726	0.9732	0.9738	0.9744	0.9750	0.9756	0.9761	0.9767
2.0	0.9773	0.9778	0.9783	0.9788	0.9793	0.9798	0.9803	0.9808	0.9812	0.9817
2.1	0.9821	0.9826	0.9830	0.9834	0.9838	0.9842	0.9846	0.9850	0.9854	0.9857
2.2	0.9861	0.9865	0.9868	0.9871	0.9874	0.9878	0.9881	0.9884	0.9887	0.9890
2.3	0.9893	0.9896	0.9898	0.9901	0.9904	0.9906	0.9909	0.9911	0.9913	0.9916
2.4	0.9918	0.9920	0.9922	0.9924	0.9927	0.9929	0.9931	0.9932	0.9934	0.9936
2.5	0.9938	0.9940	0.9941	0.9943	0.9945	0.9946	0.9948	0.9949	0.9951	0.9952
2.6	0.9953	0.9955	0.9956	0.9957	0.9959	0.9960	0.9961	0.9962	0.9963	0.9964
2.7	0.9965	0.9966	0.9967	0.9968	0.9969	0.9970	0.9971	0.9972	0.9973	0.9974
2.8	0.9974	0.9975	0.9976	0.9977	0.9977	0.9978	0.9979	0.9980	0.9980	0.9981
2.9	0.9981	0.9982	0.9982	0.9983	0.9984	0.9984	0.9985	0.9985	0.9986	0.9986

z	3.00	3.10	3.20	3.30	3.40	3.50	3.60	3.70	3.80	3.90
P	0.9986	0.9990	0.9993	0.9995	0.9997	0.9998	0.9998	0.9999	0.9999	1.0000

APPENDIX B
Table of NPV factors

Table B1

Periods (n)	Discount rates (r)									
	1%	2%	3%	4%	5%	6%	7%	8%	9%	10%
1	0.990	0.980	0.971	0.962	0.952	0.943	0.935	0.926	0.917	0.909
2	0.980	0.961	0.943	0.925	0.907	0.890	0.873	0.857	0.842	0.826
3	0.971	0.942	0.915	0.889	0.864	0.840	0.816	0.794	0.772	0.751
4	0.961	0.924	0.888	0.855	0.823	0.792	0.763	0.735	0.708	0.683
5	0.951	0.906	0.863	0.822	0.784	0.747	0.713	0.681	0.650	0.621
6	0.942	0.888	0.837	0.790	0.746	0.705	0.666	0.630	0.596	0.564
7	0.933	0.871	0.813	0.760	0.711	0.665	0.623	0.583	0.547	0.513
8	0.923	0.853	0.789	0.731	0.677	0.627	0.582	0.540	0.502	0.467
9	0.914	0.837	0.766	0.703	0.645	0.592	0.544	0.500	0.460	0.424
10	0.905	0.820	0.744	0.676	0.614	0.558	0.508	0.463	0.422	0.386
11	0.896	0.804	0.722	0.650	0.585	0.527	0.475	0.429	0.388	0.350
12	0.887	0.788	0.701	0.625	0.557	0.497	0.444	0.397	0.356	0.319
13	0.879	0.773	0.681	0.601	0.530	0.469	0.415	0.368	0.326	0.290
14	0.870	0.758	0.661	0.577	0.505	0.442	0.388	0.340	0.299	0.263
15	0.861	0.743	0.642	0.555	0.481	0.417	0.362	0.315	0.275	0.239

Periods (n)	Discount rates (r)									
	11%	12%	13%	14%	15%	16%	17%	18%	19%	20%
1	0.901	0.893	0.885	0.877	0.870	0.862	0.855	0.847	0.840	0.833
2	0.812	0.797	0.783	0.769	0.756	0.743	0.731	0.718	0.706	0.694
3	0.731	0.712	0.693	0.675	0.658	0.641	0.624	0.609	0.593	0.579
4	0.659	0.636	0.613	0.592	0.572	0.552	0.534	0.516	0.499	0.482
5	0.593	0.567	0.543	0.519	0.497	0.476	0.456	0.437	0.419	0.402
6	0.535	0.507	0.480	0.456	0.432	0.410	0.390	0.370	0.352	0.335
7	0.482	0.452	0.425	0.400	0.376	0.354	0.333	0.314	0.296	0.279
8	0.434	0.404	0.376	0.351	0.327	0.305	0.285	0.266	0.249	0.233
9	0.391	0.361	0.333	0.308	0.284	0.263	0.243	0.225	0.209	0.194
10	0.352	0.322	0.295	0.270	0.247	0.227	0.208	0.191	0.176	0.162
11	0.317	0.287	0.261	0.237	0.215	0.195	0.178	0.162	0.148	0.135
12	0.286	0.257	0.231	0.208	0.187	0.168	0.152	0.137	0.124	0.112
13	0.258	0.229	0.204	0.182	0.163	0.145	0.130	0.116	0.104	0.093
14	0.232	0.205	0.181	0.160	0.141	0.125	0.111	0.099	0.088	0.078
15	0.209	0.183	0.160	0.140	0.123	0.108	0.095	0.084	0.074	0.065

INDEX